D1133285

THREE TRADITIONS OF MORAL THOUGHT

THREE TRADITIONS
OF
MORAL THOUGHT

BY

DOROTHEA KROOK

Research Fellow of Newnham College
Assistant Lecturer in English in the
University of Cambridge

CAMBRIDGE
AT THE UNIVERSITY PRESS
1959

PUBLISHED BY
THE SYNDICS OF THE CAMBRIDGE UNIVERSITY PRESS
Bentley House, 200 Euston Road, London, N.W. 1
American Branch: 32 East 57th Street, New York 22, N.Y.

Printed in Great Britain at the University Press, Cambridge
(*Brooke Crutchley, University Printer*)

To

ENID WELSFORD

'Who shall deliver me out of the body of this death?'

(Rom. vii. 24)

'Were they, this pair, of the "great world"?—and was he himself, for the moment and thus related to them by his observation, *in* it? Then there was something in the great world covertly tigerish, which came to him across the lawn and in the charming air, as a waft from the jungle.'

(HENRY JAMES, *The Ambassadors*, bk. v, ch. 2)

PREFACE

THE material of this book is based on a course of lectures given at Cambridge under the title *Three Traditions of Moral Thought: Platonic-Christian; Utilitarian; Humanist* for students reading for the paper called 'The English Moralists' in Part II of the English Tripos. Since the form of address in which it was originally composed is part of the book's method, this has been substantially retained with such modifications as seemed necessary for presenting it to a wider audience.

The larger theme of the book has been developed under certain limiting conditions, the chief of these being the need to reconcile the exposition of the theme with an elucidation of the texts that would give the student audience the kind of help they normally need in their study of difficult texts. The main theme has accordingly not been developed with rigid consequentiality, but has often been put aside in the interests of pure elucidation of special problems in the text, or general points about the doctrine or the author, or the historical setting of both. A further limitation was imposed by the fact that the audience, being chiefly students of English, had little philosophical background and no formal training in philosophy. It was therefore necessary to present the material as simply and directly as possible, avoiding technical philosophical terms, speaking as nearly as possible in the language of men, and in general making their effort to follow an unfamiliar argument, at a level of generality equally unfamiliar, as easy as possible without doing violence to the intrinsic difficulty and complexity of the subject. (This was the reason also that T. S. Eliot's opinions came to be cited so frequently and on such a variety of topics. The student of English is more likely to have read and understood Mr Eliot's essays on Hobbes, Bradley and Arnold, for instance, than the more specialised scholars' works on these writers; consequently his views—whether right or wrong, but particularly when wrong—had to be taken seriously into account. But since they ought in any case to be taken seriously, it was fortunately no great hardship to be obliged to do so.)

In the treatment of the philosophical material there was, besides, the special difficulty of having to measure out with the greatest care the quantity of logic, epistemology and metaphysics that might be supposed to serve (but not to exceed) the needs of a literary student's study of moral philosophy. Vigilance was needed to make sure that they were not given a vast deal of difficult 'pure' philosophy for a ha'p'orth of moral doctrine; and this in practice generally meant reducing the philosophical framework to a rather skeletal affair, and (even more) resolutely stopping short of the finer, subtler implications of the philosophical matters actually touched upon. This was always a difficult and never a grateful task, and was especially so in the treatment of writers such as Aristotle, Hobbes, Hume and Bradley, whose philosophical systems are at least as important and interesting as their moral doctrines. The student of philosophy will have no difficulty in detecting the short cuts that have been resorted to; and I can only hope that his dissatisfaction will be tempered by sympathy for the enterprise as a whole and understanding of the difficulties it entailed.

I wish to acknowledge very gratefully the valuable help I received from Mr R. A. Becher, of the Cambridge University Press, in preparing the manuscript for publication. I wish also to thank Professor W. C. K. Guthrie and Mr Boris Ford for reading and making very helpful criticisms of the Appendix on Socrates' Dialectical Method. For fundamental criticisms of the book as a whole, I am deeply indebted to Mr Noël Annan, whose generous interest in the work in progress was as encouraging as his comments were searching and challenging. I owe a great deal also to the questions, comments and general interest of the students who attended the lectures on which the book is based.

My chief, unrequitable debt of gratitude is to the great teacher, scholar, and best of friends to whom this book is dedicated.

D. K.

NEWNHAM COLLEGE
CAMBRIDGE
April 1959

ACKNOWLEDGEMENTS

The Oxford University Press have kindly given me permission to quote from volume XI of W. D. Ross's edition of *The Works of Aristotle* (1946) and L. A. Selby-Bigge's edition of Hume's *Enquiry Concerning the Principles of Morals* (1902); and Messrs Hodder and Stoughton Ltd have allowed me to reproduce the passages from James Moffatt's *New Translation of the Bible* (1935) in chapter V. The extracts from D. H. Lawrence's *The Man Who Died* are reprinted from *The Tales of D. H. Lawrence* (Heinemann, London, 1934) with acknowledgements to the Estate of the late Mrs Frieda Lawrence, and from *The Later D. H. Lawrence*, edited by William York Tindall, by permission of the publisher, Alfred A. Knopf, Inc. The quotations from Hobbes's *Leviathan* are taken from the edition by Michael Oakeshott in the series of Blackwell's Political Texts (Oxford, 1946), by permission of Sir Basil Blackwell.

CONTENTS

NOTE ON THE TEXTS

The following translations and editions of the principal texts discussed in the book have been used:

1 Plato's *Gorgias*: W. R. M. Lamb's translation, Loeb Classical Library (Heinemann, 1946), supplemented by Jowett's translation (3rd ed., Oxford, 1892). I have generally used Lamb's translation for the arguments, Jowett's for the discursive and declamatory passages.

2 Aristotle's *Nicomachean Ethics*: H. Rackham's translation, Loeb Classical Library (Heinemann, 1945), supplemented by J. A. K. Thomson's translation (Allen and Unwin, 1953) and D. P. Chase's, Everyman's Library (Dent, 1911).

3 St Paul's Epistles: James Moffatt's *New Translation of the Bible* (Hodder and Stoughton, 1935), supplemented by the Revised Version (C.U.P., 1949). In some passages, I have combined Moffatt's rendering with that of the Revised Version to obtain what I thought was the best reading version.

4 Hobbes's *Leviathan*: Michael Oakeshott's edition, Blackwell's Political Texts (Basil Blackwell, Oxford, 1946).

5 Hume's *Enquiry concerning the Principles of Morals*: L. A. Selby-Bigge's edition, second edition (O.U.P., 1902).

6 J. S. Mill's *Three Essays on Religion* (Longmans, Green, Reader and Dyer, 1874).

7 Matthew Arnold's *Literature and Dogma*: fourth edition (Smith, Elder and Co., 1874).

8 F. H. Bradley's *Ethical Studies*: second edition (O.U.P., 1927).

9 D. H. Lawrence's *The Man Who Died*: in *The Tales of D. H. Lawrence* (Heinemann, 1934).

CHAPTER I

INTRODUCTION

THE object of this book is twofold. Its main object is to develop a theme concerning the nature of the moral life, and an interpretation of the history of English moral thought based on this view of the moral life. Its subsidiary object is to indicate how the skills of literary criticism may be found useful in the study of philosophical works; and though this forms no part of the explicit subject-matter of the book, it is throughout implicitly present in the treatment of the subject-matter.

In developing my main theme, I propose to trace three broadly distinct and equally fundamental interpretations of moral experience, the Christian-Platonic or religious, the Utilitarian or secular, and the Humanist. The first two are historically speaking fundamental; the third is a relatively modern development out of the other two. It is not for that reason less fundamental in another sense—in the sense that it is as total an interpretation of moral experience as the other two. But, viewed historically, what I call the Humanist tradition is derivative from the other two, and is therefore best understood in relation to those two older traditions. These accordingly need first to be briefly characterised.

What is chiefly to be remarked about these two parent traditions, the Platonic-Christian and the Utilitarian, is that they are radically distinct interpretations of moral experience, in essential respects, indeed, mutually exclusive interpretations of moral experience. As such, they diverge upon many vital points, but pre-eminently upon a single, central point, which is love—the nature and importance of love in the moral life.

On one side of the dividing line stand those moralists who believe in the transforming power of love as an intrinsic constituent of moral experience, and in man's capacity to be transformed by love as an intrinsic constituent of human nature. These moralists accordingly give to love a decisive place in their moral systems; and in the history of European moral thought they happen to be the moralists in the Platonic and Christian traditions, for instance, Plato himself, St Paul and St Augustine. On the other side stand those moralists who do not believe in the reality of love as any part of man's moral nature; and this view is represented by what one may call the secular tradition of moral thought, which stems from Aristotle and includes at least some of the so-called utilitarian moral systems. The most complete and most impressive instance in English moral philosophy of a moral system that totally rejects the power of love as a constituent of moral experience is the *Leviathan* of Thomas Hobbes; and I will treat Hobbes's *Leviathan* for that reason with the fullness (and the respect) that it deserves. But there is to be found in this tradition of moral thought also another, more qualified, form of the rejection of love. This appears not to reject it outright, but seeks instead to offer a *substitute* of one kind or another—a substitute for, an approximation to, the thing itself; and this qualified type of rejection is particularly well exemplified by Aristotle and Hume. Aristotle's conception of 'friendship', set out in Book VIII of the *Nicomachean Ethics*, and Hume's eighteenth-century notion of 'social sympathy' may be taken as their respective approximations to the idea of love; and since both kinds of substitute are typical of the kind of dilution that the idea of love undergoes in the secular or utilitarian moral philosophies, it will be instructive to examine the ethical systems of Aristotle and Hume for an understanding of the effects of this kind of dilution on the analysis of moral experience.

These, then, will be my main representative authors for the two parent traditions: Plato, St Paul and (for more limited purposes) St Augustine for the first, the Platonic-Christian tradition, representing what may be called loosely the religious view of the place of love in the moral life; Aristotle, Hobbes and Hume for the second, the secular or utilitarian tradition, representing what may be called (very loosely again) the anti-religious, or even irreligious, view of love in the moral life.

It is unavoidable—indeed, a necessary part of the whole analysis—that, in tracing these fundamentally divergent views of the nature and importance of love in the moral life, I will at the same time be tracing two fundamentally divergent views of human possibility itself; two distinct views of what human nature is capable of at its furthest reach; two distinct ideals of human nature. Those who affirm the transforming power of love as an intrinsic constituent of man's nature are taking a 'high' (or 'exalted') view of human possibility; those who deny, or minimise, it are taking a 'low' (or 'base') view of human possibility. The first pitch their ideal of man as high as possible, the second pitch it as low as possible.

To use the terms 'high' and 'low', 'exalted' and 'base' in this way is, of course, to simplify rather drastically the differences between these views of human possibility. For it is impossible that these simple terms should do justice to the complexity of the particular systems we shall be examining; and they are, besides, rather invidious and rather polemical in intention and in effect. But I propose all the same to use them, partly for the sake of simplicity, chiefly because I believe them to be substantially accurate; and I will try to correct in my treatment of the particular systems, the high and the low, any impression of over-simplification that these terms may convey.

The third tradition I have called the Humanist tradition. This tradition I conceive to be distinctively modern; and the authors I have chosen to discuss as in different ways representative of it are John Stuart Mill, Matthew Arnold, F. H. Bradley, and D. H. Lawrence.

Since I propose to use the term Humanist in a rather special sense—a sense different from, though not wholly unrelated to, the various current senses in which it is used—it would perhaps be unwise to attempt to define it too positively at this stage; its full meaning will emerge in the course of my discussions of the representative authors. For the present I wish only to indicate as briefly as possible the nature of its relation to the two parent traditions and to my main theme concerning the moral life.

In respect to the religious tradition, the Platonic and the Christian but particularly the Christian,[1] it takes the simple straightforward view that it is to this tradition that we owe whatever spiritual wisdom we may possess, and that its principal, and most precious, contribution to the spiritual development of the human race is Christ's gospel of love. This is the vital common ground between the Humanist and the Christian: their common recognition of a superior or transcendent order of values, of which the supreme value is love; their common belief in the absolute unchanging reality, the absolute unchanging validity, and the absolute binding force upon men's conduct of these values; and their common rejection of the inferior perishable values by which 'the world' —the worldly world—is governed.

These transcendent values, which stand squarely opposed to the values of the world, include all the great virtues that Christ preached for the salvation of mankind: charity, or loving kindness (which is not the same as mere kindness); humility, which presupposes self-knowledge (for how should man, being what he is, not be humble if he really knows himself?); the desire to serve our fellow-men before ourselves; the readiness to forgive those who have done us injuries; the power to renounce pleasure for the sake of the good, and the power to endure suffering where there is no other way of affirming the good; and, above everything, the belief in the power of love to conquer and transform all the tragic disa-

[1] For reasons to be explained later (ch. vii below), Humanism is more directly and intimately related to the Christian side of the religious tradition than to the Platonic.

bilities which belong to man by the condition of his humanity. The Humanist, in short, affirms with the same fullness of conviction as the Christian the three great Christian virtues, faith, hope and charity: faith in the redemptive power of love and in the capacity of all men to be redeemed by love; hope for the final salvation of the world by love; charity as the universal means by which the faith and the hope are at once practised and sustained.

As a necessary consequence (or condition) of sharing the Christian scheme of values, the Humanist shares also in all essential points the Christian and Platonic view of man's moral nature. In defiance of all modernist attempts to minimise out of existence the elements of division and conflict in moral life, he stands firmly with the religious moralists, from Plato and St Paul onwards, in postulating a 'higher' self and a 'lower', and viewing all moral life as a perpetual effort of the higher to appropriate and transform the lower. The lower, for the Humanist, as for the Christian and Platonist, subsumes all the base and destructive impulses in man's nature—all those impulses that may be seen as forms of fear, vanity and greed; and the higher subsumes the Christian virtues or powers already mentioned, of which the great encompassing virtue or power is love. It is a view of man's nature that has no room in it for either a facile optimism or a facile pessimism. Man is not naturally good; on the contrary, there is much in man's nature that is vile seemingly beyond the hope of redemption. Yet he is capable of giving and receiving love; and by believing absolutely in the redeeming power of love and persistently seeking to conform his life to the law of love, he can redeem—transcend and transform—what is vile in his nature. The formula that perhaps best expresses the Humanist's attitude is that applied by T. S. Eliot to the Catholic: in respect to the moral life he, too, like the Catholic, has 'high—indeed, absolute—ideals and moderate expectations'.

This is the common ground between Christianity and

Humanism, which establishes its continuity with the first of the two parent traditions, the religious or Platonic-Christian. On the other side, however, it is linked also with the secular—the utilitarian, rationalist, scientific—tradition, in a way that the historic Christian is bound to find disappointing and even desolating. It is linked with this other, anti-religious and anti-Christian tradition in denying the reality or the necessity of a supernatural sanction for that transcendent order of values of which the crown is love. The Humanist denies both the metaphysical reality and the logical necessity of the supernatural sanction postulated by historic Christianity as the only certain foundation of this order of values which transcends the inferior perishable values of the world. For the Christian, to recognise the reality and the validity of these transcendent values is necessarily to presuppose an order of existence different in kind from the human order, which is therefore called 'divine', a Supreme Being who is the single supreme source of these transcendent values, and a divine providence by the grace of which these transcendent values are made available to men for their salvation. For the Christian, in short, the transcendent order of values I have been speaking of is transcendent only in so far as it derives from an order of existence and experience distinct from and independent of the human.

For the Humanist this is not so. For the Humanist, this order of values, whose redemptive power he affirms equally with the Christian, is transcendent within the human order alone. These values for the Humanist are absolutely real, absolutely valid and absolutely binding because, and only because, they can be proved in human experience to exceed in dignity and power the inferior perishable values of the world. They can be proved in human experience—in our day-to-day moral experience—to be productive of peace, power and joy in a way that the values of the world demonstrably are not; and such a proof, claims the Humanist, being so intimate and immediate, so thoroughly empirical and experimental, is therefore conclusive, and needs no supernatural sanctions—no God, no divine order, no divine providence, no miracles and no theology—to confirm it.

The Humanist accordingly denies the existence of God in the sense in which the historic Church has defined God; and denies also, again in the sense in which the historic Church has defined them, the existence of a divine order, a divine providence, and the divinity of Christ: he denies what the Church understands by the divinity of Christ while affirming the greatness and the uniqueness of Christ's gospel of love. And in so far as Humanism denies all that the historic Church affirms as central to its teaching, it is of course anti-Christian; and if 'Christian' is synonymous with 'religious', it is also anti-religious.

Yet the Humanism I am speaking of may, I believe, legitimately be called religious if the term 'religious' is understood in a sense broader, though not less precise, than that derived from its common historic usage. For (to argue first from what it is not) it is not merely naturalistic, like (for instance) the Humanism of Bertrand Russell and the Rationalist Press Association, whose Humanism is remarkable chiefly for what it ignores of vital human experience and for the lucid confusions of its doctrinal pronouncements. Nor is it merely scientific, since it does not share the faith of the scientific Humanist, that the redemption of man is to be sought in the methods of observation and analysis employed by the physical sciences. It has nothing in common with the so-called 'perennial philosophy' of the type popularised in recent years by Aldous Huxley, which seeks to merge all religious faiths into one and becomes as a consequence what F. H. Bradley would have called a 'bloodless abstraction'—useless for the ends of an operative faith since it commits one to nothing specific in belief or practice, and is in fact merely a painless way of enjoying the varieties of religious experience at the smallest cost. It has also nothing in common with that species of Humanism which is constituted merely of good intentions, good manners, and an agreeable disposition to reflect upon serious matters in an agreeably haphazard way, about which the kindest thing that can be said has been said by T. S. Eliot in another connexion: 'Such people confuse morals with their own good habits, the result of a sensible upbringing, prudence, and the absence of any very powerful temptation.' Such a Humanism can never have the character of a living faith; and since the Humanism I am discussing must be a living faith—for if it is not a living faith, it would be an impertinence to speak of it in the same breath with the redemptive vision of the *Gorgias*, the Epistle to the Romans and (even) the *Leviathan*—it must on no account be confused with this other variety.

So the Humanism I have in mind when I speak of 'the Humanist tradition' in English moral thought is not merely naturalistic or scientific, nor a meaningless abstraction like the perennial philosophy, nor a series of exhortations to the practice of kindness and good manners like the Humanism of the Cambridge Humanists. It is, I want to claim, a redemptive view of human possibility, a redemptive view of human destiny, and a redemptive rule of life. The phrase 'rule of life'—that which regulates human life and conduct—is one of the strict meanings of the word 'religion'; and if it can be shown that the Humanism I am speaking of is, or can be, such a redemptive rule of life, its claim to be regarded as, in this strict sense of the word, *religious* will, I think, be established. In my discussions of John Stuart Mill, Matthew Arnold, F. H. Bradley and D. H. Lawrence, I will accordingly try to explain the sense in which their Humanism is a religious as distinct from a scientific or naturalistic Humanism.

One last point perhaps needs to be stressed. Since the Humanist tradition is so modern a phenomenon as to be still (in the Platonic phrase) in a state of 'becoming' rather than of 'being'—still incompletely and imperfectly 'realised', still an ideal rather than an actuality—the authors I have chosen as representative of this tradition all exhibit its ideal characteristics in an imperfect and incomplete way. It will therefore be necessary in my treatment of these authors to show not only how each is representative of the Humanist position but also how each, in his own interesting and instructive way, falls short of the Humanist ideal.[1]

The second, subsidiary object of this book has to do with the literary aspects of philosophical writing; and what I hope to show is that it is of the first importance in the reading of a philosophical work to give the closest attention to the strictly literary features of the philosopher's statement of his doctrine. By this I mean not only such obvious matters as the use of imagery, fable, rhetorical figures and other common poetic devices, but also (and more important) those more elusive features of tone, emphasis, personal accent belonging to the writer's 'voice'—what in literary criticism proper we are accustomed to recognising as the special signs of the individual, the distinctive, the unique in poetic expression. What I want to argue, in short, is that it is as necessary in the reading of a philosophical work as in the reading of a poem, a play or a novel to give the closest attention to everything that is usually huddled together under the name of 'style'.

Now style in philosophical writing is commonly treated in a rather perfunctory way; and it is so treated for the reason

[1] The most complete and perfect religious Humanist of the last age is Henry James, who has provided (among so much else) the best definition of the religious spirit as the Humanist understands it. This occurs in one of his autobiographical works called *Notes of a Son and Brother*, in which he seeks to define the religious spirit of his father, the elder Henry James, a distinguished theologian and moralist. It consisted, writes James, in 'the recognition of an order of goodness and power greater than any that this world can show', yet (he adds) 'unaccompanied with a single one of the outward or formal, the theological, devotional, ritual, or even implicitly pietistic signs by which we usually know it'. If it is understood that this recognition of an order of goodness and power greater than any that this world can show implies also a total submission to it, and that by the phrase 'this world' James means, not this world as opposed to another, divine world, but, simply, the worldly world and its values, the formula may be taken to express as exactly and felicitously as may be desired the fundamental position of a religious Humanism. James's Humanism, however, is too large a matter to be undertaken in this study, and its treatment has accordingly been reserved for a separate work.

that it is taken to be strictly extrinsic to what is understood to be the content or substance of the writer's doctrine. This is not to say that qualities of style are entirely ignored by professional philosophers. Even the least aesthetically developed of the writers of philosophical text-books have not failed to notice and commend some of the more striking examples of good style in philosophical writing—Hume's eighteenth-century elegance, for instance, the dramatic intensity that Plato achieved by means of the dialectical method, the fine metaphorical vivacity of Hobbes's *Leviathan*, and so on. Nevertheless, the tendency of professional philosophers is to regard the style of a philosopher as hardly more than an agreeable ornament to the content or substance of his doctrine, which, on this view, is assumed to be independent of the writer's way of expressing it and therefore amenable to paraphrase without significant loss of meaning. On this view, any preoccupation with the details of expression or style in a philosophical work must accordingly seem a trifle gratuitous since it cannot be supposed to contribute anything of significance to our understanding of the doctrine itself.

Against this view I want to urge the claims of style in its widest sense as an important source of illumination to us in our effort to understand the doctrine itself, and the consequent importance of bringing to bear upon the reading of a philosophical text the same literary—or, rather, literary-critical—skills that we exercise in the reading of poems, plays and novels. In urging this, I do not wish in the least to minimise the differences between works of poetry and works of philosophy. These are, of course, real and important; and nothing is gained for the better understanding of either by any attempt to approximate poetry to philosophy or philosophy to poetry. I wish only to draw attention to the significant common ground that may be seen to exist between poetry and philosophy when both are viewed as products of the creative imagination. For it is only when they are viewed in this way that the importance in philosophical study of a developed literary sensibility (with all that this implies) may be most readily understood and appreciated.

Viewing poetry and philosophy, then, as equally products of the creative imagination, what essentially they have in common is not difficult to discern. A philosophical system, in the same way as a poem, a play or a novel, expresses its author's interpretation of reality—his 'vision' of reality, as we call it, when it is especially comprehensive and coherent and intense; and when the philosophical system in question happens to be a system of moral philosophy, what it essentially expresses—what it essentially *is*—is a systematic rendering or interpretation of the author's fundamental moral experience, his vision of human possibility. Now since it is *his* interpretation, *his* vision, *his* system, it is necessarily as individual an affair as a play, a poem or a novel: *Leviathan* is as intensely personal a statement of Hobbes's vision of human life as *King Lear* is of Shakespeare's; and every argument, every passage of ratiocination, in the *Gorgias* or the *Republic* is as intimate an expression of Plato's interpretation of his life's experience as the most concrete image and the most evocative cadence in a poem by Blake or by Hopkins or by Yeats is an intimate expression of Blake's or Hopkins' or Yeats' vision of life.

To insist in this way on the individual or personal aspect of a philosophical system is not, of course, in the least to threaten its objectivity. For what the word 'objective' means in this context is, simply, 'possessing the widest validity'—in some instances, a universal validity. In a poem, a play or a novel, to possess this sort of objectivity is, we know, never incompatible with its being an intensely individual or personal statement; and what is true in this respect of a poem, a play or a novel is equally true of a philosophical system: its objectivity, its universal validity, is never incompatible with its being a projection of a personal vision of reality. Every product of the creative imagination is individual or personal—'subjective'—in so far as it is, and must be, the projection of a personal vision; and it is at the same time thoroughly objective in so far as it has a validity transcending the merely individual and personal.

If it is granted that every philosophical system, just like any poem, play or novel, is a statement of a highly personal interpretation of reality, it must also be granted that the distinctive quality—the individual, the unique quality—of a philosophical system, as of a poem, a play or a novel, will lie in the rendering of that vision of reality, in other words, in the details of the execution. For it is in the details of the execution that the interpretation or vision is 'realised', as we say in literary criticism; it is the execution, and this alone, that gives us access to the kind and quality of the life's experience in which the whole system is grounded, and, where the system happens to be a system of moral philosophy, to the kind and quality of the writer's sense of human possibility and so of his whole view of life. And since the validity of the whole system is tested ultimately by the kind and quality of the writer's 'sense of life', and since the quality of that sense of life is rendered accessible to us only in and through the details of the execution, it follows that we will only discover the full meaning of the system—of the doctrine, that is—by giving the closest attention to the details of the execution; and if this is not, in some sense, an exercise in literary discrimination and judgment, it will be very difficult to say what it is.

If this analysis is correct, the conclusion would seem to be inescapable, that to discover the full meaning of a philosophical doctrine, or specifically a moral doctrine, it is necessary to attend to the details of the execution, and that this, being in a wide but exact sense a literary phenomenon, invites a literary response analogous to that which we give to a poem, a play or a novel. But to say this is to bring us up against our first difficulty. For there is indeed this difference between a work of philosophy and a work of poetry, that a great deal more of the substance of a philosophical work can in fact be grasped and adequately reproduced without much reference to the literary features of the style of presentation. This is true, most conspicuously, of that part of almost every philosophical system that consists in its system of definitions and distinctions. For these definitions and distinctions are usually expressed in a terminology more or less technical or scientific, and as such would seem to fall outside the province of literary response and judgment. Indeed, at their most technical they would seem to be no more amenable to literary criticism than the symbolic language of a mathematical system: Plato's theory of Forms in the *Republic*, Hobbes's materialist doctrine of perception in the opening sections of *Leviathan*, Locke's elaborate doctrine of 'ideas' in the *Essay concerning Human Understanding* are instances of the kind of philosophical material upon which literary skills would seem to have little bearing.

This is all quite true, yet with certain important qualifications. In the first place, it is true chiefly of those branches of philosophy that are not our chief concern, namely, logic and epistemology. It is much less true of moral philosophy, where the basic distinctions and definitions are rarely technical in the sense in which they are so in logic and the theory of knowledge. They may indeed be expressed in language which involves extensions or modifications of the common meanings of words; and sometimes, in our study of the earlier writers in our tradition in particular, some special knowledge, historical and etymological, may be needed to grasp nuances of meaning that would otherwise be missed, often with disastrous effects upon our understanding of the doctrine. But such special knowledge is, after all, not different in kind from the similar knowledge that is needed for reading Chaucer or Shakespeare or Donne or Milton, and it cannot therefore be regarded as a difficulty peculiar to the study of philosophy.

The argument, then, that the technical or quasi-technical language of philosophy puts it out of the reach of the 'literary' approach that I am urging, has no serious force. The rendering or 'style' of execution of a philosophical system remains a literary phenomenon in the sense I have indicated, and as such demands an attention to the details of the philosopher's style very similar to that which we give to the literary details of a poem, a play or a novel.

The details themselves, however, are different; and this is the next point of difference between poetry and philosophy to be considered. In poetry, the basic elements of the poet's art (to reduce it to the briefest formula possible) are imagery and musical rhythm—what we think of as material primarily sensuous and concrete; and in every work of poetry what gives us access to the poet's meaning is the organisation of imagery and the patterning of musical rhythm. In one sense, indeed, the organisation of imagery and the patterning of musical rhythm together *create* meaning in poetry. In philosophy, on the other hand, the elements are *arguments* or ratiocinations. The single argument in a piece of philosophy may be said to correspond to a single image in a poem, a sequence of arguments to a complex of images organically held together by the rhythmic pattern; and in philosophy it is therefore the organisation of the arguments—the *logical* movement from premises to conclusions, from the basic definitions to the logical implications of those definitions—that creates philosophical meaning.

This is a real and important difference; but it is not absolute and irreducible. The history of English poetry alone yields plenty of instances of poets who have made poetry out of ratiocinations: Shakespeare and Donne among our older poets, T. S. Eliot among contemporary poets, are sufficiently familiar examples. And, on the other side, there have been philosophers—Plato, Hobbes and F. H. Bradley are among these—who have contrived to do much of their ratiocination in and through images; and have even in the presentation of their argument sought the aid of rhythm, in an enlarged sense of the word—in the sense that their systems exhibit, both in the parts and as a whole, something that it is difficult not to see as a dramatic structure, a kind of patterned movement.

This (in Plato, for instance, and in Hobbes) may be as intensely and intricately organised as the dramatic movement of a Shakespeare tragedy or a Hopkins sonnet or a late novel of Henry James; and the point about their use of rhythm and imagery is that it is not used merely for ornament, nor even merely to reinforce their meaning, but actually to express their meaning.

So the difference between poetry and philosophy in this respect is not as absolute and irreducible as is commonly supposed. Nevertheless, this difference between what may be called the poetic mode of rendering experience and the philosophic mode remains real and important. The poet, in so far as he is a poet, is perpetually transmuting all his life's experience, the intellectual as well as the sensuous, into images and musical rhythm; and the philosopher, in so far as he is a philosopher, is perpetually generalising all his experience into matter for ratiocination.

This difference must not be ignored or minimised; and it leads us to the largest, most fundamental, difference of all—that between the so-called 'concreteness' of poetry on the one side, the so-called 'abstractness' of philosophy on the other. Poetry, in the comprehensive sense in which the term is used here, is concerned, we know, with life in the concrete. Whatever else it may or may not do as well, it must, if it is to succeed as poetry, exhibit—render, recreate—the immediate quality of life. It must give us the sense of life in its felt particularity, the quality of life as it is known in immediate experience. Philosophy, on the other side, is abstract. It is concerned to make generalisations *about* life, not to exhibit the particularities *of* life. Like poetry, it is of course concerned with life; yet not life as it is known in immediate experience, but life mediated by concepts or ideas, transfixed, immobilised, within the categories of thought.

Another way of putting the same point is to say that philosophy seeks to penetrate to the causes, the grounds or the reasons of things, not (again) to render the qualities of things;

and what the philosopher finally creates is a system of such causes or reasons, a structure of theory, which is abstract in the sense that it is (or seems to be) wholly removed from those concrete realities that form, directly and immediately, the material of poetry. Consequently, while the fundamental criterion of poetic achievement is the vividness and the intensity with which it renders the quality of life, the measure of philosophical achievement is, or seems to be, merely the comprehensiveness and coherence of its system of causes or reasons, its system of abstractions.

This difference is certainly real and important; yet it, too, is not absolute and irreducible. What we find, on closer examination, is that this well-established antithesis of concrete and abstract raises our central problem rather than resolves it; and the particular problem that it raises is that of the generalising power of the poetic mind itself. Coleridge, speaking somewhere about what he calls 'the subjective genius' of the poet, has something brilliantly apposite to say on this point. The 'subjective genius' consists in the power or disposition of the poetic mind to be 'intensely watchful of its own acts and shapings, [to] think while it feels in order to understand, and then to generalise that feeling'; and this defines, with admirable precision, what must be recognised as the philosophic aspect of the poetic mind. It reminds us that we in fact habitually praise the great poets, not only for the vividness and the intensity with which they are able to render the quality of life, but also for their depth of insight, the largeness, or comprehensiveness, of their understanding, the coherence of their vision of life, and sometimes even their grasp of the reality underlying the appearances of things. These surely are qualities that no man can possess unless he does possess the power (in Coleridge's phrase) 'to generalise his feelings'; unless he has, to some extent, in some sense, engaged in the philosopher's business of seeking the true wisdom, which is to see reality, or some part of it, in its largest, most general, light. This aspect of the great poet's achievement is, in the widest sense, philosophical; and it is inseparable from his strictly poetic achievement.

On the other side, the best philosophers, though they labour all the time with generalities, frequently surprise us by intimations of their sense of the qualities of things. Indeed the best of them—Plato again, and Hobbes and Bradley, and even Aristotle and John Stuart Mill—are, like the best poets, a perpetual threat to the conventional distinction between the abstractness of philosophy and the concreteness of poetry. For they give us, so intensely, the sense of being in touch with the concrete, indeed of never having lost touch with it, but only of having, as Coleridge says, generalised the particulars of experience, and generalised in such a way as to involve ultimately no loss of particularity. When such a philosopher sets out his system of abstractions, this sense of the concrete quality of life lingers about it like a fragrance, recalling to us—even, in its own implicit and indirect way, recreating for us—that immediate sense of life which the philosophic passion for abstraction has been powerless to exorcise.

I do not suggest that all philosophers achieve this poetic dimension, any more than all poets achieve the philosophical dimension I spoke of just now. But it is in this connexion precisely that I conceive the ultimate value of a developed literary sensibility to be capable of showing itself in the study of philosophy. For as in the study of poetry the special task of a developed literary sensibility is to discriminate between the great and the good, between the good and the not-so-good, the not-so-good and the downright bad, and the downright bad and the wholly non-existent (for there is much that passes as poetry that is in fact wholly non-existent as poetry), so in the study of philosophy the developed literary sensibility has a similar function to perform. Its function is likewise to discriminate between one kind and quality of philosophic achievement and another; between those philosophic systems that are in fact dry-as-dust because emptied of all traces of the concrete from which once they were derived, and those that evoke for us a living sense of the qualities of things out of the very heart of the distinctions and definitions that make up the system as a system.

This I conceive to be the ultimate task of a developed literary sensibility in the study of philosophy. But the ultimate task fortunately is reducible in practice to a number of more modest tasks; and it is to these that I will address myself in the discussion of my selected authors and texts, with the object of showing what may be gained for the understanding of philosophical works by reading them with one's literary senses as wide awake as possible.

PART I

RELIGIOUS AND SECULAR

CHAPTER II

VIRTUE FOR LOVE

PLATO'S 'GORGIAS'

ONE reason for choosing the *Gorgias* as my representative Platonic text was that it seemed especially well suited to showing what may be gained for the understanding of a philosophical work by the kind of literary reading I spoke about in the last chapter. This applies in particular to the dialectical method itself, which I propose to treat, at least partly, as a dramatic convention in a sense of the term 'convention' analogous to that in which we speak of the 'poetic convention' of Elizabethan and Jacobean drama or the 'naturalistic convention' of Ibsen's drama; and I will try to elucidate the organisation of Plato's argument in the *Gorgias* in such a way as to suggest its intimate dependence upon Plato's use of the dialectical method—in the same way as (for instance) the complex organisation of a Shakespeare tragedy can be shown to depend on Shakespeare's use of the conventions of the poetic drama, or that of *A Doll's House* upon Ibsen's use of the conventions of the naturalistic drama. As a part of this task of exhibiting the dialectical method as a dramatic technique or convention, it will be necessary to give special attention to the dramatic characters of Socrates' opponents in the *Gorgias*, namely, Gorgias himself, Polus and Callicles. For it is of the utmost importance to understand Plato's dramatic intention with each of these characters in order to understand the dramatic structure of the whole argument; and this is likely to remain obscure unless one is fully receptive to the literary evidences that alone make it accessible to the attentive reader.

My main reason, however, for choosing the *Gorgias* is that

I believe it to be the greatest of Plato's Dialogues before the *Republic.* Indeed, among the Dialogues that show us Plato as strictly a moralist, it is perhaps the greatest of them all. For its interest is overwhelmingly moral and religious. There is as little as possible of explicit metaphysical or epistemological or ontological matter to deflect the course of the moral argument—no theory of 'reminiscence', for instance, as in the *Meno*, no doctrine of 'forms,' as in the *Republic.* There is, of course, a good deal of this more purely philosophical matter present by implication; and at least one of the great Platonic distinctions, the distinction between knowledge and opinion, which is to be more fully developed in the *Republic*, is explicitly touched upon here, as it had already been touched upon in some of the earlier Dialogues. But predominantly the *Gorgias* is concerned with moral and religious problems, and can be read and understood with as little reference as possible to Plato's purely philosophical system.

The *Gorgias* is interesting also for our purpose for the way in which it combines the peculiar virtues of the earlier Dialogues on the one hand and those of the *Republic* on the other. In point of Plato's handling of the famous dialectical method, the *Gorgias* stands closer to the earlier Dialogues than to the *Republic.* In the *Gorgias*, as in the earlier Dialogues, the dialectical method is used as a genuine instrument of enquiry. Socrates has the air of genuinely not knowing the answer before he starts, of working his way through to an answer by the give-and-take of the dialectical exchanges with his three adversaries. Consequently each of the three adversaries really gets a fair innings; each is allowed to state his case as forcibly as possible, and in the argument itself to make things as difficult as possible for Socrates. The result is that they all emerge as full dramatic characters; and the development of the theme has all the tension of a genuine drama and all the freshness of a genuine process of exploration and discovery.

In this respect the *Gorgias* stands out in contrast to the *Republic*, where the dialectical presentation of the arguments gives the impression, after about the Second Book, of being a somewhat artificial, even a somewhat mechanical, device rather than an instrument of enquiry. Plato, one feels, now *knows* all the answers, and really only wants to make positive affirmations, to set out his mature doctrine as fully and persuasively as possible. The adversaries in the *Republic* are accordingly more or less puppets, who are there for the most part only to express assent or dissent as Plato's exposition of his doctrine requires; and the structure of the whole is commensurately less dramatic than that of the *Gorgias*—though not less brilliant in its own literary mode, which one might call the expository and declamatory as distinct from the dramatic.

On the other hand, the *Gorgias* stands closer to the *Republic* in being much more affirmative, and about a greater range of fundamental matters, than the earlier Dialogues. In such a Dialogue as the *Protagoras*, for instance, Socrates seems not to mind coming to no conclusions at all, so long as the several points of view of the contestants are fully exhibited and the several possibilities of a solution suggested. Indeed, in the *Protagoras*, Socrates takes a special delight in showing how the dialectical method can lead to a complete reversal of positions between the adversaries. Protagoras finds at the end of the Dialogue that he has been led round to the position that Socrates proposed at the beginning, and Socrates finds that he, in his turn, has come round to the position that Protagoras had started with. The *Protagoras* among the earlier Dialogues is therefore one of the best or 'purest' examples of the functioning of the dialectical method as, strictly, a method of enquiry. In the *Gorgias*, however, Socrates does mind about the conclusions; he does wish to affirm positive doctrines about the moral life and the political life; and Plato accordingly takes care so to arrange the dialectical exchanges that he shall have every opportunity to make these affirmations at full and conclusive length.

What is the *Gorgias* about? It is not easy to give a summary account of its multifold theme; but it may help to consider first what it is that Socrates particularly desires to expose in this Dialogue. This is, in the first instance, the art of rhetoric as it is taught by the Sophists, of whom Gorgias, famous teacher of rhetoric, and Polus, his disciple, are here the chosen representatives.

The art of rhetoric, which is the art of persuasive discourse in the public assemblies, is shown in the *Gorgias* to exhibit all the vicious characteristics of what would now be called 'propaganda' in the most opprobrious sense of the word, or—more opprobriously still, and more colloquially—the art of sales-talk, the art of ballyhoo, as practised by the vendors of moral and political merchandise. Socrates chooses to make his attack on rhetoric the point of departure for his broader attack on the whole morality that it presupposes, namely, the morality of worldly success—that view of the moral life that takes worldly success for its chief good and recognises no other measure of the good life. This broader theme emerges when Socrates, having disposed of Gorgias and Polus, takes issue with Callicles, his most formidable opponent, who has put into practice the moral philosophy of the Sophists, has found that it works to admiration, and is therefore able to argue the case with a special confidence and a special authority.

The specific false doctrines that Socrates undertakes to discredit as the main part of his attack on the morality of worldly success may be reduced to two. The first is the doctrine that Might is Right, the view, that is, proposed first by Polus and afterwards by Callicles, that power is identical with virtue, and that the acts of the powerful are the sole measure of what is right. The second false doctrine that Socrates undertakes to expose is necessarily implied by the first, and is that proposed by Callicles, namely, that the pleasant is the measure of the good, that the good is identical with the pleasant, and that the just or virtuous life is that which takes the pursuit of pleasure as its final good.

THE DIALECTICAL METHOD[1]

The method by which Socrates exposes the morality of worldly success is the dialectical method; and the exposure consists in showing that this morality is self-contradictory, therefore self-destructive, therefore false. This indeed is the basic assumption of the dialectical method, that a position that can be shown to be self-contradictory thereby destroys itself, is therefore false, and must therefore be abandoned. If (as is at least conceivable) the 'answerer' in a dialectical exchange (as the opponent in a dialectical exchange is technically called) should choose to repudiate this assumption: if he should choose to say 'I grant that my position is self-contradictory, but I deny that it is therefore false'; or (with a different emphasis, which would normally be called cynical), 'I know that my position is self-contradictory but *I don't care if it is*, and I will continue all the same to maintain it'—in either case the dialectical method is immediately rendered inoperative. For as it takes two to make a quarrel, so it also takes two to make a rational argument; and rational argument is obviously impossible when either party to the argument denies the very condition of rational discourse itself.

So the dialectical method proceeds upon this as its first assumption, that a false doctrine will expose itself *as* false by exposing itself as self-contradictory. If therefore, in the *Gorgias*, the morality of worldly success taught by the Sophists is a false doctrine, it is bound, on this principle, to collapse into incoherence once its implications have been fully understood. And Socrates, who believes that the Sophists' view of the moral life *is* false, conducts his exposure of their teaching on just this principle: he draws out, step by step, the logical implications of what each of his opponents has affirmed, or assented to, as true; and then shows that these implications cannot be maintained without self-contradiction.

[1] I have discussed the principles of the dialectical method more fully in Appendix A, 'Some Principles of Socrates' Dialectical Method'.

The second assumption, which is closely connected with the first, has to do with what may be called the *common ground* between the 'questioner' and the 'answerer', the 'common ground' of moral beliefs and attitudes between Socrates and his adversaries, upon which depends the very possibility of exposing the false and affirming the true.[1]

It soon becomes evident from a study of the Platonic Dialogues that one of the main gifts of the master of dialectic is his power to discern *in advance* what propositions—what moral truths, that is—each of his opponents would desire to affirm or be ready to concede. Now this power implies the power to discern in advance what common moral beliefs and attitudes he can assume as *shared* by himself and his adversary, and can therefore draw upon in his argument. For—and the point cannot be sufficiently emphasised—the whole dialectical method depends upon the actual existence of some such common ground between the 'questioner' and the 'answerer'. If there is none, the method is once more rendered inoperative; for it is only by appealing to this common ground that Socrates is able to expose the self-contradictory character of his adversary's position.

The way he does it is most easily grasped by the aid of a simple diagrammatic image. Imagine two overlapping circles, one representing Socrates' whole moral doctrine, the other the adversary's whole moral doctrine. The overlapping portion will then represent the common ground between Socrates' position and his adversary's—the moral beliefs and attitudes that they in fact share (though of course only Socrates, the master of dialectic, knows this: the adversary does not—and upon this hangs the whole dialectical tale). Given, then, that Socrates' position and the adversary's overlap in the way suggested, what Socrates does is to show the adversary that this area of shared moral beliefs and attitudes is *inconsistent* with the rest of his (the adversary's)

[1] This valuable point was made by R. L. Nettleship in his notes on the *Gorgias* printed in *Philosophical Remains* (ed. A. C. Bradley, 2nd ed., 1901).

moral position and *consistent* only with the moral position that Socrates himself desires to affirm. Or (reverting to our diagram of the overlapping circles) what Socrates demonstrates is that the overlapping portion belongs, logically, not to the circle representing the adversary's position but to the circle representing his own.

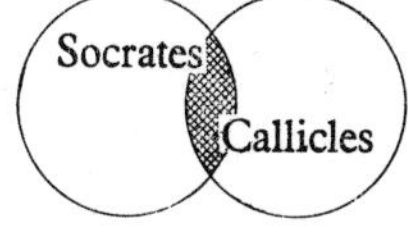

This, stated as simply as possible, is the analysis of the Socratic method of exposing the adversary's position as self-contradictory. It is, in each instance, self-contradictory in the sense that what the adversary affirms or assents to as true is seen to be in fact no part of the moral position that he believes himself to be maintaining, but turns out, on the contrary, to be a part of the moral doctrine he believes himself to be rejecting, this being the doctrine that Socrates wishes to maintain. And the reason that the adversary believes what he believes is that he is muddled, confused, unable to tell what, logically speaking, belongs where; and it is this unhappy condition that the master of dialectic undertakes to remedy.

There is one further point to make in this connexion. This vital common ground between the 'questioner' and the 'answerer' in a dialectical dispute—between Socrates and his adversaries in the *Gorgias*, for instance—can be narrow or broad. And so there is an obvious dramatic propriety in doing what Plato does in the *Gorgias*, namely, in so arranging the Dialogue that the common ground shared by Socrates with his three successive adversaries is presented in an order of diminishing magnitude. That is to say, the common ground is broadest between Socrates and Gorgias, narrower between Socrates and Polus, narrowest—indeed, diminished almost out of existence—between Socrates and Callicles. And that is why the exchange with Gorgias is comparatively brief: Gorgias, in effect (though he does not know it), shares so *much* of Socrates' position that it is comparatively easy for Socrates to convince Gorgias that the rest of his position—what he does *not* share with Socrates—must be false. With Polus, the common ground is much narrower, consequently less can be assumed as shared and more has to be proved—and the contest with Polus is therefore longer and fiercer. And it is longest and fiercest with Callicles, with whom there is the minimum of common ground, therefore as little as possible to be assumed as shared, and consequently as much as possible to be proved.

These are some of the elementary principles of the method by which Socrates conducts his great enquiries into the foundations of moral and political life in the *Gorgias*; and Socrates' adversaries, Gorgias, Polus and Callicles, having been put there by Plato on condition that they play the game according to the rules, do in fact observe the rules, and Socrates is therefore able to show each of them that the position he is seeking to maintain cannot be maintained without self-contradiction, that it is therefore false, and must therefore be abandoned. This part of his task takes up a good portion of the Dialogue for the important reason that Socrates has first to break down the resistance of his adversaries and induce in them what theologians call 'a pious disposition of the will' in order that they may be rendered properly receptive to the positive doctrine that he is presently to set out. The positive doctrine indeed already emerges in this negative process of breaking down his adversaries' positions; it is only made more fully explicit in the latter part of the Dialogue.

This positive doctrine, it will be seen, is grounded in what is in essence a religious view of life, on that wider definition of the religious spirit which stresses its recognition of, and submission to, an order of values transcending in dignity and power the values of the world. It would be going too far to say that it is the Christian view of life that Socrates is giving us in the *Gorgias*, or even, in the strictest sense, an anticipation of the Christian view. For in Socrates' scheme of salvation there is no God in the full Christian sense, there is no Revelation, and there is no Redeemer. But what can be said is that it has close affinities with the Christian view as a whole, and the closest affinities, in particular, with some of the principal teachings of the New Testament.

Socrates' main affirmations in the *Gorgias* can leave us in no doubt about the connexion. That it is better to suffer injustice than to inflict it; that the end of the moral life is the pursuit of the good, not the pleasant; that what Socrates calls 'punishment', what Christians would call 'expiation' following on 'repentance', is a means of purification, a cleansing of the soul polluted by sin—these are some of the main affirmations that make up Socrates' teaching in the *Gorgias*. They make up his 'strange doctrine', as his adversaries in the *Gorgias* several times call it, thereby expressing, besides their derision and hostility, their sheer perplexity at what Socrates is urging them to believe; and it is one of Plato's minor dramatic achievements in the *Gorgias* that he is able to convey so vividly the disquieting effects upon the pagan mind of this strange near-Christian doctrine that Socrates is preaching. In any case, we cannot forget as we read the *Gorgias* that this is the doctrine for which Socrates died, for which, in effect, he was martyred; and this adds much poignancy to a doctrine that would already command sufficient interest by the passion and the authority with which it is enunciated.

The great central argument of the *Gorgias* is developed in three distinct stages. The first round is with Gorgias himself—Gorgias, famous teacher of rhetoric, who believes, honestly and sincerely, that the art he has taught so successfully for so many years is really a beneficent art, or at least has done more good than harm, and whose worst faults are no worse than a certain self-complacency and the usual hopeless confusion of the academic as to the ultimate end to which his art is directed. Gorgias, in short, is the type of professional man one cannot help liking and respecting in spite of his obvious shortcomings; and in the exchange with Socrates, he counters Socrates' attack on his profession with firmness, moderation and some dignity.

Socrates starts off, characteristically, with a request for a definition. 'What, Gorgias, does rhetoric *mean*? What *is* this art that you profess to teach?' Gorgias makes a few false starts; he suggests, for instance, that rhetoric teaches the art of discourse; but that obviously will not do, since it plainly does not teach the art of mathematical discourse or medical discourse or nautical discourse. It must teach something else; and this, it presently emerges, is the art of persuasion. What, then (asks Socrates), does it persuade *about*? It does not, clearly, persuade about medicine or mathematics or shoe-making or ship-building: it persuades (Gorgias finally replies, after much hedging) judges in the law-courts, statesmen in the council chamber, the commons in the market-place, any audience in any assembly connected with public affairs, about what is *just* and *unjust*—that is, good and bad, right and wrong—in the particular case that is being argued.[1]

Socrates declares himself more than satisfied: that was just what he himself had suspected Gorgias' art might be about. And then, invoking a distinction familiar in Greek thought, the distinction between 'knowledge' and 'opinion', he enquires: But, Gorgias, does rhetoric concern itself to teach *knowledge* of justice and injustice, or merely *opinion* concerning these things? That is to say, is the art of rhetoric grounded in a *true* notion of justice and injustice, a *true* conception of the moral life; or is it content to rest itself merely upon the views of justice and injustice currently accepted? Gorgias, having already conceded (as no educated Greek could fail to concede) that 'knowledge' and 'opinion' are

[1] *Gorgias*, 452 E–454 B.

two different things, answers firmly that rhetoric concerns itself with 'opinion'—that is, with the currently accepted views of what is just and unjust, good and bad, right and wrong;[1] and then launches into a lengthy, and very persuasive, discourse on the art of rhetoric, which turns upon two main claims. The first is that it is the peculiar merit of rhetoric that it can successfully persuade about *all* subject-matters, even those the rhetorician knows nothing about. For instance, he can persuade men of the virtues of medicine, or of a particular course of medical treatment, even though he has no medical knowledge; and he can persuade any assembly, simply by his mastery of the art of rhetoric, to appoint him, the ignorant rhetorician, to a public office rather than a man whose 'knowledge' really qualifies him for the job. 'So great, so strange, is the power of this art', Gorgias concludes with some complacency. But, further, Gorgias argues (remembering that the Sophists had come in for a good deal of public criticism for allegedly corrupting the minds of their pupils by teaching them to make the worse cause appear the better, and in general turning out some thoroughly undesirable characters), the art of rhetoric must be regarded as no more than a *technique* of persuasion. As such, it is capable of being used well or ill—that is, justly or unjustly; and therefore (concludes Gorgias) the teacher of rhetoric is not to be blamed if at least some of his pupils use it for unjust ends, in the interest of unjust causes.[2]

The argument with Gorgias is approaching its climax. Socrates chooses to take up Gorgias' first claim. Let us allow that the master of the art of rhetoric can indeed persuade a multitude about subject-matters of which he has no knowledge whatever—medicine, for instance, and all the special arts and sciences; yet (asks Socrates) does this ignorance extend also to all that pertains to justice and injustice, good and bad, right and wrong—which is, *by Gorgias' own definition*, the subject-matter of the art of rhetoric? And (Socrates goes on), if at

[1] *Ibid.* 455 A.

[2] *Ibid.* 456 A–457 C.

least in all that pertains to justice and injustice, it is necessary to have knowledge as distinct from mere opinion, who (Socrates asks) is to teach the young rhetorician who aspires to become a master of the art of rhetoric the nature of justice and injustice, that is, the true morality? Whence is he to derive his knowledge of the avowed subject-matter of his art?

There would seem to be only two possible alternatives. The first is that he already comes to the teacher of rhetoric, like Gorgias, with the (true) knowledge of justice and injustice. In that case he is already *morally mature* when he undertakes the study of the art of persuasion; and then there can be no question of his abusing the technique of persuasion he is taught, since to be 'morally mature' *means* to be incapable of abusing the instrument to evil or unjust ends.[1] Alternatively, the pupil does not yet possess this vital knowledge; and then, presumably, the teacher of rhetoric must teach it to him. Now (asks Socrates) what does the teacher of rhetoric in fact do about this?[2] Gorgias answers (partly, no doubt, from vanity—is there anything the master of rhetoric cannot teach his pupils?) that the teacher of rhetoric does teach his pupils the knowledge of justice and injustice if they do not already possess it.[3]

This is Gorgias' fatal concession. Socrates is now able to deliver his knock-out blow, by the following characteristically 'logical' argument: He who has knowledge of building is a builder; he who has knowledge of music is a musician; he who has knowledge of medicine is a physician; therefore, he who has knowledge of justice is a just man. Therefore, he who has become master of the art of rhetoric must be a just man; therefore, he is incapable of abusing the technique of persuasion he has learnt from his teacher; therefore Gorgias' at-

[1] This is typical of Socrates' procedure. While appearing to deal only with Gorgias' first claim for the art of rhetoric, he is in fact also tackling his second claim, that rhetoric is a morally neutral technique. This other claim would be hard, probably impossible, to refute directly, but can be undermined indirectly, in the way Socrates is doing here.

[2] *Gorgias* 459 D–460 A.

[3] *Ibid.* 460 A.

tempted defence of the evil uses to which his art has been put, that it is merely a technique in itself morally neutral and capable of being used well or ill, falls to the ground.[1]

Looking back on the whole exchange with Gorgias, one can see its general direction and scope. Socrates in his genius had discerned from the start what particular true propositions Gorgias would be willing to assent to—that is, would know to be true and would sincerely acknowledge to be true. These were that rhetoric concerns itself with *morality* ('justice' and 'injustice'), that it is the business of the teacher of rhetoric to teach his pupils *true* morality (the 'knowledge' of justice and injustice), and consequently, since knowledge—real knowledge as distinct from mere 'opinion'—is virtue, to make them virtuous men. These were the parts, or fragments, of the real that Gorgias, in spite of his immersion in appearances, could still recognise and acknowledge; and Socrates had deliberately made these propositions particular, not general—not about 'the good' in general, but about the particular 'good' that the art of rhetoric was supposed to aim at—on the correct assumption that this, if any, was the good that Gorgias might be supposed to know something about and about which therefore he might be supposed to have positive convictions. And what Socrates is able to show is that Gorgias' view of his own art is confused and self-contradictory, his principal self-contradiction being, as we have seen, that he at once maintains that rhetoric undertakes to teach morality and so to make men truly virtuous, and then tries to evade the consequences of his own definition by pleading that rhetoric is a morally neutral technique. The point of exposing the self-contradiction, here as elsewhere in the Platonic Dialogues, is, of course, to suggest that Gorgias' view of his art, being confused, is to that extent false, and to the extent that it is false in theory, is likely to be bad in practice.

This, indeed, is Socrates' larger object in attacking Gorgias'

[1] *Ibid.* 460 B–461 B. This seemingly sophistical argument is further discussed in Appendix A, p. 315.

account of rhetoric, which does not emerge fully until later in the Dialogue. On its negative side, the object is to expose the debasing effect upon public life of the demagogic methods of argument and appeal practised by the politicians of the time and taught by the professional Sophists. And on the positive side Socrates is in effect affirming that this evil state of public life will not cease until those (like the Sophists) who are concerned with the education of the young do really make it their business to teach their pupils 'the knowledge of justice and injustice'—that is, true moral values—so that they may become truly *good men*, moral goodness being the only ultimate safeguard against the immoral use of an instrument as powerful as the art of rhetoric. All this is made explicit in the latter part of the Dialogue, when Socrates is drawing together the several threads of his whole argument. It comes out in particular in the great speech in which he denounces the 'elder statesmen' of Athens,[1] 'they who have filled the city full of harbours and docks and walls and revenues and all that trash, and have left no room for justice and temperance', and indicates what he conceives to be the ideal of the truly good statesman.

In the meantime, the argument enters its second stage. As Gorgias, the master, retires, Polus, his pupil, comes forward to take issue with Socrates. ('Polus' is the Greek word for 'colt' or 'filly', and the name is intended to indicate that this adversary is young, impetuous, irascible and unavoidably wrong-headed.) Polus has spotted the fatal concession upon which Gorgias foundered, and angrily taxes Socrates with having trapped Gorgias into making it. Gorgias (says Polus) was ashamed to say openly that the teacher of rhetoric has no knowledge of justice and injustice (and need have none), and that he therefore cannot (and need not) teach any such knowledge to his pupils. Moreover (adds Polus) it showed very bad taste on Socrates' part to take advantage of Gorgias' modesty on this point.[2] Socrates upon this invites Polus to

[1] *Gorgias*, 519. [2] *Ibid.* 461 c.

correct his errors by the dialectical method he himself has been using. Polus agrees to be questioner to Socrates, and begins by asking him the question he had put to Gorgias, namely, What is rhetoric?

This gives Socrates his chance to state his own positive views about the nature of rhetoric. (It is also dramatically the most appropriate point for such a statement, since Socrates has just discredited Gorgias' false view and thus cleared the ground for the true view.) Socrates' definition emphasises its character as propaganda in the modern sense, as the instrument of the demagogues who are corrupting the public life of the city. He calls it a form of *flattery*, a pseudo-art, which subsists by pandering to ('flattering') the basest appetites and most irrational prejudices of the demos for demagogic ends. At best, it is directed to the attainment of immediate, short-term political and economic ends ('filling the city full of harbours and docks and walls and revenues'), at worst, to the appropriation of personal power; but in either case, it is indifferent to the true, the ultimate, good of the people and so of the commonwealth itself. 'Flattery . . . is what I call it, and I say this sort of thing is a disgrace, Polus . . . because it aims at the merely pleasant and ignores the best. . . .'[1]

The theme of power is thus introduced; and this marks the transition to the next great stage in the argument. Polus perceives that there is an analogy between the demagogue and the tyrant: both possess absolute power, the demagogue over the minds of the people, the tyrant over their bodies as well; and both are disposed to exploit that power absolutely, without recognising any moral check other than their pleasure. Now (Polus challenges Socrates to say): is not Archelaus, the tyrant of Macedon, who has absolute power over his subjects—who can put to death anyone he pleases, deprive anyone he pleases of his property and expel him from the city—is not Archelaus the happiest of men in his possession of such absolute power? And is he not the happier as his crimes remain

[1] *Ibid.* 463 B–465 A.

unpunished, for lack of anyone more powerful than he to inflict the punishment?[1] This is Polus' challenge to Socrates; and its interest for us is that Polus speaks here not merely for a particular political theory that happened to be prevalent in fourth-century Athens, but for the perennial doctrine that underlies all totalitarian philosophies, all tyrannies and dictatorships in all times and all places: the doctrine that *might is right*, that power is self-justifying, and that the possession and exercise of absolute power is the supreme good.

Socrates accepts the challenge, and answers, No: Archelaus, the tyrant of Macedon, so far from being the happiest of men, is the most miserable of men; because—and this is Socrates' 'strange doctrine'—it is a far greater evil to do injustice than to suffer it; and the greatest of evils is to do injustice and escape punishment.

Polus is suitably staggered by this strange doctrine:

> How do you mean? If a man be caught criminally plotting to make himself a despot, and he be straightway put on the rack and castrated and have his eyes burnt out, and after suffering himself, and seeing inflicted on his wife and children, a number of grievous torments of every kind, he be finally crucified or burnt in a coat of pitch, will he be happier than if he escape and make himself despot, and pass his life as the ruler in his city, doing whatever he likes, and envied and congratulated by the citizens and the foreigners besides? Impossible, do you tell me, to refute that?[2]

Socrates answers, sensibly enough, that of two such wretched persons neither can be *happier*, but, yes, he repeats, the *more* wretched is he who establishes himself as despot and escapes punishment for his crimes. Then, perceiving that Polus is laughing, he remarks, 'Here we have yet another form of refutation—when a statement is made, to laugh it down, instead of disproving it!' To which Polus replies: 'Do you not think yourself utterly refuted, Socrates, when you make such statements as nobody in the world would assent to? You have only to ask anyone of the company here.'[3]

[1] *Gorgias*, 470D–473A. [2] *Ibid.* 473C. [3] *Ibid.* 473E–474A.

It is clear that Plato is, for dramatic purposes, deliberately prolonging the expressions of astonishment and derision with which Socrates' grand propositions are met by Polus and the rest. The doctrine is indeed very strange, very revolutionary—almost as strange and revolutionary to the pagan mind as the teaching of Christ was to be some four hundred years later; and Plato wants to make sure that we feel the full impact of this 'strange doctrine' upon the pagan mind through these reactions of Socrates' audience.

Socrates now proceeds to demolish Polus' position and establish his own. The argument by which Polus is defeated might at first sight appear to be little more than a piece of verbal fencing; but it is in fact an especially brilliant example of Socrates' skill in the use of the dialectical method, in particular (to emphasise the point again) his skill in discerning what part of the true moral order even Polus is still willing to acknowledge, and then pressing home the logical consequences of this admission by showing that it involves no less than an acknowledgement of the very propositions that Polus has denied.

It turns out that the proposition that Polus denies is that to do injustice is more *evil* than to suffer it. What he concedes, however, is that to do injustice is yet, somehow, more—the Greek word is *aeschros* and it is variously rendered in English as 'dishonourable', 'disgraceful', 'foul', 'ugly';[1] and 'ugly' is probably the best word to use because it expresses in English most sharply the antithesis that Socrates has in mind. For what Socrates has discerned is that a young worldling of Polus' type, thoroughly sophisticated but not yet cynical, will not admit that to do injustice is *evil*: that, in his emancipated view, is a lot of cant, the sort of dreary humbug that the preachers go in for. But he *is* ready to admit that to do 'injustice'—to commit acts of murder, theft, rape, acts of violence in general—is 'ugly', meaning by 'ugly' distasteful, *aesthetically* repellent. Not *morally* repellent, mind you, he

[1] Homer uses the word of Thersites: thus 'foul', 'deformed', 'ugly'.

insists on that; but, yes, aesthetically repellent; not quite decent perhaps; rather beastly, in fact; certainly, in thoroughly bad taste. (These would be the nearest Anglo-Saxon equivalents for what Polus means by the word *aeschros.*) That Polus, the young man whose moral taste is better than his moral principles, will admit; and that is enough for Socrates. For Socrates, the master of moral wisdom, knows (though he does not, of course, let on that he knows) that the good, the true and the beautiful are, in the end, all one; and their opposites, the evil, the false and the ugly are also, in the end, all one. They are, that is, in the end, reducible to one another; therefore, if it is known that a certain thing is 'beautiful', it *must* also be 'good', if 'ugly', then also 'evil'; and therefore if a man has admitted that a certain thing is beautiful (or ugly), it is possible, *must* be possible, to prove that the same thing is also good (or evil). This is the secret assumption that guides Socrates in his argument against Polus and directs it to a triumphant conclusion.

Before embarking on the demolition of Polus' position, however, Socrates deliberately makes it as difficult as possible for himself by getting Polus to affirm quite explicitly that the good and the beautiful, the evil and the ugly, are not the same:

Soc.: Now again, which is uglier—doing wrong or suffering it? Answer.

Pol.: Doing it, I say.

Soc.: And also more evil, if uglier.

Pol.: Not at all.

Soc.: I see: you hold, apparently, that beautiful and good are not the same, nor evil and ugly.

Pol.: Just so.[1]

Then Socrates proceeds to his demonstration, as follows:

If injustice, as Polus has granted, is more ugly or foul (though not more evil) than justice, then justice must be more beautiful (though not more good) than injustice.

Now a thing is beautiful (Socrates suggests) if it is pleasant or useful (beneficial) or both. Yes, says Polus; and adds, significantly,

[1] *Gorgias*, 474C–D.

'This time, Socrates, your definition is quite fair when you define what is beautiful by pleasure and *good* ('beneficial')'. Polus, in other words, *identifies the useful with the good,* and so enables Socrates to propose the new equation, that the beautiful is the pleasant or *the good* or both.

Now, if the beautiful is the pleasant or the good or both, the ugly is the painful or the evil or both.

Therefore, if of two things, *A* and *B*, *A* is more beautiful and *B* less beautiful, *A* is more beautiful than *B* in being more pleasant or more good or both; and if *A* is more ugly and *B* less ugly, *A* is more ugly than *B* in being more painful or more evil or both.

Applying this to the disputed proposition, let *A* be the doing of injustice and *B* the suffering of injustice.

Then *A*, the doing of injustice, is more ugly, and *B*, the suffering of injustice, less ugly (which is exactly Polus' contention); and *A*, the doing of injustice, is more ugly than *B*, the suffering of injustice, in being more painful or more evil or both.

But—Polus has insisted (with Archelaus, the tyrant of Macedon, in mind) that it is infinitely *more pleasant* to do injustice than to suffer it;

therefore, *A*, the doing of injustice, cannot be more ugly than *B*, the suffering of injustice, by virtue of being *more painful* (unpleasant);

therefore, the doing of injustice cannot be more ugly than the suffering of injustice by virtue of being *both* more painful *and* more evil;

therefore, the doing of injustice must be more ugly than the suffering of injustice by virtue of being *more evil.*

Now (asks Socrates), Would Polus, in any situation, choose the greater evil rather than the less? Polus answers—*has* to answer—No; and so has to admit that he would rather choose to suffer injustice, which has been shown to be the less evil, than to do injustice, which has been shown to be the greater evil.[1]

It is worth remarking the point at which Polus fatally undermines his own position. It is when he himself proposes that the 'useful' is the 'good', and thereby exposes to view the intimate link that may so often be found to exist between the most refined aestheticism and the plainest, most vulgar utilitarianism. And this identification of the useful with the

[1] *Ibid.* 474D–475E.

good, though it proves fatal to Polus' position, is nevertheless perfectly consistent with the general character of his type of cynicism: he will grant that the useful is the good, though he would certainly not grant the converse, that the good is the useful, being reluctant to commit himself to any definition of the good as such, except that it consists in the exercise of power. And Socrates, the master of dialectic, does not, of course, fail to take advantage of Polus' slip. He avoids throughout a head-on collision about the nature of the good (the 'moral'), and confining himself to the beautiful and the useful (the 'aesthetic' and the 'utilitarian') succeeds in forcing Polus to admit the proposition that he had at the start so vigorously denied.

He refutes Polus' remaining contentions by arguments on similar lines—by drawing out the implications of the definitions that Polus grants, and showing that the propositions he grants logically imply the propositions he denies, and that he cannot therefore without self-contradiction grant those and deny these. This is how Socrates forces Polus' assent to all parts of his 'strange doctrine'—that it is not only a greater evil to do injustice than to suffer it, but that it is the greatest evil to do injustice and to escape punishment, and that Archelaus, the tyrant of Macedon, who has done the greatest injustices and escaped all punishment, is therefore the most miserable of men. The whole exchange with Polus ends with a passionate exhortation from Socrates as to the proper uses of rhetoric, turning upon the suggestion that when we have been guilty of an act of injustice, we should turn our powers of persuasion, not to exculpating ourselves in order that we may escape punishment, but, rather, to *asking* for the punishment we deserve. For 'punishment' (Socrates contends) is to the diseased soul as the surgeon's knife is to the diseased body; and we must seek its aid, when, burdened with the guilt of an unjust act, we have need of it.[1] 'Repent ye that ye may be saved': this, in effect, is Socrates' message in this exhortation

[1] *Gorgias*, 480D.

to Polus; and it is, so far, quite the strangest part of his strange doctrine.

The argument of the *Gorgias* now enters upon its third and last stage. The new adversary is Callicles; and he is the most formidable of them all. Gorgias after all was only a rather simple-minded, rather muddle-headed academic, whose success as a teacher of rhetoric had no doubt given him a vested interest in the profession, but who believed, quite sincerely, that he was doing some real good by teaching the rising young politicians the art of putting things across in the public assemblies. And Polus after all was only a headlong youth, still unspoilt enough to feel the aesthetic appeal of virtue, but also spoilt enough already to be dazzled by the cult of power expressed in the might-is-right doctrine and exemplified in the history of Archelaus, the tyrant of Macedon.

In Callicles, however, we meet an adversary altogether more dangerous than either Gorgias or Polus. He is the type of the successful man of affairs, full of the personal confidence and easy Philistinism that success in the world of affairs inspires, and full also of the cynicism that experience of the world produces in such men. Callicles *knows* all about human nature. He has knocked about in the greater world of politicians and lawyers and big businessmen, the world in which top-level decisions concerning national policy, administration and so on, are daily made and unmade—the world, in short, in which the appropriation and exercise of *power* is the thing that counts for everything, and a man must know what's what to keep his head above water. So Callicles, who has successfully kept his head above water in this greater world, knows all about men and life; and what precisely he knows is disclosed to us in his long opening address to Socrates,[1] from which the dramatic character of the man emerges with a wonderful vividness.

He knows, for instance, all about the difference between

[1] *Ibid.* 482C–486D.

men's apparent motives and men's real motives. He knows that they will say one thing for appearance's sake, but will privately think quite another thing; and will, of course, always *act* from their real private motives, which are always base, never from their apparently virtuous public motives. For while for appearance's sake they may be willing to pay their tribute to virtue (Callicles calls this acting according to 'convention')—to admit, for instance, that to do injustice is a greater evil than to suffer it—what they really believe (according to 'nature', as distinct from convention) is exactly the opposite: they believe that to suffer injustice is much the greater evil, and would many times rather do injustice than suffer it—if only they had the power. Socrates simply doesn't know men (Callicles intimates) if he thinks that they care, at bottom, for anything but power and pleasure—if he thinks that anything but power and pleasure are the measure of human happiness and the end of all human endeavour.

And why (Callicles goes on) doesn't Socrates know these elementary truths about human nature? Why, because he's a philosopher: because he wastes his substance pottering about with philosophical problems, searching for what he calls the truth of things, whatever that may be; the sort of thing (says Callicles) that's well enough for boys, bright young lads who need to exercise their minds as they need to exercise their bodies; but it is distinctly not the thing for a grown man. Indeed, in a man like Socrates, the impropriety of it is quite embarrassing.

No (Callicles continues): what a man like Socrates wants to do is to get out of his ivory tower, learn to know life and men, come to grips with the realities of the practical world—the real world, from which alone the true wisdom of life is to be learnt. And what, besides everything else, this might teach him would be how to take proper care of himself in this real world, in which, whatever his high-minded pretentions, he was actually living. For (Callicles hints), if he should ever, for one reason or another, get into trouble with the authorities and be brought to trial for his life, he might (among other things) find himself a good deal less ready to despise that useful art of rhetoric that he had just been so cleverly exposing.

Plato, writing, of course, after Socrates' death, is here using the historical fact of Socrates' trial and death to give the maximum dramatic point to Callicles' derision and to Socrates' own defence of his life, which comes later in the Dialogue. Indeed, this latter part of Callicles' opening speech, in which he is exposing the absurdity of dedicating one's life to philosophical enquiry, is one of Plato's most characteristic dramatic achievements in the *Gorgias*. What makes the attack so convincing, so persuasive, and so disturbing is Callicles' tone, which is as good-humoured and cordial as it is pleasantly condescending. Callicles *likes* Socrates (he insists on that)—he likes him and wishes him well, and for that very reason so much hates to see him making a fool of himself with all this stuff about philosophy and the search for truth.

The whole sketch of Callicles is masterly; and, again, it is a perennial type that we are invited to recognise: the cynical man of the world, who, being so thoroughly at ease in Zion, is therefore the most dangerous kind of Philistine. For he has, or appears to have, such excellent grounds—such sensible, such solid, grounds—for his Philistinism; and it is this, more than anything, that gives him the power, skilfully emphasised by Plato, to present the philosophic temper in the worst possible light, as peculiarly inept, naïve and foolish, and not, distinctly not, to be taken seriously by those who really know men and life.

So this is Callicles' opening challenge to Socrates; and Socrates, in his own opening speech,[1] acknowledges Callicles' formidable character as an adversary. He praises him for his 'knowledge' (meaning his general cultivation), for his candour and his good will, and makes it clear that he positively looks forward to engaging with an adversary who so clearly

[1] *Gorgias*, 487 A.

knows what he is about, and from whom it will be impossible not to learn a great deal. This Socratic irony is intended to make it plain to us that Callicles is going to be quite the toughest of the three adversaries, and that this last stage of the argument will be especially fierce and protracted.

The contest actually begins with Callicles' reaffirmation of the might-is-right doctrine in his opening speech.[1] He has accused Socrates of taking advantage of the 'modesty'—by which he means the hypocrisy—of Gorgias and Polus; and, invoking the crucial distinction between nature and convention, Callicles argues that the concessions they made were concessions only to convention, not dictated by nature. When Polus granted that to do injustice was more ugly than to suffer it, he was granting only what was true by convention, not what was true by nature; and since Socrates must have known this (Callicles adds), it was only by a logical trick that he was able to rout Polus: by effectively taking advantage of the ambiguity of the terms, and pretending that Polus meant that to do injustice was *really* uglier, uglier *by nature*, when in fact he meant only *apparently* uglier, uglier *by convention*.

For—and now Callicles sets out his doctrine of 'might is right': it is only by convention that to do injustice is more ugly than to suffer it; by nature it is clearly more ugly—that is, more evil—to suffer injustice. The conventional attitude (he goes on to explain) has arisen from the fact that most men are too weak to inflict injustice upon others, and have for that reason, as a measure merely of self-preservation, invented the slavish doctrine that it is more evil to inflict injustice than to suffer it. The tyrant, however, who has the power to indulge his desires without fear of punishment, scorns and repudiates all such conventional checks, and thereby affirms the truth established by nature, that to do injustice is not an evil at all, and that its general condemnation is merely a necessity imposed upon the weak. This is the might-is-right doctrine:

[1] *Gorgias*, 482D–484C.

that it is always the 'stronger' that prevails by nature; and that by nature—though not by convention—it is the stronger that *ought* to prevail.

As the argument proceeds, it becomes evident that the might-is-right doctrine rests upon a particular view of the moral life which it is Socrates' main endeavour, here and elsewhere, to expose. This is the view that pleasure, being the final end that all men do pursue and cannot but pursue, is the supreme good and the only measure of the good. This point in the argument is reached by several stages of the normal dialectical enquiry, in the course of which Socrates succeeds in showing Callicles that his use of some of his basic terms—the 'stronger', the 'superior', the 'wiser', and so on—is confused and contradictory.[1] The gratifying result of these preliminary skirmishes is that Callicles' self-confidence is already undermined before the main contest properly begins with Callicles' open and explicit affirmation of an out-and-out hedonist position: that (as he puts it) 'luxury and licentiousness..., if they have the support of force, are virtue and happiness, and [everything else]—the unnatural covenants of mankind—are all mere stuff and nonsense.'[2] This, according to Callicles, is happiness, the perpetual gratification, to the furthest limits of one's power, of all the desires that can possibly be felt. Happiness and pleasure are the same thing; and the pursuit of pleasure, the gratification of desire, is the final end of all moral endeavour, and the definition of morality itself. This is the moral doctrine which has been implicit in all the false doctrines that have already been considered, which Socrates now undertakes to expose in this the last and greatest contest in the Dialogue.

It is not difficult to see why this, and no other, should be the fundamental, the bed-rock, issue between Socrates and those who are upholding the morality of worldly success, and why Socrates should reserve his heaviest artillery, so to speak, for the attack upon Callicles' hedonism. The reason is that

[1] *Ibid.* 488 B–491 C.

[2] *Ibid.* 492 C.

this kind of absolute hedonism, which recognises no qualitative differences between pleasures, which does not so much as acknowledge that some pleasures are 'good', others 'bad', destroys the very possibility of making *any* moral distinctions and *any* moral judgments. The word 'good' loses all intelligible meaning when what is merely pleasant is taken to be the measure of what is good. For then the word 'good' becomes merely a synonym for 'doing as one likes' (as Matthew Arnold called it in a similar connexion); and the doctrine of doing as one likes is only another name for that totally subjectivist and relativist view of morality which declares that all moral judgments are, in the end, a matter of personal taste, and that a man's personal taste in the matter of moral judgments is, in the end, entirely relative to those circumstances—psychological, historical, cultural, economic and so on—by which they happen to have been formed. The doctrine of doing as one likes, in short, is only another name for moral chaos.

Now Socrates discerns not only that all this is implied in Callicles' absolute hedonism, but also that Callicles' hedonist position rests ultimately upon his refusal to allow that there are any qualitative differences between pleasures. Consequently he directs his whole effort to forcing Callicles to acknowledge that some pleasures are good, others bad, or (more simply) that at least *some* pleasures are bad: to acknowledge, that is, that basic fact of our moral experience by denying which the hedonist falsifies our moral experience, and so undermines at its foundations the very possibility of moral life. The moment Callicles concedes this, that we do in fact distinguish, merely distinguish, between good and bad pleasures, he can no longer maintain his hedonist doctrine. For to make this distinction at all necessarily implies the recognition of a moral standard other than pleasure itself; every particular pleasure has then to be judged good or bad by reference to a standard which is not itself pleasure; and if this standard, which is the measure of the good, is *not* pleasure, Callicles' hedonist position must necessarily fall to the ground.

This is Socrates' task in this last stage of the argument of the *Gorgias*; and he accomplishes it in two distinct stages, which it will be of special interest to us to analyse. Each stage represents a distinct method of 'proof', a distinct method of commanding the mind's assent to a given proposition. In the first stage, Socrates proceeds by what may be called the poetic mode. He appeals directly, in a series of images of cumulative intensity, to what he knows to be the common ground of moral belief between himself and Callicles. His aim is, literally, to shock Callicles out of his hedonism by exhibiting, through a succession of linked images, the sheer loathsomeness of what it entails. Not by argument, not by ratiocination, but by concretely 'picturing' to him the concrete consequences of his hedonism, he seeks to induce in him that revulsion from moral evil which is the beginning of salvation.

This first 'proof', then, is in the nature of a direct assault upon Callicles' moral sensibility—his sensibility, as distinct from his merely rational mind, or merely logical faculty, or whatever it is we think of as the merely intellectual part of the soul when we distinguish this from that total organ of response that we call the sensibility.

Socrates starts off with the image of the leaking jar or colander (which, he says, he got from an old fable by some Sicilian or Italian writer).[1] Is not a life devoted to the pursuit of pleasure like a leaking colander—pleasures constantly being poured in and constantly pouring out? Yes, says Callicles. Socrates presses the image: Is not the life of such a man like the life of a cormorant, always hungering and always eating, always thirsting and always drinking? Yes, says Callicles still. Is he not then like a man with a skin-disease, always itching, always scratching; and will Callicles maintain that such a man is happy? 'I answer', says Callicles

[1] *Gorgias*, 493 A.

defiantly, 'that the scratcher would live pleasantly.' Socrates then relentlessly brings his little demonstration to its climax: 'And what if the scratching is not confined to the head?' The image he is now inviting Callicles to consider is the exceedingly unpleasant image of a catamite. 'And what if the scratching is not confined to the head?' Is not such a man like a catamite; and will Callicles deny that the life of a catamite is terrible, foul, miserable?[1]

Callicles does not deny it. He expresses anger and disgust (how can Socrates be so shameless as to bring in such matters in a discussion between gentlemen?); but he does not deny it. Whereupon Socrates reminds him that it had been his boast at the start of their colloquy that he, Callicles, would not be guilty of the 'modesty' (as he called it) that had undone Gorgias and Polus. And (Socrates adds) if Callicles can be so shameless as to affirm that the pleasant is the measure of the good, why, then he, Socrates, has no alternative but to show him the shameless consequences of such a doctrine.[2]

The main point, however, is that Socrates does in fact succeed by this lightning method of 'proof' in shocking Callicles into a recognition of the loathsome implications of admitting no distinction between good pleasures and bad which was the basis of his hedonist position. Callicles capitulates; and expresses his capitulation in a way that permits Socrates to make the transition to the other type of proof. Socrates presses Callicles with the question: 'But come . . . and tell me [again] whether you say that the pleasant and the good are the same thing, or that there is some pleasure which is not good.' To which Callicles answers: 'Well, then, for the sake of consistency, I will say they are the same.'[3]

'For the sake of consistency'; 'for the sake of the argument', that is: Callicles, it is clear, has already been persuaded. Yet it is clear also that he desires something more, some other

[1] *Gorgias*, 494 E.

[2] For further discussion of the catamite image, see Appendix A, pp. 316–19.

[3] *Gorgias*, 495 A.

kind of 'proof', for the final completeness of the demonstration. Socrates accordingly abandons what I have called the poetic mode for the more strictly philosophic, the logical or formal, mode—proof by ratiocination as distinct from proof by cumulative imagery; and this brings us back to the familiar procedures of the Socratic dialectic, the analysis of terms and propositions, which destroys the adversary's position by showing that it is self-contradictory.

The logical proofs that follow (there are three of them) are very extended; and it is not merely trivial to observe that the 'proof by images' occupies less than three pages of the Loeb text, the proofs by ratiocination nearly ten pages.[1] It points, in a simple and obvious way, at least one of the fundamental differences between the poetic mode of demonstration and the logical. To put it as briefly as possible: the poetic or metaphorical mode tends to *simultaneity* of statement; a metaphor or image tends to say several things at once, to achieve a fusion of disparate or heterogeneous elements. We remember Mr Eliot's definition of the metaphysical metaphor or conceit: 'heterogeneity of material compelled into unity by the operation of the poet's mind'; or, as Dr Johnson preferred to put it, 'the most heterogeneous ideas. . . yoked by violence together'; and it is this fundamental feature of metaphorical statement that accounts for the immediacy of its impact, for its tendency to significant ambiguity, and for its economy—even in the trivial matter of the space it occupies on the page. The ratiocinative or logical mode tends to *discursiveness*; its tendency is constantly to break up, to separate into its elements, the complex wholes of experience, and to present the elements singly and successively—as steps in an argument, as a series of deductions drawn out of the premises, or inferences derived from the first definitions. And because it is discursive, it is extended; and therefore ten pages are needed to prove by logic what the series of images had proved in less than three.

These extended logical proofs are very intricate and very

[1] *Ibid.* 495 C–499 B.

subtle,[1] and so exasperate Callicles that he threatens at one point to withdraw from the whole argument if Socrates continues with them. But he is coaxed back by Gorgias, and is in the end brought to the desired admission that the pleasant is not the measure of the good. He makes this final concession very irritably, and with an effort to save his face by pretending that he had of course meant this all along: 'So you suppose that I or anybody else in the world does not regard some pleasures as better, and others as worse! . . .'[2] Socrates, however, pays no attention, and proceeds from there to draw out the main consequence of Callicles' admission, namely, that to allow qualitative differences between pleasures is to admit a standard of the good other than pleasure itself, or (as Socrates puts it) 'that the good is the end of all our actions, and it is for its sake that all other things should be done, and not it for theirs.'[3]

This virtually marks the end of the dialectical portion of the whole Dialogue. The false doctrines proposed in turn by Gorgias, Polus and Callicles have been discredited; and Socrates is now in a position to draw out the full implications of all that his opponents have been forced to concede, in other words, to set out explicitly the positive doctrines that have emerged from the dialectical enquiries.

One of the first points to emerge is the double-reference of all the false doctrines that have been exposed and all the true doctrines that have been affirmed in the course of the dialectical enquiry. This double-reference is, on the one hand, to the morality of the individual, morality in its personal or private aspect, and, on the other, to the morality of the state or commonwealth, to morality in its public, its social and political, aspect. In the dialectical enquiry the emphasis has been all on the individual: What is it to be *a good man*? What must *a man* do to be saved? What must the teacher of rhetoric teach his pupils? Why is Archelaus, the tyrant of Macedon,

[1] The first of these logical proofs is discussed in Appendix A, pp. 313–14.
[2] *Gorgias*, 499 B. [3] *Ibid.* 499 E.

the most miserable of men? Is not the man who pursues pleasure for its own sake like a leaking colander, like a cormorant, like a man with a skin disease, like a catamite? But the implications of these enquiries and these discoveries for the polity—the state, or commonwealth—have all the time been hovering over the discussion; and in this latter part of the Dialogue the connexion is established, explicitly and firmly. The conditions of personal salvation, it is now clearly seen, are simultaneously and inseparably the conditions of the well-being of the commonwealth. The commonwealth is the individual soul writ large, and the laws of moral health of the one are *mutatis mutandis* also the laws of moral health of the other. Indeed, we can now see how throughout the dialectical discussion itself Socrates has constantly moved back and forth between the two, between the private and the public, the individual and the social, showing how, in his mind, the two realms are continuous with one another, how the single vision of the good that fills his mind comprehends both inseparably. To put it in more familiar terms: what Socrates is maintaining is that politics and ethics, public morality and private morality, are inseparable, that there is *no double standard*, one for the individual, another for the state, as the practical men—the politicians, the demagogues and the dictators—of his time as of all times were intent upon maintaining in order to ensure their own survival.

With this double-reference present to our minds, it is possible to restate the whole theme of the *Gorgias* with a fresh emphasis. The two principal disorders which persistently threaten the life of the commonwealth are tyranny and demagoguery: this is Socrates' grand political insight. And it is inseparable from his grand moral insight, namely, that these diseases of the commonwealth, tyranny and demagoguery, are grounded in a particular view of the moral life, the view that power and pleasure are, together, the highest good. These two principal disorders of the commonwealth (with the moral philosophy that they imply) find a common emblem, as it were, in the art of rhetoric, or political propaganda—the art of putting across successfully a doctrine, a point of view, or a plan of action irrespective of its intrinsic goodness or badness and its effects upon the health of the individual soul and of the commonwealth. Rhetoric is the emblem of demagoguery as it operates by what Socrates calls 'flattery'—by appealing to, and gratifying, the basest impulses and the most irrational prejudices of the multitude; and it is the emblem of political tyranny as it strengthens and reinforces those base impulses and irrational prejudices, thus rendering the multitude an easy prey to the physical oppression of the tyrant. That is how the two disorders of the commonwealth, tyranny and demagoguery, find a common expression in the art of rhetoric. And that is why the Dialogue is called the *Gorgias*, after the master rhetorician of Socrates' time; and that is why the whole enquiry starts off with an exposure of the art of rhetoric as practised and taught by the master rhetoricians.

In the latter portion of the Dialogue this grand double theme is brought to a climax in Socrates' anatomy of the politician. What he insists upon there is that all the supposedly great and good statesmen in Athenian history, Pericles and Miltiades not excepted, were neither great nor good. For none of them fulfilled the condition that defines the character of the true statesman, that he shall make men better than he found them; and must therefore use the art of rhetoric, the all-powerful instrument of persuasive discourse, not for self-aggrandisement, or even for the achievement of limited political and economic ends, but solely for advancing men in the study of perfection. The good statesman, the true shepherd of his people, does not say, We will have as much virtue as may be compatible with having the ships, the walls, and the revenues we want. He says instead, We will have only the ships and walls and revenues that are compatible with that perfect justice which comprehends perfect wisdom, courage, temperance and piety.[1]

[1] *Gorgias*, 515 A–519 A.

This is Socrates' fundamental political teaching, which his pupil Plato was to expand and refine into the monumental system of the *Republic*; and it is the only political doctrine compatible with the morality Socrates opposed to that of the Sophists, the morality which subordinates power and pleasure to an absolute good, and refuses to allow that power and pleasure are the measure of that absolute good. Its deepest presupposition is a faith in the capacity of men to be transformed, to be 'made better than they are' by example and instruction in the way of perfection. This perfection was not indeed, for Socrates and Plato, to be sought through love—not love, at any rate, as the Christian or the Humanist understands it. It was to be sought through virtue, which was the consummation of the philosopher's quest for reality and truth. Perfect knowledge issued in perfect virtue; the ascent of the soul through the great abstract studies culminating in the study of dialectic at once illuminated the intelligence and purified the motive; the final vision of the supreme form of the Good was simultaneously a circumcision of the mind and of the heart. So it is virtue for love in the Socratic scheme of salvation; but a virtue so full of the power to transform, sanctify and redeem as to bring it remarkably close to the love that speaks with the tongues of men and angels. And it is this faith in the redeeming power of the perfect virtue that issues from perfect knowledge that places the Socratic moral and political doctrine at the opposite extreme to that other tradition of moral and political thought, which stems from Aristotle and finds its most formidable exponent in the English secular tradition in Thomas Hobbes. This takes its stand upon a fundamental lack of faith in the power of men to be made better than they are, and accordingly reduces—is compelled to reduce—morals to *mores* and politics to the institution and enforcement of positive law.

The larger reference of the dialectical enquiries in the *Gorgias* extends, however, even beyond the nature of commonwealth to the universe itself. What binds everything together (Socrates tells Callicles) is the principle of order or harmony: 'And philosophers tell us, Callicles, that communion and friendship and orderliness and temperance and justice bind together heaven and earth and gods and men, and that this universe is for that reason to be called cosmos or order, not disorder or misrule....'[1]

And finally, beyond this larger reference to the universal order is the largest of all, the reference to a divine order, the invisible, eternal and immutable source of all that is orderly and harmonious, good and beautiful, in the universe, in the commonwealth, and in the individual soul. The intimations of a divine order and a life after death are almost as clear and explicit in the *Gorgias* as in the great passage in the *Republic* in which Plato invokes the image of the sun as the source of light and life to express his visionary experience of the supreme 'form', the Form of the Good, and speaks of the Good as that which 'transcends even being in dignity and power'. Here, in the last sections of the *Gorgias*, we receive similar intimations of 'an order of goodness and power greater than any that this world can show'; and these are nowhere more powerfully or more movingly expressed than in Socrates' *apologia pro vita sua*, in which he seeks to answer the personal charges directed against him by Callicles at the beginning of their exchange, in particular the charge of a ridiculous ineptitude in practical affairs and an unmanly meekness of spirit.

Socrates' grand plea, in answer to this charge, is that self-preservation, mere personal survival, is not the sole or even the chief object of a good man's life. He addresses Callicles with a most passionate earnestness:

> I tell you, Callicles, that to be boxed on the ears wrongfully is not the worst evil that can befall a man, nor to have my face and purse cut open; but that to smite and slay me and mine wrongfully is far more disgraceful and evil; aye, and to despoil and enslave and pillage, or in any way at all to wrong me and mine, is far more disgraceful and evil to the doer of the wrong than to me who am the sufferer....[2]

[1] *Gorgias*, 508 A (Jowett). [2] *Ibid.* 508 E (Jowett).

And presently again:

> Do you think that all our cares are to be directed to prolonging life to the uttermost, and to the study of those arts which secure us from danger always; like that art of rhetoric which saves men in courts of law, and which you recommend me to cultivate?[1]

This is followed by the parable of the ship's pilot.[2] The ship's pilot (says Socrates), having a true sense of values, takes no special pride in 'saving' the lives of his passengers; for he knows that he has made them neither better nor worse by merely steering them safely across the sea from Aegina to Athens. Yet Callicles claims for the rhetoricians in the courts of law that they do something positively good in saving people from death or punishment:

> O my friend! I want you to see that the noble and the good may possibly be something different from saving and being saved, and that he who is truly a man ought not to care about living a certain time. He knows, as women say, that we must all die, and therefore he is not fond of life; he leaves all that with God, and considers [only] in what way he can best spend his appointed term....[3]

And what *is* the way a man can best spend his appointed term? The answer is enunciated with the utmost clarity and force in the *Gorgias*, in the *Republic*, and in all the other Dialogues in which Plato bodied forth the moral teaching of his master Socrates. The way in which a man best spends his appointed term is in the whole-hearted and single-minded pursuit of the good for its own sake. For its own sake: not, that is, for the sake of pleasure—the pleasure, or happiness, that may (and indeed often does) add the bloom of perfection to the good man's life. Nor for the sake of power—though power (as Plato himself insists in the *Republic*) may be a necessary means to establishing and maintaining the good in the life of the commonwealth. Yet the good is to be pursued not for the sake of pleasure, or for the sake of power, or for

[1] *Gorgias*, 511 C (Jowett).
[2] *Ibid.* 511 D
[3] *Ibid.* 512 D–E (Jowett).

the reputation of virtue, or because honesty is the best policy. It is to be pursued only for its own sake; for the sake of its own inherent loveliness; for the sake of the power and the glory intrinsic to itself, by which the lover of the good is drawn to his redemption.

This (Socrates intimates) is how a man should spend his appointed term. And this also, in the *Gorgias*, brings Socrates to the final defence of his life, which forms the last section of the whole Dialogue. Socrates speaks here for all the great moral and religious teachers who have had to give up their lives in order that the Word, or some part of it, might be made flesh. Since this kind of pursuit of the good (he tells Callicles), this whole-hearted and single-minded pursuit of the good, may involve the rooting out of evil, not only in the hearts of individual men but in the life of the commonwealth as well; and since those in public life do not take kindly to preachers like Socrates, whose strange doctrines puzzle and perplex them, make them uncomfortable and even ashamed, and fill them with a fear of the radical alteration in their way of life that they seem to threaten—since the men of affairs do not take kindly to such preachers and their doctrines, 'there is no telling', says Socrates, 'what may happen to such a man'.

In this connexion, there is point in remembering the tribute that Alcibiades pays Socrates at the end of the *Symposium*. Alcibiades is the brilliant young man of affairs who happens also to be a devoted friend and admirer of Socrates. He arrives at the end of the dinner-party, and, being sufficiently tipsy to be free of false inhibitions, speaks his mind about Socrates with what one must suppose to be unusual force and candour. This is what he says:

> There's one thing I've never felt with anybody else—not the kind of thing you'd expect to find in me either—and that is a sense of shame. Socrates is the only man in the world who can make me feel ashamed. Because there's no getting away from it, I know I ought to do the things he tells me to; and yet the moment I'm out

of his sight I don't care what I do to keep in with the mob. So I dash off like a runaway slave, and keep out of his way as long as I can; and then next time I meet him I remember all that I had to admit the time before, and naturally I feel ashamed. There are times when I'd honestly be glad to hear that he was dead....[1]

To have this little speech of Alcibiades present to one's mind is perhaps to appreciate in an especially intimate way the poignancy of Socrates' own speech in the *Gorgias* in which he anticipates his own trial and death:

I think, Callicles, that I am the only, or almost the only, Athenian living who practises the true art of politics; I am the only politician of my time. And seeing that when I speak I speak not with any view to pleasing, and that I look to what is best and not to what is most pleasant, having no mind to use those arts and graces which you recommend, I shall have nothing to say in the court of justice.... If anyone says that I corrupt young men and confuse their minds, or that I speak evil of old men, and use bitter words towards them, whether in private or public, it is useless for me to reply, as I truly might: 'All this I do for the sake of justice, and with a view to your interest, your good, my judges, and to that only.' It would be useless for me to speak thus; and therefore there is no saying what may happen to me....[2]

The intimations of immortality that we have already received earlier in the *Gorgias* appear in their strongest light in the closing parable of the Day of Judgment, in which Socrates tells how every soul shall be impartially judged after death.[3] And it is in the comment that follows upon this parable that we have disclosed to us a last significant aspect of the whole Socratic teaching. 'Now I, Callicles', Socrates begins, 'am persuaded of the truth of these things, and therefore I consider only how I shall present my soul whole and undefiled before the judge on that day....'[4] Then, suspecting that Callicles will dismiss his parable as an old wives' tale, he

[1] *Symp.* 216B–C (*Five Dialogues of Plato*, Everyman's Library, trans. Michael Joyce).

[2] *Gorgias*, 521D–E, 522B–C (Jowett).

[3] *Ibid.* 523A–526D.

[4] *Ibid.* 526D (Jowett).

reminds Callicles of the 'proof' that he himself has given him of the truth of his faith; and it is the form of this last statement of his that is so revealing and so touching. 'But', says Socrates, 'you see, Callicles, that you and Polus and Gorgias, who are the three wisest Greeks of our day, *have not been able to show that we ought to live any life which does not profit in another world as well as this*....'[1]

The negative form of the statement is not accidental. Socrates can say so much, but no more; for he has neither the knowledge nor the authority to say more. It is perfectly true that Gorgias, Polus and Callicles—the wisest of the Greeks of his day, as Socrates calls them, the wisest Gentiles, replete with the wisdom of the world, as St Paul might have called them—cannot maintain their doctrine, cannot prove Socrates' doctrine to be false. But it is also true that Socrates, on his side, cannot prove his doctrine to be true. He cannot prove it, he can only affirm it, and leave it, presumably, to the experience of mankind to confirm it.

Now this may be proof enough for some men, for those, in particular, who may be called men of the Humanist temper. For such men, a fundamental moral or religious truth is sufficiently proved if it can be shown that moral life is impossible without it. A truth in morals and religion is, for the Humanist, always and only that which can be proved in our most intimate experience to be a necessary condition of moral life.

But this, which is enough for the Humanist, is not enough, one feels, for the religious temper of a man like Socrates; and what Socrates lacks, one comes to see, is a revelation. Nor is the sense in which he lacks it (in the first instance, at any rate) a sense either psychological or emotional, that his heart aches for the knowledge of a revealed God and his bowels yearn for the voice from the burning bush. It is rather in a strictly *logical* sense that his doctrine requires and demands a revealed God and a revealed Gospel to complete it.

[1] *Gorgias,* 527 B (Jowett).

Socrates' whole system is pressing, logically pressing, towards the conclusion which was not to be reached historically until some four hundred years later, when a man was born in Bethlehem who proclaimed himself to be the Word—the whole, the complete, the perfect Word—made flesh.

The sense of this last lack, this last gap, in Socrates' vision of the moral life is most compellingly present in the closing sections of the *Gorgias*; and it is not the Christian alone who will recognise the loss it must have been to Socrates to be without a revealed God and Gospel, while seeing at the same time how much this very lack magnifies his stature as a moral and religious teacher. It is with Socrates in mind that I will try to show in my discussion of the Epistles of St Paul how it may profit a man of the full religious temper to possess a revealed God and a revealed Gospel.

CHAPTER III

SELF-SUFFICIENCY FOR LOVE

ARISTOTLE'S 'NICOMACHEAN ETHICS'

I have chosen Aristotle's *Nicomachean Ethics* as the fundamental text for the study of the second of our three traditions of moral thought, which I have called the secular or utilitarian tradition in an attempt to suggest what it is that sets it apart from the Platonic-Christian on the one hand and the Humanist on the other. Neither term, however, is exact. Of the moralists I have chosen to represent this tradition, only Hume may properly be thought of as both secular and utilitarian. Hobbes, though secular enough, is not a utilitarian in the way Hume, and Bentham and Mill, are; and the Catholic might well raise an eyebrow at the suggestion that Aristotle, whom St Thomas Aquinas was so easily able to accommodate to Christian uses, is secular. A fuller definition of those aspects of each of these moralists that may be seen as secular or utilitarian or both will emerge from the discussion of the texts. For the present, it may be enough to say that these terms, when given a wider interpretation than is usual in the histories of thought, do suggest at least some of the great common features that hold together moral systems as diverse as those of Aristotle, Hobbes, Hume and Bentham. Aristotle, we will find, is, as a matter of historical fact, the ultimate source and inspiration of all the utilitarian moral philosophies in the history of English moral thought; and his view of man's nature, which is the foundation of his moral doctrine, is as intimately similar to that of Hobbes, Hume and Bentham as it is radically different from Plato's and St Paul's.

Indeed, it is this, their common view of man's nature, that more than anything holds them together as moralists in a single tradition. I propose to call it the *low* view of man's nature, in a sense of the word 'low' to be explained. It is a view of man's nature that sometimes goes by the name of moral realism; or it might be called *Realsittenlehre*, that which in moral philosophy corresponds to *Realpolitik* in political philosophy. It is, in any case, fundamental to the moral teaching of this group of moralists, and every other aspect of their moral doctrine is more or less intimately and directly related to it. Their utilitarianism, for instance, is logically grounded in this view of man's nature; and their empirical approach to moral problems—which is common at least to Aristotle, Hume and Bentham, though absent in Hobbes—is also closely linked with their low or realistic view of man's nature. Consequently it is of vital importance for the understanding of their moral systems as a whole to grasp the main features of this view of man's nature, and to learn to recognise it in all its variant forms; and since the *Nicomachean Ethics* contains one of the classic expositions of this view, it deserves to be closely examined as the Aristotelian variant of the moral realism that Aristotle shares with Hobbes, Hume and Bentham.

To receive the distinctive flavour of Aristotle's moral realism, its exact pitch and accent, it will be helpful to turn aside for a moment from the *Nicomachean Ethics* and look into another of his works called the *Rhetoric*. The *Rhetoric* was written as a sort of text-book guide to human nature for the use of the young political orator wishing to make his mark in the public assemblies, and as such it contains a great deal that significantly illuminates the Aristotelian view of man. Indeed, the evidences for Aristotle's view of man are, by the nature of his undertaking in the *Rhetoric*, more full, direct and explicit than in the *Nicomachean Ethics*, and therefore supplement and confirm in an invaluable way what we find in the *Nicomachean Ethics*. Besides this, the *Rhetoric* happens to be a work that has influenced some of the most important English moralists in the tradition we are now considering. Hobbes, Hume and Bentham are among these, but particularly Hobbes, who translated it, obviously admired it, and showed, in his own account of human nature in *Leviathan*, how much he had learnt from it. There is accordingly a special point in citing the evidences for the Aristotelian view of man's nature contained in the *Rhetoric*.

The chief of these are the famous sketches of the Youthful Man, the Elderly Man and the Man in his Prime,[1] these being, according to Aristotle, the main types of character that the political orator must be acquainted with and constantly take account of. The sketches are full, and unusually concrete and vivid, and the most revealing of them is the sketch of the Elderly Man—the man past his prime, as Aristotle calls him. The sketch of the Young Man, which precedes it, is really only an introduction to the other. All that we find engaging in the young (Aristotle intimates) is due entirely to their innocence and ignorance and inexperience; they are, indeed, really engaging—always passionate and brave, generally also noble and disinterested; but they are so only because they do not yet know life *as it is*. This, precisely, is what the Elderly Men do know; and in his portrait Aristotle brings out very vividly the desolating effects upon human character of knowing life as it is.

They [the Elderly Men] have lived many years; they have often been taken in, and often made mistakes; and life on the whole is a bad business. The result is that they are sure about nothing and *under-do* everything.[2] They 'think' but they never 'know'; and because of their hesitancy they always add a 'possibly' or a 'perhaps', putting everything this way and nothing positively.

They are cynical ; that is, they tend to put the worst construction on everything. Further, their experience makes them distrustful and therefore suspicious of evil. Consequently they neither love warmly nor hate bitterly, but following the hint of Bias they love as though they will some day hate and hate as though they will some day love. . . .

[1] *Rhetoric*, Bk. II, chs. 12–14.

[2] It was characteristic of the Young to *over-do* everything.

They are small-minded, because they have been humbled by life: their desires are set upon nothing more exalted or unusual than what will help them to keep alive. They are not generous, because money is one of the things they must have, and at the same time their experience has taught them how hard it is to get and how easy to lose. They are cowardly, and are always anticipating danger; unlike that of the young, who are warm-blooded, their temperament is chilly; old age has paved the way for cowardice; fear is, in fact, a form of chill. . . .

They are too fond of themselves; this is one form that small-mindedness takes. Because of this, they guide their lives too much by considerations of what is useful and too little by what is noble—for the useful is what is good for oneself, and the noble what is good absolutely.

They are not shy, but shameless rather; caring less for what is noble than for what is useful, they feel contempt for what people may think of them. . . . Old men may feel pity, as well as young men, but not for the same reason. Young men feel it out of kindness; old men out of weakness, imagining that anything that befalls anyone else might easily happen to them, which is a thought that excites pity. . . .[1]

Their fits of anger are sudden but feeble. Their sensual passions have altogether gone or have lost their vigour: consequently they do not feel their passions much, and their actions are inspired less by what they do feel than by the love of gain. Hence men at this time of life are often supposed to have a self-controlled character; the fact is that their passions have slackened and they are slaves to the love of gain. . . .[2]

This is Aristotle's picture of the Elderly Man as set out in the *Rhetoric.* Then, having shown us in the Young and the Elderly the two extremes of human character, the Young representing the excess, the Elderly the defect, of the major virtues, Aristotle gives us, characteristically, the mean between these extremes, what he calls the Man in his Prime.

The sketch of the Man in his Prime is brief, and suggests a

[1] Compare with Hobbes's definition of pity (*Leviathan,* ch. 6); and see below, ch. IV, p. 118.

[2] *Rhetoric,* 1389b–1390a (trans. W. Rhys Roberts, in *The Works of Aristotle translated into English,* ed. W. D. Ross, vol. XI). The items have been slightly rearranged.

strong family resemblance to the Magnanimous Man in the *Nicomachean Ethics*:

> As for Men in their Prime, clearly we shall find that they have a character between that of the young and that of the old, free from the extremes of either. They have neither that excess of confidence which amounts to rashness, nor too much timidity, but the right amount of each. They neither trust everybody nor distrust everybody, but judge people correctly. Their lives will be guided not by the sole consideration either of what is noble or what is useful, but by both; neither by parsimony nor by prodigality, but by what is fit and proper. So, too, in regard to anger and desire; they will be brave as well as temperate, and temperate as well as brave; these virtues are divided between the young and the old; the young are brave but intemperate, the old temperate but cowardly. To put it generally, all the valuable qualities that youth and age divide between them are united in the prime of life, while all their excesses or defects are replaced by moderation and fitness. The body is in its prime from thirty to five-and-thirty; the mind about forty-nine.[1]

The anatomy of human nature contained in these three sketches of human character is indeed impressive. The acuteness of the insight is matched by the formidable confidence of the manner; the dispassionate tone does much to enhance the force of the penetrating observation; and the phrasing is so sharp and economical as to give each sketch the air of a series of brilliant aphorisms. It is, in short, very much the work of Aristotle's Man in his Prime, who is able to 'judge people correctly', who neither rejoices extravagantly in their virtues nor deplores extravagantly their vices and weaknesses, but sets them all down 'as they are', bestowing praise and blame in exactly 'the right amount' and with exemplary 'moderation and fitness'.

So it is impossible not to be impressed by Aristotle's realistic view of man's nature as it is exhibited in these sketches in the *Rhetoric*. Yet, at the same time, one marvels at all that Aristotle has failed to take account of in man's nature; and though it is perhaps not easy at first glance to see what is

[1] *Rhetoric*, 1390a–1390b.

missing (for there *is* so much truth in it, and it *is* so persuasive, and if we resist the view of human possibility that it implies, are we not resisting it precisely because it is so true—so disagreeably, so dishearteningly, true?), yet the sense that it is, in some way, wrong persists, inviting a closer examination of the whole Aristotelian picture. And what this discloses is the fact that the Aristotelian scheme touches neither the highest nor the lowest reaches of man's moral experience. These, the highest and the lowest extremes of human possibility, are totally excluded from it; and it is in this sense that the Aristotelian view of man's nature is a low view, a disastrously limited and incomplete view of man's nature.

What specifically it excludes is, at one extreme, the quality of sanctity, using the term in a general sense to denote the furthest reach of moral perfection, in particular moral heroism, that the human spirit is capable of. There is too evidently no place in Aristotle's scheme for this quality of sanctity, of which nevertheless the history of the human race offers some indisputable instances, and at least one, in the person of his master's master Socrates, that was not very remote from Aristotle in place and time. This quality, if it were recognised and given a place in Aristotle's moral universe, would transcend immeasurably in the rank of virtues that 'nobility' which Aristotle praises as the supreme virtue of his Young Man in the *Rhetoric*, and would transcend by the same measure the magnanimity of the Magnanimous Man in the *Nicomachean Ethics*, the liberality of the Liberal Man, the *sophrosyne* of the Temperate Man, and even the wisdom of the Contemplative Man. But sanctity is absent in the Aristotelian scheme of moral virtues, and it accordingly falls short of the highest reach of human goodness.

And it falls correspondingly short at the lower end. For it takes no account of the quality of depravity, where the term is used, again, in a general, not theological, sense to denote the quality of absolute evil that exists, at least as a possibility, in human nature. Depravity has many forms, and among the most terrible is that absolute cruelty, that wanton destructive cruelty, of which the history of the human race has yielded many examples and the history of our own time some of the most memorable. Like the quality of sanctity, this quality of depravity, if acknowledged and given a place in the Aristotelian scheme, would, in the rank of vices, fall far below the mere meanness and cowardice of Aristotle's unsavoury Elderly Man—and far below, also, the three conventional vices, murder, theft and adultery, that Aristotle names in the *Nicomachean Ethics* as the lowest reach of human badness. For compared to the depravity I am speaking of, murder, theft and adultery are not the lowest reach of human possibility in the way of evil; yet the Aristotelian scheme takes human evil no further down than this; and because it goes only so far down, it is as defective at the lower end as at the upper.

This, we will find, is the special mark of what I have called the low view of man's nature—that it goes neither high enough nor low enough, that it reaches neither to the heights nor to the depths of human possibility; and it is for this reason that it must be accounted a fatally limited, incomplete, defective view. All the moral philosophers in the tradition which stems from Aristotle have it in common, and it will be instructive presently to compare Aristotle's variant with those of Hobbes and Hume, who are his chief heirs in the English moral tradition. The particular moral doctrines, however, that each of them derives from this common view of man's nature differ greatly, and their total systems of which these doctrines are the constituent parts differ correspondingly; and it is in the *Nicomachean Ethics* that we may trace the effects upon Aristotle's moral philosophy of the view of man's nature that I have tried to sketch on the evidences supplied by the *Rhetoric*.

In the *Nicomachean Ethics* the evidences for Aristotle's low view of human nature are on the whole less full, and less direct and explicit, than in the *Rhetoric*. Indeed, some of his most revealing pronouncements occur as parenthetical asides, or afterthoughts, as if they were of no special importance, much less of central importance. But the casual air is deceptive; these pronouncements are crucial, and must receive their proper emphasis in any reading of the *Nicomachean Ethics* that is to be genuinely illuminating.

A typical instance of this kind of remark occurs in the Tenth Book, where Aristotle is discussing the claim of ethical theory, as distinct from practice, to influence moral conduct. Ethical theory, he says, has indeed the power to influence the few, but never the many. For—and this is the significant parenthesis—'it is the nature of the many to be amenable to fear but not to a sense of honour, and to abstain from evil not because of its baseness but because of the penalties it entails'.[1] And again, in the same chapter, 'The many are more amenable to compulsion and punishment than to reason and to moral ideals.'[2]

No sane man would wish to deny that this is at least partly true of 'the many'; if it were not, there would be no need of laws or law-courts or police officers or prisons. But the fact that it is part of the truth does not make it the whole truth, or even the most important part of the truth, about man's nature. Yet that Aristotle does take it to be the most important part of the truth about man's nature is shown by some of the main doctrines of the *Nicomachean Ethics*, which make sense only on such a low view of 'the many' and would make sense on no other. And (to point the connexion with Hobbes) it is worth noting that when this view of 'the many' is taken to its logical conclusion, what we get is the moral and political doctrine of Hobbes's *Leviathan*. There, in Hobbes's *Leviathan*, not most but *all* men are exclusively 'amenable to fear' and to 'compulsion and punishment'; and because they are thus dominated by fear (and also, in Hobbes's scheme, ferociously competitive), it becomes necessary to create, by the mutual consent of the subjects, the great Leviathan, that most absolute

[1] *Nic. Ethics*, x. ix. 4. [2] *Ibid.* x. ix. 9.

of sovereigns who will save them all from tearing each other to pieces by the exercise of his absolute power in the way of compulsion and punishment. Hobbes's doctrine in *Leviathan* is, in short, Aristotle's taken to its logical conclusion; and though Aristotle himself does not take it to the Hobbesian extreme, he comes very close to Hobbes in some of his specific ethical and political doctrines.

The chief of these is the subordination of ethics to politics: the subordination, that is, of the moral life of men to—indeed, its incorporation into—the life of the state. The *Nicomachean Ethics* (Aristotle effectively tells us in the last chapter) is merely a prolegomenon to the *Politics*; the good life, for Aristotle, is completely dependent upon political institutions, having no existence and no meaning apart from political institutions; and the main business of the moralist becomes accordingly substantially the same as that of the political philosopher.

What, then (it may be asked), is the difference on this vital point between Aristotle's view and Plato's and Socrates'? Do not Socrates in the *Gorgias* and Plato in the *Republic* take a similar view of the relation of the moral life and the political? No one, it seems, could be more insistent upon the need of good institutions to make men good than Plato in the *Republic*; and Socrates' exposure of the rhetoricians in the *Gorgias* was, as we saw, at once and equally an exposure of bad political practices and institutions. Yet the Socratic and Platonic view, though apparently similar to the Aristotelian, is nevertheless radically different from it. In the *Republic*, the vision of the Form of the Good, which is for Plato the ultimate source of all *political* as well as moral wisdom, is not in any sense dependent upon political institutions. On the contrary, the laws of the ideal commonwealth and the proper administration of these laws depend upon *it*—upon the virtue and the wisdom that the philosopher-king receives from his direct experience of the ultimate source of all goodness and wisdom. Similarly, in the *Gorgias*, we remember Socrates' explicit reference to an eternal immutable law that transcends the temporal law of the state, by which Socrates himself hopes ultimately to be judged. But for Aristotle there is no Form of the Good and no eternal immutable law by which a man may guide his life when the polity is corrupt. For Aristotle, moral goodness is wholly dependent upon, and wholly derivative from, good institutions; and this is what makes the qualitative difference between his view of the relation between the moral and the political and that of Socrates and Plato.

The main evidence, however, for Aristotle's view of human possibility and its radical divergence from the Platonic (and the Christian) view is to be discovered in his analysis of the virtues in the middle Books of the *Nicomachean Ethics.* What emerges from this detailed analysis of the virtues—courage first, then temperance, liberality, magnanimity, and so on—is an ideal of worldliness that stands squarely opposed at once to the Socratic-Platonic ideal and the Christian; and the supreme expression of the Aristotelian worldly ideal is the portrait of the Magnanimous Man,[1] the Man of 'Justifiable Pride', as Professor Thomson translates the Greek word *megalopsuchia,* more commonly translated *magnanimity* after the Latin *magnanimitas.*

The Magnanimous Man, it must be understood, is Aristotle's Perfect Man. He is the man perfected in the exercise of the practical reason, which, in the Aristotelian psychology, has the function of controlling the appetites and thereby ensuring the perfection of moral virtue. On the intellectual side, the crowning moral virtue is *phronesis,* or practical wisdom, on the practical ('practising') side it is *sophrosyne,* that is, temperance or self-command; and both are functions of the practical reason. The Magnanimous Man, being the man of perfected practical reason, is therefore the man perfected in the supreme moral virtues of *phronesis* and *sophrosyne,* and as such stands as one Aristotelian ideal of perfected human nature—the perfect Ethical Man, one may call him. How this

[1] *Nic. Ethics,* IV. iii.

ideal is to be reconciled with that other Aristotelian ideal of perfected human nature, the Contemplative Man, described in Book x of the *Nicomachean Ethics*, is a matter for separate enquiry, to be taken up in its place.[1]

The main interest for us of the Magnanimous Man is that he is deficient, with a most exemplary consistency and completeness, in all those virtues to which the religious everywhere tend to attach a supreme value, the irreligious and worldly to despise and reject; and of these religious or 'Christian' virtues of which the Magnanimous Man is so completely innocent, humility is the most conspicuous. His very title, the Man of Justifiable Pride, already declares that humility is no part of his moral constitution. He has *no cause* (that is Aristotle's grand point) to be humble, *being what he is*: being the man of perfected practical wisdom and perfected self-command, being, that is, in a superlative degree morally self-sufficient, he has no cause—cannot, by definition, ever have cause—to be humble.

These accordingly, his practical wisdom and his self-command, are the 'internal goods', as Aristotle calls them, that, possessed in the perfection in which they are in fact possessed by the Magnanimous Man, yield one aspect of his splendid self-sufficiency. But, besides these, he possesses also not a mere sufficiency but a splendid amplitude of 'external' goods; consequently he is splendidly self-sufficient also in this respect, and splendidly capable therefore of exercising the supreme worldly virtue of magnanimity. And such a man must of necessity (says Aristotle) seek *honour* above everything: 'For honour is the greatest of external goods,... [and] it goes without saying that he concerns himself with honour; it is what he claims, and claims justly, above all.'[2]

There is a characteristic (and, I believe, deliberate) ambiguity in Aristotle's use of the phrase 'concerns himself with honour' or 'pursues honour'. The Magnanimous Man, in one sense, pursues honour in claiming *to be* honoured, to receive

[1] Pp. 88–93, below. [2] *Nic. Ethics*, IV. iii. 11 (Thomson).

the highest honours from others. But he pursues honour also in the sense that he is himself honourable—having (Aristotle explains) *no cause to be otherwise.* Thus he will never run away in battle or be guilty of cheating, since (asks Aristotle significantly) 'what motive for base conduct has a man *to whom nothing is great*?'[1]

What this means is that the Magnanimous Man is brave in battle and honourable in his dealings with other men, not because he sees cowardice and dishonesty as evils, not because he has a fear and horror of being cowardly or dishonest, not from a moral repugnance to vice, but because he *scorns* to do as other, inferior men do. He scorns to do that which he, in his perfect superiority, *has no need to do*, and, if done, would place him on a level with those other, inferior men. He acts honourably and nobly, in short, not in order that the good may be affirmed, but in order that he may maintain unimpaired his superiority over his fellow-men. The Perfect Lifeman, the man perfected in the art of Lifemanship—that, in the current phrase, is Aristotle's Magnanimous Man: he who is always *one up* on his fellow-men; who knows all the best ploys and gambits for keeping himself securely, unassailably, in this agreeable condition of superiority. And what gives him his pre-eminence among Lifemen is his discovery of the nicest, subtlest gambit of all, namely, the exercise of virtue itself—courage, honesty, and the rest—in the interests of a perfected Lifemanship.

In this connexion it is interesting to remark another link between Aristotle's moral scheme and Hobbes's. What we discover is that Hobbes, who found so much in the *Rhetoric* and the *Nicomachean Ethics* to confirm his own, very low, view of human nature, was able to find in the Magnanimous Man's 'pursuit of honour' in particular something that he could admire without reservation. It is not often in *Leviathan* that Hobbes finds cause to rejoice in any part of man's nature; but of the few occasions on which he does, one of the most

[1] *Nic. Ethics.* IV. iii. 15.

conspicuous is that on which he singles out for praise a quality that he actually calls *magnanimity* or, alternatively, *gallantry*. And the defining mark of Hobbes's Gallant Man, we find, is significantly similar to that of Aristotle's Magnanimous Man: he is one (says Hobbes) who '*scorns to be beholden for the contentment of his life to fraud or breach of promise*'.[1] The Magnanimous Man, we remember, also scorned to be beholden for the contentment of his life to cowardice in battle or dishonesty (Hobbes's 'fraud') in his dealings with his fellow-men; virtue, in other words, in Hobbes's Gallant Man as in Aristotle's Magnanimous Man, is grounded, not in the love of the good, but in scorn of that which will dishonour him by placing him on a level with those masses of his fellow-men who are neither gallant nor magnanimous but only mean, base, craven, and amenable to nothing but compulsion and punishment.

There is, however, also the other sense in which the Magnanimous Man 'concerns himself with honour', in the sense of claiming the honour that is due to him; and, in 'pursuing honour' in this sense, his conduct is again perfectly consistent with the character of the Man of Justifiable Pride. He is one (Aristotle tells us) who likes to confer benefits but hates to receive them.[2] Not, however, for the pious Christian reason that it is more blessed to give than to receive, but for the reason that he cannot bear to be under an obligation to another. For to be in the position of a debtor would, of course, diminish his superiority, and that, above all things, is intolerable to the Man of Justifiable Pride. That is why (Aristotle says) 'when he does repay a service, it is with interest, for in this way the original benefactor will become the beneficiary and debtor in his turn'.[3] That is why also he has a 'better memory for benefits conferred than benefits received. . . and likes to be reminded of what he gave and not what he got'.[4] And that is why, finally (and more subtly),

[1] *Leviathan*, ch. xv, p. 97 (under 'Justice of men and justice of actions, what').
[2] *Nic. Ethics*, IV. iii. 24.
[3] *Ibid.* IV. iii. 25 (Thomson).
[4] *Ibid.* IV. iii. 25 (Thomson).

he is so consistently candid in his treatment of other men. 'The superior man', Aristotle says, 'is bound to be open in his likes and dislikes, and to care more for the truth than for what people may think, and to be straightforward in word and deed'; and this again sounds splendid—until we learn, in the next sentence, that it is 'the poor opinion he has of other men [that] enables him to speak his mind freely'.[1] The reason for his candour, in other words, is, again, not the intrinsic virtue of candour, but the scorn proper in such a man of concealing his real feelings towards his inferiors. For such concealment could only be due to fear; and fear, everyone knows, is the craven passion of inferior men. But the Magnanimous Man, being the perfectly superior man, has no cause for fear; therefore he has no cause to conceal his feelings; and is therefore always open and candid in his dealings with other men.

These are the main features of Aristotle's Man of Justifiable Pride; and it is not difficult to find another, more incisive, name for him. This other name is the Man of Perfected Self-Righteousness: he who is by definition so assured of his own perfect virtue and so secure in it, that he can, on the one hand, justly demand the highest honour in recognition of his perfect virtue and, on the other, justly despise as inferiors those who are obliged to honour him in this way. Having no sense of his own radical imperfection, he knows no humility and no gratitude. Having no fear of doing wrong, he never has need of forgiveness, or of repentance and expiation. He never even (in Jowett's famous phrase) explains and never apologises, never having cause to do either; and in his perfect self-sufficiency is accountable neither to other men, nor to the God whom Aristotle occasionally mentions in the *Nicomachean Ethics* and elsewhere, but only to himself.

This is the Man of Perfected Self-Righteousness, representing the Aristotelian ideal of moral perfection; and, as such, he stands at the opposite extreme to the ideal that we have already met with in the *Gorgias*, and are to meet again,

[1] *Ibid.* IV. iii. 28 (Thomson).

much intensified, in the Epistles of St Paul. 'I tell you, Callicles', says Socrates in the *Gorgias*,

> that to be boxed on the ears wrongfully is not the worst evil that can befall a man, nor to have my face and purse cut open; but that to smite and slay me and mine wrongfully is far more disgraceful and evil; aye, and to despoil and enslave and pillage, or in any way at all to wrong me and mine is far more disgraceful and evil to the doer of the wrong than to me who am the sufferer.[1]

What is this, in the Aristotelian scheme of moral values, but a perfect instance of that slavish, craven *poor-spiritedness*—that quality (which Aristotle calls the 'defect' of 'justifiable pride' or 'magnanimity') which leads a man persistently to make a fool of himself in the eyes of the world? What is Socrates but a perfect example of Aristotle's Poor-Spirited Man, who stands at the opposite extreme to the Magnanimous Man: the kind of man (says Aristotle) who, 'though not undeserving deprives himself of such advantages as he deserves, the effect of his failure to claim his deserts being to convince people that there must be something bad about him'.

There must be 'something bad about him'—'something wrong with him', as we would say. And 'such men', adds Aristotle, 'like the vulgar and paltry are not generally thought of as evil (for they do no evil) but as wanderers from the straight path'[2]—meaning by the last phrase, one must suppose, moral cranks or eccentrics of a type not harmful but only tiresome.

That is Aristotle's judgment upon men such as Socrates: sorrowful rather than angry; pitying, as the worldly always pity the aberrations of the unworldly; in fact, the judgment of Callicles in the *Gorgias*, only more coolly analytical, less passionate, than that of Callicles. Viewed in this light, the portrait of the Magnanimous Man may be taken as the strongest proof to be found in the *Nicomachean Ethics* of Aristotle's implacable hostility to the moral philosophy of Socrates and Plato; compared, at any rate, with those rather wearisome

[1] *Gorgias*, 508 E (Jowett). [2] *Nic. Ethics*, IV. iii. 35 (Thomson).

logical arguments directed against the Form of the Good in the Sixth Chapter of the First Book of the *Nicomachean Ethics*, it is an attack incomparably more powerful and more radically undermining.

But if the Aristotelian ideal of magnanimity or justifiable pride is such an implicit criticism of Socrates, how much more is it—by anticipation, as it were—a criticism of St Paul? For consider Paul in the light of Aristotle's wisdom: a man of such parts as Paul; a man so clearly not undeserving of the highest honours; a man, if ever there was one, who could justly lay claim to the Aristotelian virtue of justifiable pride; yet a man who could so wantonly, so cravenly, so slavishly, deprive himself (in Aristotle's phrase) 'of such advantages as he deserved'. As we hear in a famous passage in the Epistle to the Philippians:

> What things were gain to me, these have I counted loss for Christ. Yea, verily, and I count all things to be loss for the excellency of the knowledge of Christ Jesus my Lord: for whom I suffered the loss of all things, and do count them but dung, that I may gain Christ.... I would know him in the power of his resurrection and the fellowship of his sufferings, with my nature transformed to die as he died, to see if I too can attain the resurrection from the dead. Not that I have already attained this, or am already perfect. But I press forward to appropriate it, because I have been appropriated myself by Christ Jesus.[1]

The distance that separates the Aristotelian view of human possibility from the Platonic and the Christian cannot be more strongly marked than by placing side by side the portrait of Aristotle's Magnanimous Man and these passages from the *Gorgias* and the Epistle to the Philippians.

Returning briefly to Socrates and the Magnanimous Man, there are evidences to suggest that Aristotle's account of the Magnanimous Man is intended as something more than an attack upon the Socratic and Platonic morality in general. It would seem to be directed specifically against the historic

[1] Phil. iii. 7–13.

Socrates himself; and since this is not a view commonly held, it is perhaps worth mentioning the evidences that appear to support it.

The chief of these is characteristically oblique and inexplicit but not therefore less striking. It turns upon Aristotle's curious insistence on the fact that the Magnanimous Man 'pursues honour' in the sense of *claiming that which is due to him* by virtue of his being the Perfect Man. But (it occurs to one to ask): if the Magnanimous Man is the Perfect Man, the man of *justifiable* pride, would not all honour *by definition* be due to him, and would he not by definition receive it, *whether or not he claimed it*? And if this is so, why this seemingly gratuitous emphasis on the fact that he claims it, and *justifiably* claims it?[1]

The emphasis would indeed be gratuitous—logically superfluous, that is, and therefore illogical—if Aristotle did not have a special reason for it. This reason, I suggest, is Socrates, his character and personality, and in particular his 'poor-spiritedness' and the *refusal* to claim what was due to him that this implies.

'It is a greater evil to do injustice than to suffer it', said Socrates in the *Gorgias*, thereby exposing himself to the scorn and derision of Polus and all the bystanders; and, 'Better to suffer tortures on the rack than have a soul burdened with the guilt of wrong-doing', said Socrates in the same exchange with Polus, leaving Polus speechless with astonishment and disgust at this slavish doctrine. Now there are certain significant asides in the *Nicomachean Ethics* which strongly suggest that Aristotle in the end stands with Polus (and Callicles) in his attitude to these central Socratic teachings. In one of these, he finds occasion to remark: 'People who maintain that, if only a man be good, he will be happy *even on the rack or when he is involved in some black disaster* are talking nonsense, whether they know it or not.'[2] Again, in discussing the claims of virtue (moral goodness) to be regarded as the Supreme Good, he

[1] *Nic. Ethics,* IV. iii. 11–14. [2] *Ibid.* VII. xiii. 3 (Thomson).

says, 'The virtuous man may meet with the most atrocious luck or ill-treatment; and *nobody who was not arguing for argument's sake would maintain that a man with an existence of that sort was "happy"*.'[1] (Aristotle forgets—or chooses not to remember—that Socrates had not said that the man on the rack was 'happy', only that he was 'less wretched' than the man who had committed injustices and escaped unpunished. But this little distortion of Socrates' doctrine might be taken as one of the signs of Aristotle's exasperation: he so much wants to undermine it that he does not mind if he *is* a little unscrupulous about the means he employs.[2])

These are the references to the man on the rack. As for the doctrine that it is better to suffer injustice than to do it: Aristotle, it transpires, cannot, any more than Polus in the *Gorgias*, deny that there is something morally unsavoury about the doing of injustice. Yet at the same time, the suggestion that it may therefore be better to suffer injustice is to him, as to Polus, thoroughly repugnant. Therefore, being Aristotle, he seeks a compromise, and produces it in the surprising definition of Justice as *a mean between doing injustice and suffering it*. For 'to do injustice' (he explains) 'is to have more than one ought, and to suffer it is to have less than one ought';[3] and since to have less than one ought—that is, to *claim* less than one ought—is the very definition of the despised quality of 'poor-spiritedness', we are back, through this definition of Justice, to the irreconcilable difference between Plato's Socrates and Aristotle's Magnanimous Man. And it is, of course, perfectly logical—perfectly consistent with his moral premises—that Aristotle should single out this and no other

[1] *Ibid.* I. v. 6 (Thomson).

[2] Another conspicuous instance of this kind of distortion occurs in Aristotle's attack on Plato's Form of the Good (*Nic. Ethics*, I. vi. 16), where he dismisses its claim to be considered the Supreme Good on the ground (among others) that 'it is not easy to see how knowing that same Ideal Good will help a weaver or carpenter in the practice of his own craft, or how anybody will be a better physician or general for having contemplated the absolute Idea'—a position never maintained by Plato.

[3] *Nic. Ethics*, v. v. 17 (Thomson).

feature of the Socratic character as the fundamental point of divergence between them. For the quality that Aristotle calls poor-spiritedness (and the Christian calls humility) is the quality that the religious will always affirm and strive to practise and the worldly and irreligious will always despise and reject; and if, on the hypothesis proposed, the portrait of the Magnanimous Man is intended (among other things) as a deliberate attack on the religious temper of the historic Socrates, Aristotle's seemingly gratuitous insistence on the fact that the Magnanimous Man not only deserves all honour but positively and insistently *claims* the honour that is due to him ceases to be illogical.

It now remains to discuss briefly those elements in the *Nicomachean Ethics* that appear to modify the anti-Platonic and anti-Christian character of Aristotle's view of man and so to redeem his low view of human possibility. These mitigating elements, it is claimed, are, first, Aristotle's recognition of a *summum bonum* or Supreme Good; second, his account of Justice; third, his account of Friendship; fourth, his praise of the Contemplative Life. The question to be asked about each is whether it does or does not in fact modify, mitigate and redeem in the way suggested.

(1) The account of the *summum bonum*, with which the *Nicomachean Ethics* opens, has been taken to set Aristotle apart from those other anti-Platonic and anti-Christian moralists in the tradition we are considering who deny, explicitly or implicitly, the existence of anything in the nature of an absolute or final end to which human effort is, and ought to be, directed. The chief of these is Hobbes, who denies it with the utmost explicitness. 'The felicity of this life', writes Hobbes in chapter XI of *Leviathan*, 'consisteth not in the repose of a mind satisfied':

For there is no such *finis ultimus*, utmost aim, nor *summum bonum*, greatest good, as is spoken of in the books of the old moral philosophers. Nor can a man any more live whose desires are at an end than he whose senses and imaginations are at a stand. Felicity is a continual progress of the desire from one object to another; the attaining of the former being still but the way to the latter.[1]

Felicity is 'a continual progress of the desire from one object to another', or (as he puts it in another place) 'a perpetual and restless desire of power after power, that ceaseth only in death.'[2] This is indeed to deny the existence of an absolute or final end; and Aristotle's affirmation of such an end in the opening sections of the *Nicomachean Ethics* would seem to set him apart from Hobbes, and place him, on this vital point at least, in the same camp with Plato and St Paul.

This would be true if Aristotle's affirmation of a Supreme Good could be taken at its face value. But its face value is not its real value; and what is affirmed about the Supreme Good in the whole lengthy discussion contained in the First Book of the *Nicomachean Ethics* amounts to very much less than is generally supposed.

The supreme Good, says Aristotle, is Happiness, meaning by this that Happiness is the ultimate end to which all human activity is directed. But in saying this, Aristotle surely says nothing different from Hobbes, who also insists that the end to which man's endeavours are directed is what he calls Felicity. The only difference, so far, is that Hobbes refuses to call this Felicity or Happiness the *summum bonum* or Supreme Good, since, as he puts it (probably with Aristotle himself in mind), 'There is no such *finis ultimus*, utmost aim, nor *summum bonum*, greatest good, as is spoken of in the books of the old philosophers.'

Now Aristotle does affirm what Hobbes denies, namely, that there is a *summum bonum* or Supreme Good. But since bare affirmation and bare denial are as meaningless in philosophy as in ordinary discourse, everything hangs upon Aristotle's demonstrating, or at least arguing, the real existence of the Supreme Good and defining its real properties. What we find, however, is that Aristotle neither demonstrates

[1] *Leviathan*, ch. 11, p. 63. [2] *Ibid.* ch. 11, p. 64.

it nor even argues it, but merely asserts it in the baldest way; and asserts it, moreover, in a form that seriously calls in question its real existence.

The crucial statement runs as follows:

> If. . . among the ends at which our actions aim there be one which we wish for its own sake, while we wish the others only for the sake of this, and if we do not choose everything for the sake of something else (which would obviously result in a process *ad infinitum*, so that all desire would be futile and vain), it is clear that this one ultimate End must be the Good, and indeed the Supreme Good. . . .[1]

What Aristotle is saying here is that *if* there existed an end 'which we wish for its own sake', a final end beyond which there are no other ends, then its proper *name* would be the *summum bonum* or Supreme Good. *If* it existed: but Aristotle does not here, or anywhere else in the *Nicomachean Ethics*, affirm that it does exist; he only proceeds, in the rest of Book I, to enumerate the properties of the Supreme Good—finality, self-sufficiency and so on—*supposing that it did exist.*

This is the first point, that Aristotle nowhere affirms the real existence of the Supreme Good. The second is that he merely affirms, but nowhere demonstrates, that it is even logically necessary to suppose that it exists. He *appears* to demonstrate the logical necessity in the parenthetical remark in the passage quoted above; what he there seems to say is that if we do *not* assume the existence of a Supreme Good, the result is an infinite regress of frustrated desire—or, as Hobbes put it, 'a perpetual and restless desire of power after power that ceaseth only in death'. But to say this is surely to argue only the need, the merely psychological need, for assuming the existence of a Supreme Good. It does not prove, or even argue, the fact that it does exist. And since the fact is not proved or argued, it can legitimately be denied—as, we have seen, Hobbes does deny it in his definition of Felicity.

What is interesting, however, is that Hobbes does not merely deny it as Aristotle merely asserts it. He does attempt

[1] *Nic. Ethics*, I. ii. 1.

to demonstrate, that is, to argue the validity of, his denial of a *summum bonum* or Supreme Good. And he argues the validity of his position in the only way open to a systematic philosopher, by showing that this and no other position is consistent with the rest of his philosophical system. He invokes the whole of his philosophical doctrine—materialist, nominalist and psychological—in support of his denial of a *summum bonum* or Supreme Good; he shows that to deny it is rigorously consistent with every part of his philosophical system, and is therefore entailed by the whole of it; and to show this *is* to demonstrate in the only proper philosophical sense of the word.

But it is Hobbes's reason for taking all this trouble to demonstrate the validity of his denial that is significant for the present argument. The reason is, of course, that it is vitally necessary to his moral and political doctrine that there should exist no such *summum bonum.* It is as necessary for Hobbes's doctrine of man and doctrine of commonwealth to deny the existence of a Supreme Good as it is necessary for Plato's and St Augustine's to affirm its existence. Why this should be so is a question to be pursued elsewhere;[1] the relevant point for the present argument is merely the fact that it is so. For it is this fact that accounts, I believe, for the difference between Hobbes's treatment of the *summum bonum* and Aristotle's, and explains why Hobbes's should be so thorough, Aristotle's so perfunctory. Aristotle's perfunctoriness in the treatment of a matter as vital as the Supreme Good may be taken as a measure of its lack of importance in Aristotle's moral system. Compared with the kind of importance that the Form of the Good has in Plato's system, or the Living God in St Augustine's, it is of no *real* importance whether Aristotle affirms or does not affirm a Supreme Good; it is (in the philosophical sense of the word explained below) of purely *nominal* importance. And this suggestion—that Aristotle treats the matter of the Supreme Good so perfunctorily

[1] See ch. IV, pp. 119–21 below.

because it is of merely nominal importance in the moral system of the *Nicomachean Ethics*—is supported by the significant fact that Aristotle never returns to it in that treatise. He never finds occasion to refer to it again, either explicitly or implicitly; he has, in fact, no further use for it in his ethical system; and when he does return to it, in Book VII of the *Politics*, it is only to say again what he said in the First Book of the *Nicomachean Ethics*, that the Supreme Good is Happiness, that this is what all men seek as their ultimate good, and that the Good State must therefore pursue Happiness as its ultimate end.[1] And this is to take the matter not a step further than it was taken in the First Book of the *Nicomachean Ethics*.

There is more to say about Aristotle's treatment of the Supreme Good, particularly in explanation of the view that the whole account of the Supreme Good in Book I is purely nominal in the philosophical, not the popular, sense. This is not the place to argue this point in detail, or (even less) to attempt to establish a larger hypothesis concerning the submerged nominalism of the whole Aristotelian logic, which (on this hypothesis) would be seen to infect the Aristotelian method of analysis throughout the *Nicomachean Ethics* and the *Rhetoric*, and would establish another profound link between Aristotle and Hobbes. The point can only be mentioned here, with a brief indication of the way in which it confirms the suggestion that Aristotle's analysis of the Supreme Good in Book I is not what it appears to be. It is not, as it appears to be, an analysis of the real, concrete properties of the real, concrete *experience* that we call happiness; it is merely a logical or linguistic analysis of the meaning of the *term* (the *name*) 'Supreme Good' or 'Happiness'.[2] To say, for instance, that the defining properties of the true happiness

[1] *Politics*, VII. xii. 2.

[2] Aristotle himself appears to emphasise the nominal character of his definitions: for instance, 'By the term "absolutely final", we denote that which is an object of choice always in itself, and never with a view to any other' (*Nic. Ethics*, I. vii. 4); and 'We define that to be self-sufficient "which taken alone makes life choiceworthy, and to be in want of nothing" '(*ibid.* I. vii. 7).

are peace, power and joy is to give the real, concrete properties of the experience that we call happiness; and each of these properties is amenable to further real, concrete specification. To say, on the other hand, as Aristotle says in the First Book of the *Nicomachean Ethics*, that the defining properties of Happiness are 'finality', 'self-sufficiency', 'that which we pursue for its own sake', 'that beyond which there is no further end' and so on, is to give the abstract, logical properties of an entity that is not an experience but a concept: it is to define, not the nature of the '*thing*' Happiness, but the meaning of the *word* or *name* 'Happiness'. And because (it can be argued) nominal definitions in moral philosophy, whatever may be true of logic and epistemology, are never a legitimate substitute for real definitions, Aristotle's analysis of the Supreme Good in Book I of the *Nicomachean Ethics* may well give the impression of offering only the stones of logical analysis to those who come to it for the bread of moral wisdom.

(2) Of Aristotle's treatment of Justice in Book V of the *Nicomachean Ethics* the main criticism is substantially the same as that of the Supreme Good in Book I. The definition of Justice in its largest sense, as synonymous with Righteousness, which (some have thought) suggests a close affinity between Aristotle's moral doctrine and Plato's, is in fact as nominal as the definition of the Supreme Good. It is so general and abstract, so 'empty' or 'tautological', as logicians call it, that it is compatible with almost any particular political system. It is as compatible, for instance, with Hobbes's political system in *Leviathan* and Plato's system in the *Republic* as with Aristotle's own Best State, as he calls the ideal commonwealth in the *Politics*; and a definition of Justice or Righteousness that is so catholic as to be equally applicable to systems as fundamentally opposed as Plato's and Hobbes's is, in the ordinary, as well as the strict, sense of the word, 'empty'—empty or meaningless.

The crucial definition is as follows:

> It is clear that, since the lawless man is. . unjust and the law-abiding man just, all lawful things may be regarded as just, *where by 'lawful' we mean what is plainly prescribed by the legislative power.* (We imply that these ordinances are every one of them 'just'.) . . . So here we have one meaning of the word 'just'. It is applied to *whatever creates or conserves for a political association its happiness or the happiness of some part thereof.* Besides this the law imposes certain regulations about the way a man should behave. For instance, he must prove his courage by refusing to leave his post in battle or run away or discard his accoutrements; prove his continence by refraining from adultery, outrage, etc.; prove his gentleness by (for example) not wounding others by words or blows. And so with the rest of the virtues and vices—law deals with all of them, *enjoining the former, prohibiting the latter. If it has been rightly enacted, it will do this rightly*; *not so rightly, if it is a hastily devised expedient.*
>
> Now justice in this sense of the word is complete virtue. . . .[1]

What is chiefly remarkable about this definition of Justice or Righteousness is that it succeeds in begging all the really important questions. It begs all the questions which, if left unanswered, leave us quite unable to determine Aristotle's precise political doctrine, and quite unable, in particular, to decide whether it stands with that of the *Republic* or that of *Leviathan*. For this whole account of Justice is seen, on closer examination, to be only another example of Aristotle's famous propensity to circular definitions—definitions, that is, of the meanings of words, not of the properties of things; and as such it is another interesting example of the submerged nominalism mentioned just now in connexion with the Supreme Good in Book I.

What, we ask, is the just? That which is lawful, answers Aristotle. And what is the lawful? That which is plainly prescribed by the legislative power. Again, What is political justice? That which creates or conserves for a political association its happiness or the happiness of some part of it. When is a law just? When it has been rightly enacted. When unjust? When it is 'a hastily devised expedient'—that is, has

[1] *Nic. Ethics*, v. i. 12–15 (Thomson).

been *wrongly* enacted. Each of these so-called definitions is, too plainly, merely a definition of the meaning of the word or term 'just', 'unjust', 'law', 'lawful', and so on. Each of these so-called definitions, being entirely circular or tautological, is equally compatible with any concrete political system, with the system of Hobbes's *Leviathan* no less than with that of Plato's *Republic*; and if this is so, there is nothing, I suggest, in Aristotle's definition of Justice to modify the essentially anti-Platonic (and anti-Christian) character of the doctrine of the *Nicomachean Ethics* which I have tried to establish on other grounds.

The remaining two elements in Aristotle's system that would appear, at last indisputably, to redeem his low view of man's nature and place him much closer to the Platonic and Christian positions than has so far seemed possible are his account of Friendship in Book VIII of the *Nicomachean Ethics* and his account of the Contemplative Life in Book X.

(3) Aristotle's account of Friendship would indeed seem to suggest that here, if nowhere else, he is approaching a recognition of the transcendent quality of love. He distinguishes, it will be remembered, three principal kinds of friendship, that kind which has for its object the useful or profitable, that which has for its object the pleasant, and that which has for its object the good. The first, friendship for the sake of utility, says Aristotle (recalling to our minds his portraits of the three types of character in the *Rhetoric*) is the kind most commonly practised by the old: for Elderly Men, as he showed in the *Rhetoric*, do everything for the sake of the useful, for what they can get out of it, as we would say.[1] And friendship for the sake of the pleasant is the kind of friendship that the young go in for; for their main object in life, according to Aristotle, is to keep themselves amused, and they do everything for the sake of the fun they can get out of it.[2] But friendship for the sake of the good, that which has for its

[1] *Nic. Ethics*, VIII. iii. 4. [2] *Ibid.* VIII. iii. 5.

object the goodness of the friend, not his pleasantness or his usefulness, which takes a delight in the friend for his own sake and is therefore truly disinterested, truly self-less—this kind of friendship (says Aristotle) is the best kind and can only be enjoyed by the truly *good man*.[1]

The emphasis upon the disinterestedness of this kind of friendship, which makes it the best and most perfect kind, is quite explicit in the following passage:

> So then it appears that from motives of pleasure or profit bad men may be friends to one another, or good men to bad men, or men of neutral character to one of any character whatever: *but disinterestedly, for the sake of one another, plainly the good alone can be friends*; because bad men have no pleasure even in themselves unless in so far as some advantage arises;[2]

and this recognition of disinterested friendship, which is as near as Aristotle comes anywhere in his whole moral philosophy to the recognition of love as a constituent of man's nature, would indeed seem to be a large concession, and would indeed seem to make a breach in Aristotle's low view of human possibility.

But the breach is apparent rather than real. 'Plainly the good alone can be friends', says Aristotle; and this sounds admirable. But, remembering Aristotle's account of the moral virtues earlier in the *Nicomachean Ethics*, and remembering in particular that the most splendid of the moral virtues is 'magnanimity' or 'justifiable pride', and that the exemplar of perfect virtue is the Magnanimous Man; remembering, in short, that *the Good Man is the Magnanimous Man*, what are we to infer from this but that the Magnanimous Man and he alone is capable of perfect friendship? And the Magnanimous Man being the man who does everything out of pride and nothing out of love, what (we have to ask ourselves) will be the real nature of this disinterested friendship of which only the truly Good Man—that is, the Magnanimous Man—is capable?

[1] *Nic. Ethics*, VIII. iii. 6.
[2] *Ibid.* VIII. iv. 2 (Lindsay).

It will be disinterested indeed; but it will be so because the Magnanimous Man is too consciously proud of his own virtue to be anything else—because, characteristically, he would scorn to be anything else. He would scorn to be anything but disinterested in friendship because to pursue friendship for the sake of pleasure or utility would place him on a level with other men; and this above everything, we have already learnt, the Magnanimous Man will desire to avoid. He will be a disinterested friend out of pride, not out of love; because he, of all men, can best afford to be disinterested; because he, being perfectly self-sufficient, has no need of anything any man can give him of pleasure or utility. Like Hobbes's Gallant Man he 'scorns to be beholden for the contentment of his life' to the baser forms of friendship, and for this reason, and this reason alone, engages only in the most superior kind.

To establish the difference between the Aristotelian conception of Friendship and the Platonic conception of Love, it is only necessary to recall Diotima's definition of love in the *Symposium*.[1] Love (Diotima tells Socrates) is the child of Penury and Contrivance; and what she means by the lover's 'penury' is his *need* (to be 'filled with that which he lacks', as she puts it)—his total *lack* of the Aristotelian self-sufficiency, his total *dependence* upon the beloved. It is out of penury, out of need, out of the absence of self-sufficiency, that Love springs; it is this, his condition of absolute penury, that drives him on, unceasingly, to seek the ultimate object of his love, which is the form of Beauty itself; and (Diotima adds) it is by contrivance or resourcefulness, that is, by his native intelligence and resolution, that he succeeds in attaining to the final goal of his aspiration.

If the difference between the Platonic conception of love and the Aristotelian conception of friendship is absolute and irreducible, how much more is this true of the difference between the Aristotelian conception of friendship and the

[1] *Symp.* 203 B–E.

Christian conception of love. There are many ways of defining the difference, but what perhaps proves it most conclusively is that Aristotle's friendship has no power to transform the world that the Magnanimous Man inhabits. It has no power even to alter or modify, much less to annihilate, the wisdom of the world (as St Paul was to call it) figured in the Magnanimous Man. Aristotle's friendship coexists peacefully with courage and temperance and liberality and magnanimity as just another of the several 'goods' that the man perfected in all the worldly virtues will enjoy. It is not, of course, the less a virtue for being merely co-ordinate with the other virtues; but it is not to be compared for splendour and efficacy, for the power to transform and glorify, with the love that, according to the New Testament story, descended upon the disciples on the day of Pentecost in the shape of cloven tongues of fire.

(4) The same kind of difference as that between Friendship in the Aristotelian scheme and love in the Platonic and Christian schemes is, I believe, to be discerned between Aristotle's view of the Contemplative Life and Plato's. Aristotle's account of the Contemplative Life is generally taken to be his closest link with Plato; and it is certainly true that he is quite as explicit as Plato about the supreme value of the life of contemplation. In Book x of the *Nicomachean Ethics*, he enlarges, with uncharacteristic vivacity, upon the perfections of the life of pure contemplation.[1] Among other things, it can be enjoyed with only a moderate endowment of worldly goods. It is of all human activities the most perfectly self-sufficient since it alone 'aims at no end beyond itself'. It also yields the highest and most durable pleasure. Indeed the Contemplative Man, in his perfect exercise of his contemplative powers, participates most fully in the divine nature, enjoying a life akin to that of the gods; and consequently (Aristotle concludes, quite explicitly), 'perfect hap-

[1] *Nic. Ethics*, x. vii. 1–9.

piness [that is, the highest good] is some form of contemplative activity'.[1]

To claim all this for the Contemplative Life (one might well argue) is surely to claim hardly less than Plato himself claimed for it—in the allegory of the Cave and (even more) in his image of the Sun, in which he seeks to express the visionary experience of the Form of the Good. Yet Aristotle's claim for the Contemplative Life is not the same as Plato's. It is different; it is less; and it is too little. It is different, to begin with: so different, indeed, that to apply the word 'contemplative' both to Plato's and Aristotle's conception is positively misleading. It is not difficult to see that Plato's conception of the contemplative activity has the closest affinity with the Christian's. As for the Christian mystic the contemplative activity has for its ultimate end the beatific vision, so for Plato it has for its ultimate end the direct visionary experience of the Form of the Good. In both instances contemplation ends in an experience that is supra-rational, supra-intellectual—immediate, intuitive, not discursive or ratiocinative at all.

Now it is certain that Aristotle has nothing of this in mind when he praises what the translators write as 'the contemplative life'. The word that is much nearer to Aristotle's meaning is the word *speculative*. For Aristotle's Speculative Man, the man perfected in what he calls the intellectual virtues, is simply the professional philosopher—the analytical philosopher, the logician, the schoolman: the man whose characteristic activity or function is to analyse and classify, to construct systems of true distinctions, to perfect himself in the art of ratiocination. It is this and nothing more. Nowhere is there any suggestion that this Speculative Man ever transcends the ratiocinative, that his speculative power is directed to any supra-rational end comparable with Plato's Form of the Good. Aristotle's Speculative Man is accordingly something quite different from Plato's Contemplative Man and from the Christian mystic. He is the analytical philo-

[1] *Ibid.* x. viii. 7.

sopher; and is to be thought of as close kin to Bertrand Russell and G. E. Moore rather than to St John of the Cross or even St Thomas Aquinas.

This is the principal point about Aristotle's so-called Contemplative Man. And now there arises the pleasantly tantalising question of the relation of the Speculative Man to the Magnanimous Man and the Perfect Friend. These three, the Speculative Man, the Magnanimous Man and the Perfect Friend, represent three apparently distinct and apparently contradictory ideals of human perfection in the *Nicomachean Ethics*; and the question is whether they are in fact contradictory; and if not contradictory, how they are reconciled.

I have already suggested that the Magnanimous Man and the Perfect Friend are mutually reconcilable, and I indicated the grand fundamental characteristic in which they meet. This is their self-sufficiency. The Magnanimous Man is the perfectly self-sufficient man; and because he is so perfectly self-sufficient, he is also the Perfect Friend, being the man who, preeminently, can afford to be the Perfect Friend.

I now want to suggest that also the ideal of the Magnanimous Man and the ideal of the Speculative Man may be reconciled upon the common ground of their self-sufficiency. The Magnanimous Man, the man perfected in all the moral virtues, is self-sufficient in his possession of all the highest 'external' goods, of which the chief is honour. The Speculative Man, the man perfected in all the intellectual virtues, is perfectly self-sufficient in his possession of all the 'internal' goods, of which the highest, presumably, is the enjoyment of his own sublime analytical powers. Consequently there is no reason why the Magnanimous Man should not also be the Speculative Man. Indeed, in accordance with the doctrine of the Mean, to be both the Magnanimous Man and the Speculative Man would perhaps be the ultimate perfection—the perfection of perfections—to be aimed at: to strike the mean, that is, between the excess of either the practical or the intellectual virtues and the defect of either; neither to run to an excess of the speculative and a defect of the practical, (like that misguided man Socrates), nor to fall into a defect of the speculative and an excess of the practical (like, presumably, the vulgar men of affairs); but to pursue both, in the sensible moderation that is the mark of the Aristotelian ideal, which is perhaps best described in the phrase of a seventeenth-century English divine who, speaking in praise of the Church of England, called it (without irony) 'the way of virtuous mediocrity'.

So the Magnanimous Man, the Perfect Friend and the Speculative Man are, in the end, all one man; and the ultimate Aristotelian ideal may be pictured in the image of a somewhat profane Trinity. The Speculative Man, perfected in his God-like speculative reason, is the *logos* itself, the reason or ground of all things; the Magnanimous Man, perfected in the practical reason and firmly rooted in the world, is the Word made flesh; and the Perfect Friend, the good loving the good for the sake of the good, is the nearest thing to the Holy Spirit. And these three, the Perfect Man in the aspect of the Speculative Man, the Perfect Man in the aspect of the Magnanimous Man and the Perfect Man in the aspect of the Perfect Friend, are made one by the divine quality of self-sufficiency, which translates, or practically translates, the Perfect Man of the *Nicomachean Ethics* into God himself.

There is still one last and very important difference to be remarked between Aristotle's conception of the speculative or contemplative reason and Plato's. For Plato, we know, 'knowledge' as distinct from mere 'opinion' was accessible only to the pure or contemplative reason. The final end to which the contemplative activity was directed was the apprehension of the Form of the Good, this being at once the highest reach and the perfection of speculative knowledge. And such knowledge was also virtue, since the mind that had direct access to the Form of the Good, the single ultimate source of all saving knowledge, was by the same act also rendered perfect in goodness; and expressed that goodness, that perfected virtue, by a life dedicated to the service of the commonwealth.

For Plato, accordingly, there is an unbroken continuity between the supreme exercise of the contemplative reason, culminating in the vision of the Form of the Good, and that of the practical reason, issuing in the first instance in the perfection of personal virtue, and ultimately in the perfection of political virtue—the making of perfect laws and the perfect administration of those laws—in the service of the commonwealth. The allegory of the Cave pictures this continuity in a memorable way: it is when a man has received the light (Plato tells us), when he has seen face to face the Form of the Good, that he receives also the power to lead the best life and to teach others by his precept and example. For Plato, in other words, the contemplative reason, at its maximum reach, illuminates and renders truly efficacious the practical reason; it possesses in the Platonic system that same power to transform and transfigure that in the Christian scheme belongs to love.

It is this precisely that we miss in the Aristotelian scheme, this continuity of the contemplative reason with the practical. There is no such continuity; and because no continuity, therefore no transforming effect of the contemplative upon the practical. Or, to put it somewhat differently: what we miss in Aristotle's scheme is an internal, organic connexion between the ideal of the Magnanimous Man and the ideal of the so-called Contemplative Man. In Aristotle's scheme, the exercise of the practical reason reaches the perfection proper to itself in the Magnanimous Man, the man perfected in all the moral virtues and replete in all external goods; and the exercise of the speculative reason reaches the perfection proper to itself in the Speculative Man—the analytical philosopher, the man perfected in all the intellectual virtues, and replete in all internal goods. And there they stand, these two, totally distinct and unconnected. And the fact that the same man may in fact be both a Magnanimous Man and a Speculative Man does not affect this essential discontinuity. While in Plato's philosopher-king, the practical reason and the contemplative may be seen as internally connected aspects of a single organic whole, in Aristotle's Perfect Man the practical and the contemplative are not organically connected at all. Indeed, in Aristotle's Perfect Man they are not, properly speaking, aspects at all, but only parts—distinct and mutually disconnected parts of a whole that is never more than the sum of its parts.

This is the fundamental discontinuity in Aristotle's scheme between the practical reason and the contemplative. It explains why the contemplative reason—which, in the Aristotelian scheme as in the Platonic, is the highest power in man—can yet have no effect upon the acquisition of practical moral virtue, or indeed upon any part of the practical moral life of a man either as private individual or as citizen; and it explains also why the contemplative reason can have no transforming power. What in Aristotle's system transforms men, makes them better than they are, is neither Magnanimity nor Friendship nor Contemplation—nothing, that is, 'internal' to the nature of man; but only good laws and good institutions. Those who do not believe (with the Platonist) in the redeeming power of the perfected intelligence or (with the Christian) in the redeeming power of perfected love, have no alternative but to believe in the redeeming power of good institutions.

I have deliberately offered this as the last consequence of Aristotle's view of man's nature in order to emphasise again the fundamental affinity between Aristotle's political doctrine and Hobbes's. Both are obliged to believe in the saving power of good political institutions because both believe so little in the saving power of intelligence or love; and the doctrine of *Leviathan*, savage and extreme though it is, is only a development of the doctrine of the *Nicomachean Ethics* and the *Politics*.

CHAPTER IV

FEAR FOR LOVE

HOBBES'S 'LEVIATHAN'

IN passing from Aristotle's *Nicomachean Ethics* to Hobbes's *Leviathan* we pass from the great classic sketch of what I have called the low view of human nature to the full definitive study. *Leviathan* is the most cogent, the most impressive, and, in point of its literary accomplishment, the most masterly rendering of this view of man's nature that is to be found in the whole range of English moral philosophy.

In the total plan of *Leviathan*, the theory of man (Hobbes gives it the title 'Of Man') is only one part. *Leviathan* is not in the first instance an ethical treatise, but a treatise on what in the seventeenth century was called civil philosophy, what we would call today political philosophy or political science. The full title of the book is 'Leviathan, or the Matter, Form and Power of a Commonwealth Ecclesiastical and Civil'. But the theory of man, which is Hobbes's doctrine of human nature, receives all the prominence that is due to it in the logical structure of the whole system. For Hobbes's political doctrine, his theory of commonwealth, depends, in the strictest logical sense of the word, upon his moral doctrine, his theory of man's nature. It is because man is the kind of creature that he is (runs Hobbes's central argument) that the rule of the absolute sovereign Leviathan is the only possible—the only *logically* possible—form of commonwealth in which men may live together in peace. For man (according to Hobbes) is a creature dominated by two fundamental passions, the desire to preserve himself and the fear of violent death; these passions create his fundamental predicament, what Hobbes calls the 'state of nature', a condition of 'war of everyone against everyone', in which every man is intent upon preserving himself from destruction at the hands of every other man; and since in the 'state of nature' no man is strong enough to preserve himself by destroying everyone else, yet every man is in perpetual danger of violent death at the hands of every other man, the only way by which everyone may be saved from violent death is by the expedient of the 'covenant'—that expedient by which all men, voluntarily and simultaneously, agree to transfer to a single supreme sovereign their natural right to preserve themselves, and confer upon that single supreme sovereign the absolute right and the absolute power to protect them all from destruction.[1]

The logic of the argument is inescapable. If we grant Hobbes his basic premise, that man is as he says he is, then we have no alternative but to accept his doctrine of commonwealth, for it follows by an ineluctable necessity from his view of man's nature.

It is unlikely that we will, in the end, grant Hobbes his basic premise or assent to his view of man's nature. Our first task, however, is neither to assent nor to dissent, but to understand; and in our effort to follow the movement of Hobbes's mind and grasp the design and the details of his classic rendering of the low view, we will find that we have answered the most important questions concerning Hobbes as a moral philosopher.

The chief of these is the question of Hobbes's stature as a moral philosopher. Granted that his view of human life is as low as possible, granted even that it is 'diabolical' (as his Christian contemporaries thought it was), is it nevertheless not also a tragic view of life—a picture, as true as it is terrible, of the human condition when men have ceased to believe in the transforming power of love as an intrinsic constituent of

[1] The account of *Leviathan* in this chapter leans heavily on Professor Michael Oakeshott's Introduction to his edition of *Leviathan* (Basil Blackwell's Political Texts, 1946), which I regard as the most definitive, and most brilliant, study of Hobbes available to us. Since, however, I am here chiefly concerned with Hobbes as a moralist while Professor Oakeshott was chiefly concerned with him as a political philosopher, my account naturally differs from his in general direction and emphasis.

man's nature? This (we are likely to feel, with growing certainty as we enter more and more fully into Hobbes's world) is what the world *must* be like when the power of love is removed from it. And if the Hobbesian vision of the world is indeed in this sense tragic, it is so because Hobbes has grasped it and rendered it in the manner of the great artist. It is because he has explored it to its furthest limits, has contemplated it steady and whole, never for one moment relaxing his hold upon it and never losing his nerve, and has recorded it with a passion and a sobriety, with an intensely impersonal regard to the object, and a concreteness in the details rarely to be met with in a philosophical work, that *Leviathan* has all the authority of a great work of art and stands in English philosophy as the definitive statement of the low view of man's nature.

And for the Christian it has a special value. It has, or ought to have, the value of making him see more clearly than ever why it was necessary for Christ to be crucified in order to save the world. For if, speaking in the manner of men, it was to save men from Hobbes's state of nature that Christ was crucified, one can see the point of the Crucifixion better perhaps than one ever saw it before.

It is only fair to say that not all modern readers of Hobbes have pitched his claim to consideration as high as this. T. S. Eliot, for instance, in his essay on Bishop Bramhall, pitches it very low indeed. 'Thomas Hobbes', he writes, 'was one of those extraordinary little upstarts whom the chaotic motions of the Renaissance tossed into an eminence which they hardly deserved and have never lost';[1] and upon the logical structure of *Leviathan*, which we shall find cause to admire for its intricacy and its exemplary rigour, Mr Eliot comments with a similar brevity: '[Hobbes's] theory of government has no philosophic basis; it is merely a collection of discrete opinions, prejudices, and genuine reflections upon experience, which are given a spurious unity by a shadowy

[1] T. S. Eliot, 'Bishop Bramhall' (in *Selected Essays*, p. 345).

metaphysic.'[1] And Professor D. G. James, another hostile modern critic of Hobbes,[2] is quite as hard on Hobbes as Mr Eliot, only for different reasons. He does not indeed reduce Hobbes's stature by failing to understand what he is saying; on the contrary, he understands Hobbes very well. But all that I have urged as admirable in Hobbes as a philosopher Professor James finds wholly reprehensible, in particular the famous rigour, consequentiality and so on; he contrasts Locke of the 'humble heart' with Hobbes of the 'proud mind', thus confusing the man that suffers (if this is what Hobbes suffered from) with the mind that creates; and does not even find a good word to say for the artistic integrity, let alone the philosophic integrity, of *Leviathan*.

Mr Eliot and Professor James fail to make certain important discriminations in respect to Hobbes's tone and temper in *Leviathan*. It is important, for instance, not to mistake Hobbes's passion for mere gusto, or the ferocious, ruthless energy with which he seeks to undermine traditional attitudes and doctrines for simple destructiveness and the cocking of a snook at the bishops of the Church of England. For Hobbes is no village atheist; and his critique (in Part III of *Leviathan*, 'Of a Christian Commonwealth') of the Church viewed as a purely political institution deserves to be taken very seriously. Again, it is important not to mistake Hobbes's intense sobriety for mere coldness. His treatment of the passions in Part I of *Leviathan* is desolating indeed; but its source is not a cold personal revulsion from all that is vile in man. It is rather the impersonal, objective coldness, or 'coolness', of a man intently, intensely, concentrated upon his object, who *has* to keep cool in order that he may not fail to see the object steady and whole. Chiefly, however, judgments such as those of Mr Eliot and Professor James take Hobbes's view of the predicament of man to be not tragic but merely pessimistic; whereas the literary evidences, I have

[1] *Ibid.* p. 346.

[2] D. G. James, *The Life of Reason: Hobbes, Locke, Bolingbroke* (1949).

suggested, support the contrary view, that the Hobbesian vision is genuinely tragic, and that it is as complete, as cogent and as powerful a rendering of that vision as any that has been known.

NOMINALISM

In spite of what Mr Eliot says about Hobbes's lack of any 'philosophic basis' for his theory of government, exactly the contrary appears to be the truth. Hobbes's doctrine of commonwealth ('theory of government') is logically grounded in his theory of man's nature, and both the theory of government and the theory of man's nature are logically grounded in a philosophic doctrine that is worked out with the utmost care, and presented in a system remarkable for its completeness and consistency. This philosophic doctrine is composed of two distinct but intimately related parts. The first is an epistemological theory, being a theory about the nature and origin of human knowledge, the second a metaphysical theory, concerning the nature of the real; and these two theories find a common basis in Hobbes's materialism and nominalism. They are both thoroughly materialistic and nominalistic in character; and in both the materialism and the nominalism confirm and reinforce each other.

I take the nominalism, however, to be logically prior to the materialism, and in that sense fundamental to Hobbes's whole system; and since it is generally not so well understood as the materialism, I propose to discuss it rather more fully.

Hobbes's whole nominalistic doctrine is contained in two short, exceedingly compressed chapters in *Leviathan*, Chapter 4 entitled 'Of Speech' and Chapter 5 entitled 'Of Reason and Science.' I have taken my account chiefly from these chapters in *Leviathan*, but have also drawn upon two of his other works for supplementary evidence: an earlier work called *Elements of Law* (which is in effect an early draft of *Leviathan*) and a later work called *Of Computation or Logic*. These have the merit of stating the main doctrines more fully and explicitly, and are therefore useful for illuminating what Hobbes sets out in those two definitive chapters in *Leviathan*.

The main points of Hobbes's nominalistic doctrine can, by strenuous compression, be reduced to four in number.[1] They are, first, the view that what logicians call 'universals' are names and nothing but names; second, that truth is a property of language, and of language only; third, that knowledge or 'science' is purely deductive, purely mathematical, in character; and, fourth, that meaning and truth are both established by what Hobbes calls 'arbitrary institution'. These points, taken together in their logical sequence in Hobbes's system, yield the essential features of Hobbes's nominalism.

First, then, concerning the nature of universals. The term 'universal' is used to designate classes of objects or properties as distinct from individual, particular objects or properties. 'Man', 'horse', 'tree', for instance, are all names of classes of objects, as distinct from 'Peter' or 'John', 'this tree', 'that horse', which are names of particular, individual objects; and 'redness', 'tallness', 'justice' are the names of classes of properties as distinct from 'this red rose', 'that tall man', 'that just king', where 'red', 'tall', 'just' are the names of particular properties belonging to particular objects.

Now Hobbes's view of universals is that they are *names*, and nothing but names; and it is a great and persistent error (he repeatedly insists) to suppose that they are in any sense real existents. 'There is nothing in the world universal but names', he says in Chapter 4 of *Leviathan*, meaning by this crucial sentence that there is no such thing as a class of objects or properties *in nature*. The only 'things' in nature, the only real existents, are individual, particular things; therefore the universal terms that we habitually use correspond to nothing in nature. They are *only* terms ('names') used to designate 'class-concepts', which are themselves merely the product of the classifying activity of the human mind, and as such purely mental constructions.

[1] I have discussed Hobbes's nominalism more fully in an article, 'Thomas Hobbes's Doctrine of Meaning and Truth,' published in *Philosophy*, vol. XXXI, no. 116 (January 1956).

The nominalistic point here, as elsewhere in Hobbes's nominalist doctrine, is that reality (or nature, or the universe—the terms can be used interchangeably) is composed exclusively of discrete or mutually disconnected particular things. Nothing is 'given' in nature but discrete, disconnected particulars or singulars. There is no such thing in nature as an *ordering* of these particulars or singulars; no such thing in nature, therefore, as *classes* of particulars—a classification being, precisely, an ordering of particulars or singulars. And since classes do not exist in nature, they are merely products of the human mind, merely class-concepts; the universal terms that are used to designate these class-concepts are therefore merely names; and this is what Hobbes means by the statement, 'There is nothing in the world universal but names'.

From his account of the nature of universals, we pass to Hobbes's account of the nature of truth, which is the heart of his nominalistic doctrine. This is summed up in another crucial statement, in the earlier work called *Elements of Law*, 'Truth, and a true proposition, is all one';[1] and what this means is that the terms 'true' and 'false' can be legitimately applied to propositions and to propositions only. But a proposition for Hobbes is a purely linguistic phenomenon. It is not a statement, for instance, about a fact, or a state of affairs, in the real world; it is merely 'a speech' (as Hobbes calls it), consisting of two 'names' joined together by a 'copula'; and it is a *true* 'speech' or proposition when it satisfies the purely logical condition that the meaning of the predicate-name shall 'comprehend' (or include) the meaning of the subject-name. Thus (to take Hobbes's own example), the proposition 'Man is a living creature' is a true proposition for this reason, and this reason only, that it consists of a subject-name 'man' and a predicate-name 'living creature' linked together by the copula 'is' in such a way that the predicate-name 'living creature' includes or 'comprehends' the subject-name 'man'.[2]

[1] *Elements of Law*, I. v. 10.

[2] *Of Computation or Logic*, iii. 2; *Elements of Law*, I. v. 9–10.

This, according to Hobbes, is what makes the proposition 'Man is a living creature' a true proposition, this purely logical or nominal relation between the words or terms that constitute the proposition. There is no reference to any correspondence of the proposition with a fact or state of affairs in the real world; and this is what makes Hobbes's definition of truth radically nominalistic. The point is made even more explicitly in *Leviathan*. 'True and false', says Hobbes there, 'are attributes of speech, not of things. And where speech is not, there is neither truth nor falsehood.'[1] Again, any reference to a correspondence between our propositions or speeches and the real world is explicitly denied; truth, for Hobbes, is wholly a property of language—of propositions, statements, words, names; truth is purely nominal.

This definition of truth leads us, in turn, to the definition of knowledge, which for Hobbes is purely deductive, purely 'mathematical', in character. Every system of knowledge or 'science' begins from a set of propositions called the primary propositions (or first definitions, or axioms, or postulates) of that system; from these primary propositions are drawn out, in an orderly sequence, all the propositions that are logically implied or entailed by them and may therefore be deduced from them; and this, for Hobbes, is what a system of knowledge *is*—a system composed of the primary propositions, called the 'first definitions', and the 'derived' propositions, called the 'consequences'.[2] A system of knowledge, in other words, is nothing but a system of propositions—of *meanings*, of *language*, that is—held together by the logical relation of entailment or implication. And that is what Hobbes means when he says in *Leviathan* that what 'men call SCIENCE' is '*the knowledge of all the consequences of names appertaining to the subject in hand*',[3] or (as he puts it in *Elements of Law*) 'knowledge of *the truth of propositions*, and *how things are called*'.[4]

[1] *Leviathan*, ch. 4, p. 21.
[2] *Of Computation or Logic*, vi. 16–17.
[3] *Leviathan*, ch. 5, p. 29.
[4] *Elements of Law*, I. vi. 1.

That Hobbes's general theory of knowledge is as thoroughly nominalistic as his theory of universals and his theory of truth is sufficiently plain. But Hobbes has still to distinguish between a true and a false system of such knowledge; and in making this distinction he would seem at last to be abandoning at least part of his nominalistic position. For a true system of knowledge (says Hobbes) is one that begins from *true* definitions and *correctly* draws out the logical consequences of those definitions;[1] and a false system, presumably, is one which either begins from false definitions and draws out logically true consequences from those false definitions, or begins from true definitions and draws out logically false consequences from these true definitions, or begins from false definitions and draws out logically false consequences of these false definitions. (These alternative conditions for a false system of knowledge may be taken to show that the possibilities of error are greater than the possibilities of truth, and we need not in any case trouble ourselves further with the definition of the false since what is said about the true will apply *mutatis mutandis* to the false.)

We have already learnt that a true definition, being a true proposition, is a definition in which the subject-name is *correctly* joined with the predicate-name; and this (Hobbes has already explained) is the same as to say that the predicate-name includes or comprehends the subject-name—as, for instance, in the proposition 'Man is a living creature', the predicate 'living creature' includes or comprehends the subject 'man'.[2] The question accordingly arises, How do we know when a subject-name and a predicate-name *have* been thus 'correctly' joined together? How do we know, in other words, that the subject-name 'man' is included or comprehended in the predicate-name 'living creature'? Do we not know this (we ask) only by reference to the fact—the real, objective, *non-linguistic* fact—that the non-linguistic creature we call 'man' possesses the non-linguistic property of being a 'living

[1] *Of Computation or Logic*, vi. 16. [2] *Leviathan*, ch. 4, p. 21.

creature'? And if this is the answer, is not Hobbes then implicitly admitting that the standard of truth is ultimately not merely logical or linguistic, not merely a matter of joining one name to another, but does presuppose some kind of correspondence between language and reality, between our linguistic usages and the nature of things?

Hobbes, however, is not to be caught out on this testing point. He answers (and this is the last vital part of his nominalistic doctrine), All meaning is 'by arbitrary institution', entirely *ad placitum*. All truth, therefore, is also 'by arbitrary institution', and to say that a true proposition consists of the subject-name and predicate-name correctly joined together is to say, merely, that this particular connexion of names is an established linguistic usage or convention, and that its establishment was purely arbitrary.

Hobbes makes this point most explicitly in *Of Computation or Logic*. The first definitions of every system of knowledge, he says, are '*truths constituted arbitrarily by the inventors of speech*';[1] and, still more explicitly, the proposition 'Man is a living creature' is true for this reason 'that *it pleased men to impose both those names on the same thing*.[2] In other words, the truth of the first definitions, from which, according to Hobbes, our systems of 'science' proceed, is, like the truth of all true propositions, by arbitrary institution; it is true because and only because it pleased 'the inventors of speech' to define whatever it is they were defining in this way and not another.

This, the doctrine of meaning and truth by arbitrary institution, is the last turn of the screw that renders Hobbes's nominalistic position logically self-complete and self-consistent. Universals are names, and names only; truth is of propositions, and of propositions only; knowledge is purely demonstrative, a matter of drawing out the logical consequences of the first definitions; and both meaning and truth are by arbitrary institution: these are the main parts of Hobbes's nominalism, whose grand achievement is to reduce all meaning, truth and

[1] *Of Computation or Logic*, iii. 9. [2] *Ibid.* iii. 8.

knowledge to a matter of language. It remains now to consider some of its wider philosophical implications; and then to discuss briefly its effect upon the moral and political doctrine of *Leviathan.*

Of these wider philosophical implications of Hobbes's nominalistic doctrine of meaning and truth, the most important are those that bear upon Hobbes's view of reality and may therefore properly be called metaphysical. The point is perhaps best made by contrasting the Hobbesian position with that other philosophical position, commonly called 'realist', which stands at the opposite extreme to the nominalist.

What fundamentally distinguishes the realist from the nominalist in metaphysics is that the realist always recognises an objective order of things, an order of nature (as it is traditionally called) that is, in some sense, 'given'—in some sense pre-existent and prior to the conceptions of the human mind and the propositions of human discourse. The realist in metaphysics also believes that the nature of this objective order is discoverable, and that its relation to our mental constructions, our ideas or concepts, though not easy to determine, is yet capable of being determined.

The nominalist in metaphysics denies all this that the realist affirms; and when he is a nominalist as radical as Hobbes, he denies it absolutely and without qualification. For Hobbes, the world is simply 'a universe of disconnected singulars',[1] a world in which nothing is given but bare, disconnected sense-particulars. Everything else—all order, all significance, all intelligibility—are created by the mind of man. 'If you will be a philosopher in good earnest', writes Hobbes in the Epistle to the Reader of a later work called *De Corpore,*

> let your reason move upon the deep of your own cogitations and experience. Those things that lie in confusion must be set asunder, distinguished, and every one *stamped with its own name* set in order; that is to say, your method must resemble that of creation.

[1] This phrase is used of Ockham's nominalistic world-view by Meyrick A. Carré in his book *Phases of Thought in England* (Oxford, 1949), pp. 162–3 *et al.*

Hobbes says, for propriety's sake, that it must 'resemble' the creation, God's creation; but he means that it is itself the act of creation. The world as 'given', as 'received' by bare sense-perception, is a chaos—a meaningless, undifferentiated chaos. All differentiation, all connexion, all meaning and order are created by the conceptual powers of the human mind; they are created afresh, *ab initio*, each time a human mind capable of reflection lets its reason move upon the deep of its own cogitation and experience. The intelligible world, in other words, is not given, but drawn out of the human mind; it reflects, not any supposed order of nature, but only the conceptual order created in and by the human mind.

This is the metaphysical view of the universe implied by Hobbes's nominalist epistemology, which Professor Oakeshott has justly called a 'profoundly sceptical' doctrine;[1] and it is the most general and most important implication of that epistemology. For it informs every part of Hobbes's system, his ethics, his politics, his theology, his science; and informs it with a consistency that is unique in the history of English thought and cannot have many parallels in the history of European thought.

The best evidence of the range, rigour and audacity of Hobbes's application of his 'profoundly sceptical' philosophic doctrine is to be found in *Leviathan*; and I propose to discuss briefly two of the most important doctrines in *Leviathan* that are grounded in Hobbes's nominalism. The view that all law is 'positive' law, which is fundamental to his theory of commonwealth, is the first. For Hobbes, there is no such thing as a law of nature in the traditional sense, a system of law, that is, which is prior to, and independent of, the law made by the legislative power of the commonwealth. For Hobbes, *all* law is created, none is given; all law (like meaning and truth) is artificial, established by convention, not by nature. To the mind of one like Richard Hooker, who stands at the opposite pole to Hobbes in English moral and political

[1] Oakeshott, Introduction to *Leviathan*, p. xxv.

thought, a system of natural law is necessarily presupposed by the man-made 'positive' law of the civil power. For how could the civil magistrate know (Hooker and all the philosophers of that tradition ask) whether his positive laws were just or unjust if he were not guided by some antecedent law of nature; and how could he claim that they had any obligatory force upon men unless they were grounded in a law of nature? But Hobbes denies what Hooker affirms: he denies the logical necessity of presupposing such a law of nature, and therefore denies its existence.

Hobbes does indeed speak about laws of nature. Chapters 14 and 15 of *Leviathan* are given over to the listing of what Hobbes calls laws of nature, and there are as many as nineteen of them in the end. But Hobbes does not mean what Hooker means: he does not mean a system of law given *in nature*, antecedent to and independent of the laws created by men. In a crucial passage at the end of Chapter 13, having described the condition of man in the 'state of nature'—his condition in the total and terrible absence of all law—he goes on to say that the situation is happily not irremediable, since

> The passions that incline men to peace, are fear of death; desire of such things as are necessary to commodious living; and a hope by their industry to obtain them. *And reason suggesteth convenient articles of peace upon which men may be drawn to agreement. These articles are they which otherwise are called the Laws of Nature.*[1]

Reason, that is, does not *discover* the laws of nature as 'given', as pre-existent or prior to the constructions of the human mind; it 'suggesteth' (a deliberately ambiguous word) 'convenient articles of peace'—artificial, man-made principles (the legalistic term 'articles' should be given its full weight)—'upon which men may be drawn to agreement'. They are laws, that is, *agreed upon* to be fundamental to survival, not 'given' in nature as fundamental; and these, Hobbes adds (with an audacity that Hooker would have found stupefying), 'are they which otherwise are called the Laws of Nature', and

[1] *Leviathan*, ch. 13, p. 84.

proceeds henceforth to call all the 'convenient articles of peace' that he lists in Chapters 14 and 15 'laws of nature'.[1]

I have laid stress on this transition passage at the end of Chapter 13 because it has been thought by some students of Hobbes to mark an encouraging inconsistency in Hobbes's profoundly sceptical philosophy, in seeming to admit that there really are laws of nature in Hooker's sense of the term. But this is not the case; and the ambiguous phrasing is, I believe, deliberate (and deliberately misleading). 'Reason *suggesteth* convenient articles of peace', says Hobbes—and in the word 'suggesteth' strikes a sort of Aristotelian mean between the extremes he here wishes to avoid, namely, the word 'discovers' on the one hand and the word 'creates' on the other. The word 'discovers' is obviously to be avoided since to say that reason discovers these convenient articles of peace would instantly commit Hobbes to the view of natural law of the traditional Christian moralists like Hooker, and would flatly contradict his nominalist epistemology and metaphysic. But, equally, to say what the rest of the argument

[1] It need not be supposed, however, that the Hobbesian audacity here is intended to be merely derisive. It would be consistent with the marked positivist bias of Hobbes's thought if he might be imagined to be saying in effect, 'This is what Hooker and the rest *really mean* by the laws of nature; this is what they *must* mean if they mean anything at all—if they are not just producing insignificant sounds' (or meaningless statements, as modern logical positivists would say). The same view can be taken, I believe, of the still greater audacity with which Hobbes offers his 'second law of nature' as the equivalent of 'the Gospel law' (*Leviathan*, ch. 14, p. 85). It is difficult to suppose that Hobbes really believed that to say 'a man [ought to] be willing, *when others are so too, as far-forth as for peace and defence of himself he shall think it necessary*, to lay down this [natural] right to all things, and be contented with so much liberty against other men as he would allow other men against himself' was exactly the same as 'that law of the Gospel, *whatsoever you require that others should do to you, that do ye to them*'; or, in his definition of 'the fundamental law of nature', which comes immediately before this, that the Hobbesian law 'every man ought to endeavour peace *as far forth as he has hope of obtaining it*' is the same as the Christian law 'seek peace and follow it'. But it is not so difficult to suppose that Hobbes should genuinely have believed his laws to be fair restatements of the Gospel laws when these had been stripped of their 'insignificant sounds'; and though he must certainly have been conscious of the irony of the transmogrification (and the horror it would inspire in the bishops), he would as certainly have felt it to be free of any taint of disingenuousness.

logically requires, that reason creates these convenient articles of peace, would be to expose too blatantly their artificial, man-made character; and this also Hobbes wishes, at this vital point in the whole argument of *Leviathan*, to avoid. He accordingly compromises; and so succeeds in having his cake and eating it: by denying that there are such things as laws of nature in the sense in which Hooker and the rest use the term, he leaves his nominalist basis unimpaired; and by retaining the name 'laws of nature' for his 'convenient articles of peace', he is able to give them the status and the authority of the traditional laws of nature. This double purpose explains, I believe, the interesting ambiguity of the word 'suggesteth'; and if this is the correct explanation, the passage does not, as some have thought, convict Hobbes of a breach in the self-consistency of his nominalist position.

The other grand instance of the influence of Hobbes's nominalism upon his theory of commonwealth is his account of the generation of Leviathan himself 'by covenant of every man with every man'.[1] This expresses the doctrine that the life of commonwealth can be created and maintained in no other way than by the incorporation of all men into one great 'artificial man', the supreme sovereign; and it is not difficult to see the connexion between this central doctrine of *Leviathan* (Hobbes's contract theory, as it is sometimes called) and the doctrine of civil law just discussed.

Civil laws, which are the necessary condition of life in societies, are for Hobbes, we have seen, entirely artificial, entirely by arbitrary institution; and that they should be so follows logically from Hobbes's fundamental analysis of human nature. For, on this analysis, men are by nature completely lacking in what is called social feeling: they are completely unconnected by any *natural* bonds, such as mutual affinity, or liking of one another's society, or even mere gregariousness. ('Men', says Hobbes explicitly, 'have no pleasure, but on the contrary a great deal of grief, in keeping

[1] *Leviathan*, ch. 17, p. 112.

company.'[1]) And, in the total absence of such natural bonds, which, if present, would naturally dispose men towards social living, there is no natural motive to—indeed, no 'natural' possibility of—the creation of those civil laws which define the life of commonwealth; and the state of nature is therefore—*has* to be—a state of war of every man against every man. This (to repeat the argument) is the state in which every man is seeking to preserve himself from destruction at the hands of every other man; and because no one is strong enough to preserve himself by inflicting violent death on everyone else, yet each is in perpetual danger of violent death at the hands of every other, the only way in which everyone may ensure his own safety is by the expedient of the covenant, by which all men, voluntarily and simultaneously, agree to transfer to a single supreme sovereign their natural right to preserve themselves, and confer upon that single supreme sovereign the absolute right and absolute power to protect them all from destruction. 'This', says Hobbes, in a famous passage in chapter 17 of *Leviathan*, speaking of the generation of Leviathan,

> is more than consent or concord; it is a real unity of them all, in one and the same person, made by covenant of every man with every man, in such manner, as if every man should say to every man, *I authorize and give up my right to governing myself, to this man, or to this assembly of men, on this condition, that thou give up thy right to him, and authorize all his actions in like manner.* This done, the multitude so united in one person is called a COMMONWEALTH, in Latin CIVITAS. This is the generation of that great LEVIATHAN, or rather, to speak more reverently, of that *mortal god,* to which we owe under the *immortal God,* our peace and defence. And in him consisteth the essence of the commonwealth.[2]

This (Hobbes adds explicitly) is '*commonwealth by institution*'. As meaning is by institution, as truth is by institution, so also is commonwealth by institution. The great Leviathan, in whom 'consisteth the essence of commonwealth', is a great

[1] *Ibid.* ch. 13, p. 81.
[2] *Ibid.* ch. 17, p. 112 (Hobbes's emphasis).

artifact, deliberately created by men to establish absolute order where otherwise there would be only absolute chaos; and its principal function is the making of those positive, artificial laws which shall supply the absence of all natural laws. In the state of nature, writes Hobbes in Chapter 13 of *Leviathan*, 'the notions of right and wrong, justice and injustice have no place. Where there is no common power, there is no law: where no law, no injustice.' The defining function of the sovereign power is, accordingly, to make laws; and in exercising this supreme function (Hobbes clearly lets us understand), Leviathan, the mortal God, like the immortal God, creates *ex nihilo* all justice and injustice, all right and wrong, all good and bad—in short, all moral and political obligation, which is the necessary condition of life in any commonwealth.

This is how Hobbes's theory, that all law is positive law, is linked with his contract theory, his doctrine of the generation of commonwealth. And both theories are logically grounded in Hobbes's metaphysical nominalism, in his view of the universe as 'a universe of disconnected singulars'. For the contract theory, pre-eminently, rests upon a view of the human universe as a universe of disconnected singulars. In the moral world, as in the world of knowledge, there is no natural, organic unity or connectedness. All connexion is artificially created: in the world of knowledge, by the perfectly artificial, mechanical operation of the human reason that Hobbes calls 'reckoning' or 'computation';[1] in the human universe, by the perfectly artificial, mechanical device of the 'covenant'.

In one of those parenthetical remarks in which a philosopher (as we saw in Aristotle) may reveal more of his fundamental view of things, and often reveal it more vividly, than he does in his more deliberate statements, Hobbes throws out an image that rather nicely gives us the measure of his grimly

[1] *Leviathan*, ch. 5, p. 25.

'atomistic' picture of the human universe. He is describing the fifth law of nature, which he calls the law of 'mutual accommodation', and is speaking of the difficulties that may be caused in the commonwealth by the presence of certain intractable individuals:

> We may consider that there is in men's aptness to society a diversity of nature rising from their diversity of affections; *not unlike to that we see in stones brought together for building of an edifice.* For as that stone which, by the asperity and irregularity of figure takes more room from others than itself fills; and for the hardness cannot be easily made plain, and thereby hindereth the building, is by the builders cast away as unprofitable and troublesome: so also a man that by asperity of nature will strive to retain those things which to himself are superfluous, and to others necessary, and for the stubbornness of his passions cannot be corrected, is to be left, or cast out of society, as cumbersome thereunto....[1]

Hobbes's suggested treatment of these intractable individuals is by itself not particularly reprehensible. It is no harsher, in any event, than the sentence pronounced by St Paul in the fifth chapter of the First Epistle to the Corinthians upon the man who had taken his father's wife; he too was in effect to be cast out of the Christian commonwealth at Corinth. But it is Hobbes's image here that marks the difference between his picture of the relation of man and man and St Paul's. Their 'diversity of nature', says Hobbes, is 'not unlike to that we see in stones brought together for building of an edifice': they are, that is, as mutually isolated, as unconnected, as *dead* to each other, as stones; and whatever *life* they are to enjoy as members of a commonwealth cannot but be artificially created and artificially maintained. We will have occasion to remember this image of *the stones* in *Leviathan,* which pictures so perfectly Hobbes's artificial community of the children of pride, when we glance at the very different images, beautiful and organic, that spring naturally to the mind of St Paul when he in his turn is seeking to picture the living community of Christians in Christ.

[1] *Ibid.* ch. 15, p. 99.

MATERIALISM

Hobbes's materialism, being too unscientific to be taken seriously as science and too quasi-scientific to be taken as anything else, is probably the least interesting part of his whole philosophical system. Viewed in the most general light, it is Hobbes's answer to the question, What is the universe ultimately made of? or, What are the ultimate constituents of the universal matter? The answer, set out in the first three chapters of *Leviathan*, is 'matter and motion', or 'matter-in-motion'; and this amounts to little more than the answer of the classic Lucretian materialism brought up to date by Hobbes's studies in the new Galilean physics and the old Euclidean geometry. Within the framework of this neo-Lucretian materialism Hobbes attempts to explain the phenomena of sense-perception, memory, imagination, and dreams; but these quasi-scientific explanations, though they have an agreeable 'period' flavour, are not persuasive, and not entirely free of confusion.

Hobbes's materialism, however, does form an integral part of his system, and cannot be ignored even though its intrinsic interest is so small; and for those mainly concerned with Hobbes as a moral and political philosopher, its importance is twofold: first, that his materialistic theory of perception supports and reinforces his nominalistic theory of knowledge, which, we have seen, is fundamental to his whole system; second, that his materialistic psychology (or 'psycho-physiology') provides him with a quasi-scientific basis for his theory of the passions, which is fundamental to his moral doctrine and ultimately also to his political doctrine.

Hobbes states his theory of perception in a single paragraph in chapter 1 of *Leviathan*. A perception or sensation (Hobbes does not, like modern psychologists, distinguish between the two)—an act of hearing, seeing, smelling and so on—is caused by the pressure of an external object upon the appropriate organ of sense, producing a motion in the matter of the brain (and the heart, Hobbes says) which is the perception or sensation. Hobbes calls it, significantly, a 'seeming' (or phantasm or fancy); and it is these sense-perceptions or seemings that are the primary material out of which our knowledge is constituted. In view of what has been said about Hobbes's nominalism, the philosophical implications of this simple definition of sense-perception might seem to be crucial. For (it may be argued) in speaking of the impact of external objects upon the organs of sense, Hobbes is surely postulating the real, objective existence of an external world, which is given in nature, not created by the human mind; and if that is so, is he not giving away at least one vital part of his nominalist doctrine, his quasi-solipsistic theory of knowledge?

This inconsistency, however, is apparent, not real. For the external objects that make their impact upon the organs of sense are only the disconnected singulars of which the nominalist's universe is, by definition, composed; and since Hobbes nowhere suggests that we know anything about these objects except that they are singulars or particulars, his nominalist position is so far left intact. Indeed the nominalism is seen to be perfectly compatible with the materialism. For (runs Hobbes's argument) the singulars or particulars of which the universe is constituted are *known to us* only as seemings; and our seemings are only matter-in-motion; therefore, our knowledge of the external world is nothing but matter-in-motion.

The further implications of Hobbes's theory of perception show how his materialism, besides being compatible with his nominalism, positively confirms it. The chief of these is that Hobbes nowhere postulates a *knowable* relation between our seemings and the objects that produced them. There is only the barest causal connexion, but no knowable correspondence, between them; our knowledge accordingly is of our seemings, and of these only; and they (as the name 'seemings' is meant to intimate) give us no clue to the nature of things. And this is the darkly sceptical meaning of the Hobbesian theory of perception. Men are as *isolated* from one another ('like stones brought together for building of an edifice') at this most primitive level of their contact with the world as at every successive level; every man is completely confined to the contents of his own mind, to his own private, individual seemings, with no logical ground for supposing that his seemings bear any resemblance to any other man's and no natural way of comparing them with any other man's.

Happily, however, he possesses the means of delivering himself from this condition of a quasi-solipsistic isolation. The means are those two human faculties or powers which Hobbes calls speech and reason; and it is his materialist account of speech and reason that is of special significance here. Speech, on Hobbes's analysis, is nothing but the power to attach names, which are one kind of matter-in-motion (sounds in the air, marks on paper) to our seemings, which are another kind of matter-in-motion; and reason is nothing but the power to 'add' and 'subtract' the names we have attached to our seemings—the power, that is, to add and subtract those patches of matter-in-motion (names) that stand for or signify the other patches of matter-in-motion which are our seemings. This, reduced to its elements, is Hobbes's materialist analysis of knowledge viewed as a physical phenomenon—his physics of human knowledge, so to speak. It is most clearly expressed in his definition of reason,[1] where the emphasis, exactly as in his nominalistic analysis of meaning and truth, is all on the completely artificial, mechanical, inorganic character of the process; and this, once understood, explains how the Hobbesian materialism confirms and reinforces the Hobbesian nominalism.

The same is true of Hobbes's physiology of the passions. His materialist doctrine provides him with the three concepts, 'endeavour', 'appetite' and 'aversion', which are fundamental to his analysis of the passions. Endeavour is the basic, un-

[1] *Leviathan*, ch. 5, p. 25.

differentiated motion of the human organism towards or away from any object;[1] this divides into appetite, the motion of approaching (as Hobbes calls it), and aversion, the motion of retiring or withdrawing;[2] and these two kinds of motion, appetite and aversion, become the archetypal forms of all the human passions. Hobbes contrives, with characteristic consistency, to exhibit all the passions as variants of one or the other; and by reducing them in this way to completely material, physical phenomena, he succeeds in administering another blow to those anti-materialist doctrines of the universe that postulate spirit as well as matter as constituents of the universal substance, which he detested because of their historical association with the religious view of life that he especially desired to undermine.

This, however, is a consequence of Hobbes's materialism that cannot be pursued here, for it belongs properly to a discussion of his religious and theological doctrine. Our main interest is in the analysis of the passions as such, which make up Hobbes's psychological doctrine, and form the basis of his low view of man's nature, which in turn is the basis both of his moral and his political doctrine.

THE PASSIONS

For the purpose of establishing Hobbes's low view of human nature (and his common ground with the Aristotle of the *Rhetoric* and the *Nicomachean Ethics*), among the most revealing of his definitions of the passions are those of love and hate, pity, cruelty, and curiosity. Thus, on *love* and *hate*:

> That which men desire they are also said to *love*: and to hate those things for which they have aversion. So that desire and love are the same thing: save that by desire we always signify the absence of the object; by love, most commonly the presence of the same.[3]

[1] *Ibid.* ch. 6, p. 31.
[2] *Ibid.* ch. 6, p. 31.
[3] *Ibid.* ch. 6, p. 32.

What is significant here is the identification of love and desire (a feature of almost all utilitarian philosophies), implying a denial of the *difference* between them that is directly verifiable in our moral experience. The difference is between the kind of love that is grounded in a disinterested delight in the beloved object for its own sake, and the kind, properly named desire, that is grounded in possessiveness and cares for the beloved object primarily as an extension of itself. Although the difference is not absolute (for the first kind of love can and does issue in desire, often the most passionate, and the other kind is not incompatible with some regard for the object of its desire as separate from itself and existing in its own right), yet it is a difference so real and important that its consequences for human happiness and misery may be discovered in daily experience; and this at least one universal religion, the Christian, has recognised, and accordingly made the centre of its moral and metaphysical teaching. But Hobbes denies the difference between the two kinds of love which Christians call the *agape* and the *eros*; and this denial is one instance of his persistent effort to reduce the more exalted of the human passions to the more base, or (as Christians would say) the spiritual to the purely physical, in the interests of his low view.

The definition of *cruelty* turns out, in a curious and interesting way, to be complementary to the definition of *love*:

> Contempt, or little sense of the calamity of others, is that which men call cruelty; proceeding from security of their own fortune. *For that any man should take pleasure in other men's great harms, without other end of his own, I do not conceive it possible.*[1]

What Hobbes is saying is that he does not conceive it possible that a man should be cruel except from the motive of gaining some material advantage for himself. In other words, he can no more conceive of such a thing as *disinterested* cruelty or hatred than he can conceive of disinterested love. But in this

[1] *Leviathan*, ch. 6, p. 37.

connexion there are certain memorable lines in Shakespeare's *Othello* to remind us of the reality of disinterested hatred and cruelty. Iago's desire to destroy Cassio (we learn) was motivated, not principally by his desire for Cassio's place, but by the pure disinterested hatred expressed in the lines,

> There is a daily beauty in his life
> Which makes mine ugly.

It is clear that Hobbes, like Aristotle, also stops short at once of the lowest reaches of human depravity and the highest reaches of human virtue; and for the same reason as Aristotle—that he takes self-interest to be the ultimate spring of all human conduct. But absolute depravity, of which disinterested cruelty is one form, lies as far below self-interest in the scale of moral values as disinterested love lies above it; and Hobbes, in failing to conceive of either, shows again the ultimate incorrigible limitation of the low view.

Still another revealing instance of the Hobbesian disposition to deflate the more exalted passions is the definition of what Hobbes calls *curiosity*. By this he means intellectual curiosity—what we call variously the love of wisdom, the passion for truth, the common pursuit of true judgment; and he defines it as follows:

> Desire to know why, and how, curiosity; such as in no living creature but man;...[it] is a lust of the mind, that by a perseverance of delight in the continual and indefatigable generation of knowledge, exceedeth the short vehemence of any carnal pleasure.[1]

The only difference, in other words, between our noble intellectual passions and the carnal passions that we share with the lower animals is that the pleasure of the first lasts longer: a view that anticipates by several centuries that of some of the cruder schools of modern psychology, which also tend to reduce the more advanced intellectual passions to 'substitute-gratifications' for the more primitive sensual. The difference is only

[1] *Ibid.* ch. 6, p. 35.

that Hobbes expresses this view with a metaphorical vivacity not often to be met in modern books of psychology.

Finally, there is *pity*; which (says Hobbes) is

> grief, for the calamity of another. . and ariseth from the imagination that the like calamity may befall himself; and therefore is called COMPASSION, and in the phrase of this present time, a FELLOW-FEELING.[1]

Upon this account of pity the best comment is Bishop Joseph Butler's, who makes it the centre of a brilliant attack upon Hobbes's whole moral philosophy.[2] Butler's main criticism is substantially the same as that which can be made against the Hobbesian definition of love and desire. As Hobbes identified love and desire, though our moral experience insists that they are distinct, so Hobbes here identifies pity with fear. Pity, for Hobbes, *is* fear—fear for ourselves projected outwards; 'com-passion' means 'feeling with' *ourselves* through the spectacle of another's suffering or misfortune; the emotion of pity, in short, is, in a strict sense of the word, *self-centred*, not, as we had always supposed, centred upon an object outside of and other than ourselves, without reference to ourselves but with reference only to *it*self.

Against this identification of pity and fear Butler appeals, first, to common experience to testify to the difference between the emotions we call fear and pity; next, to our linguistic usage, which confirms that difference in experience (we do use the two terms 'fear' and 'pity'—and why two terms if we are talking about the same thing?); and, finally, to the grand metaphysical principle, 'Whatever is, is', or (as he himself phrases it), 'Everything is what it is and not another thing.' Our moral experience and our linguistic usage (he argues) are together irresistible proof of the fact that fear is one thing, pity another; and any man therefore who seeks to identify them would (to adapt a phrase of Aristotle's) stand in need either of perception or of punishment.

[1] *Leviathan*, ch. 6, p. 37.

[2] Joseph Butler, *Fifteen Sermons*, Sermon v (Upon Compassion: Introductory).

These representative definitions of love, cruelty, curiosity and pity illustrate Hobbes's consistent practice of giving the lowest account possible of those basic human impulses that modern psychologists call 'emotional drives' and the older moralists called 'the passions'. The same is true of his treatment of the 'manners', the term he uses to signify, broadly, the social passions of man—in his own words, 'those qualities of mankind that concern their living together in peace and unity'.[1] This account of the social passions, which is fundamental to the doctrine of commonwealth in *Leviathan*, centres on Hobbes's definition of *felicity*; and Professor Oakeshott has rightly said that Hobbes's whole account of the predicament of man in the state of nature is, logically speaking, 'a deduction from the nature of felicity'.[2] If, as Hobbes says, 'there is no such *finis ultimus*, utmost aim, or *summum bonum*, greatest good, as is spoken of in the books of the old moral philosophers', and if 'the felicity of this life consisteth not in the repose of a mind satisfied' but in 'a continual progress of the desire from one object to another, the attaining of the former being still but the way to the latter', then indeed it follows that the life of man must be 'a perpetual and restless desire of power after power that ceaseth only in death'.[3] And since every man's desire of power after power conflicts with every other man's; and since men are by nature equal, and no man therefore has the strength to overpower all the rest and so put an end to the competitive struggle for power, which is for all of them the only means of self-preservation; therefore, the state of nature is 'a state of war of every man against every other man'—a condition in which self-preservation is perpetually threatened and violent death rendered imminent for every man at the hands of every other man. This is the predicament that cannot be resolved in any other way but by the creation of a sovereign power, to whom shall be transferred every individual's natural right to protect himself from destruction at the hands of his fellow-

[1] *Leviathan*, ch. 11, p. 63.

[2] Oakeshott, *op. cit.* p. XXXIV.

[3] *Leviathan*, ch. 11, pp. 63–4.

men, and upon whom shall be conferred absolute power 'in those things that concern the common peace and safety'.

All this follows by necessary consequence from Hobbes's definition of felicity. Nor can we logically refuse him a single step in his argument unless we refuse his definition; and this we can refuse only by affirming that there *is* a Supreme Good, a *summum bonum*, a single ultimate end of human endeavour. We might say, with the mystical Christian and Platonist, that this Supreme Good is the loss of self in the soul's union with God; or, with the less mystical Christian, that it is the imitation of Christ in perfect love and service of our fellow-men; or, with the Humanist, that it is the love and service of our fellow-men without reference to the greater glory of God. Whichever of these conceptions of a Supreme Good we choose to affirm, the result is the same: Hobbes's argument is immediately and fatally undermined. For what is common to all these conceptions of a Supreme Good is the postulation of a constituent in man's nature that binds all men together, organically not artificially, by nature not by covenant, and the belief that this vital constituent transcends in dignity and power the destructive passions that Hobbes has placed at the centre of man's nature.

This power must be love. It cannot be mere sympathy or kindliness or good manners or the avoidance of such mildly reprehensible vices as priggishness and bad temper. None of these is strong enough to be set against the terror of violent death by which Hobbes believes men to be dominated. Nor will Aristotle's *sophrosyne* do, nor Hume's 'social sympathy', nor Bentham's 'enlightened self-interest'; for these at best can only mitigate the rigours of Hobbes's state of nature, but cannot annihilate it.

Only the quality of love has the power to annihilate Hobbes's state of nature by rendering it absurd. When love is postulated as the *summum bonum* and the exercise of perfect love as man's highest felicity, 'the perpetual and restless desire of power after power' becomes logically impossible; for love casts out fear, and fear, as we have seen, is the reason for the ceaseless pursuit of power in Hobbes's scheme. And if there is no perpetual and restless desire of power after power, there is no competition in Hobbes's sense—no anxiety about self-preservation and no fear of violent death; and if no anxiety about self-preservation and no fear of violent death, then no war of every man against every man; and if no state of war, then no Leviathan. But when love is absent, the predicament of man is exactly as Hobbes says it is; the life of man is solitary, poor, nasty, brutish and short; and there is no logical alternative to the solution he proposed.

It is indeed pre-eminently the logic of Hobbes's system that challenges the anti-Hobbist, whether he be a Platonist, a Christian or a Humanist. It challenges him to meet Hobbes's low view of man's nature with another view not only more comprehensive—more completely true, that is, to our moral experience in taking in at least some of those important facts that Hobbes fails to take into account, such as the experience of disinterested love, disinterested pity, disinterested passion for knowledge—but also as rigorously self-complete and self-coherent as Hobbes's. For when, as in *Leviathan*, it is no less than the whole world that is being viewed *sub specie timoris*, under the aspect of fear, there is no way to meet it but by another view as totally explanatory, the whole world viewed *sub specie amoris*, under the aspect of love.

The reason for insisting upon this is that it is a point not generally well understood, and less well understood by Hobbes's modern critics than by his contemporaries. The criticism of the doctrine of *Leviathan* tends too often to be so wide of the mark as to suggest that Hobbes's central argument has been more or less completely misunderstood. But surely (the critics argue) Hobbes can *see* that things are not as bad as he paints them? Surely he *knows* that there are plenty of decent chaps about in the world who do not in the least want to be at other chaps' throats; who are not all the time morbidly brooding about self-preservation and violent death; who positively like the society of their fellow-men, and cannot be conceived of as living in Hobbes's gruesome state of nature. And surely (the argument continues) there are enough, and have always been enough, of these decent chaps about in the world to show up Hobbes's 'state of nature' for what it is—an absurd fantasy, a philosopher's fiction, introduced merely as a piece of special pleading to give an air of plausibility to Hobbes's totalitarian political philosophy.

There is one compendious answer to this kind of criticism. Of course Hobbes knew that there were plenty of nice chaps about in this world; he himself happened to know intimately some of the nicest and most distinguished of them, like his patron the Duke of Devonshire and Mr Sidney Godolphin, to whom *Leviathan* is affectionately dedicated. So we may imagine Hobbes replying to his hypothetical critics: Certainly the world as we know it, *being in a state of commonwealth*, is full of chaps who are decent, sociable, and not at all inclined to cut each other's throats. But are they not so precisely *because* they are living in a state of commonwealth, in a world, that is, in which there are laws made by a sovereign power and backed by a police force? Consider, however (Hobbes goes on), these decent chaps in the total absence of laws, a sovereign power and a police force. Remember (Hobbes might say to his contemporaries in 1651) what these decent chaps were like in the recent civil wars, when law and order were only temporarily and only partly suspended. Did they not then virtually fall into the state of nature, with one half of the nation at the throats of the other half, and the life of man, in the space of a mere five years, becoming ever poorer and nastier and more brutish and more short? Imagine, then, our common experience of the recent calamities of our country taken to its logical extreme; imagine the condition of men in the *total* absence of a sovereign power to make laws and maintain them; and what would you have but the state of nature as I have described it in chapter 13 of *Leviathan*?

I am not saying (Hobbes may be supposed to add, a little wearily perhaps) that there ever was, as a matter of historical fact, such a state of nature.[1] I am not even saying that this state of nature is a historical hypothesis about the original state of primitive man—analogous, say, to a geological hypothesis about the original state of the earth's surface. The state of nature in Chapter 13 of *Leviathan* is not a historical phenomenon at all; it is a purely logical phenomenon. It is a logical construction, an analytical diagram of human nature in a hypothetical condition of life—a condition of life logically (not historically) antecedent to the condition of commonwealth, and defined by the total absence of civil laws and of a properly constituted power to make laws and maintain them. (At this point Hobbes may perhaps be expected to add an ironical apology, to the effect that he is sorry that he described the state of nature in Chapter 13 of *Leviathan* so vividly, in such concrete pictorial detail, as to mislead his critics into thinking that he intended it as something other than a mere logical diagram.) And can you deny (Hobbes might conclude) that my logical analysis is *true*? Can you deny that men, in the total absence of laws and lawgivers and a police force, would in fact be savages, dominated exclusively by the need to preserve themselves and the fear of violent death; and not choosing, or even desiring, but *compelled* to be at each others' throats in their efforts to save themselves from destruction? Can you deny this?

This is the challenge of *Leviathan*; and the question is indeed, Can we, the Christians and the Humanists, the angelic host of the anti-Hobbists, deny what Hobbes affirms? The answer is that we can and we do. But we can give this answer, with the proper kind and degree of assurance, only if we first consent to meet Hobbes on his own ground. This means that we have to grant him his method of arguing from a logical construction that he calls the state of nature, which is the condition of man viewed in abstraction from the actual

[1] *Leviathan*, ch. 13, p. 83.

conditions, concrete, multiple and complex, in which we find him as a member of a civil society. Having conceded the validity of the method, we, too, must abstract man from civil society, and picture him in a hypothetical state of nature; and then, and only then, can we answer, No: man in this state will not be as Hobbes says. Or, rather, he will not be *only* as Hobbes pictures him; and the qualification makes all the difference. The destroying passions will be there, and the ceaseless battle for self-preservation and the perpetual terror of violent death. And they will be there in the very intensity in which Hobbes, in his genius, depicts them. They will appear as grim and as terrible as in Hobbes's state of nature; and men will seem, as to Hobbes, beyond the possibility of redemption.

But there will be not only that. In the very midst of the powers of destruction, and inseparably bound up with them—indeed embedded in them, as the indestructible powers of the spirit are everywhere embedded in the mutabilities of flesh and bone—will be the redemptive power of love; and it is by this power (we will maintain against Hobbes) that men are delivered from the deadly predicament created by their fear, vanity and greed. Not, as Hobbes says, by that efficient mechanism, the purely instrumental 'reason', which 'suggesteth convenient articles of peace upon which men may be drawn to agreement'; but by the organic bond of love, which draws men into community, by nature, not by covenant; and not, or not only, from the desire that they might be delivered from the fear of violent death, but from the desire to enjoy one another and serve one another in a fellowship of love.

And if there is to be a Redeemer, a single sovereign Person appointed to create and maintain the life of commonwealth, he will not be that artifact Leviathan, created by covenant of every man with every man, to rule over the children of pride who are the children of Satan. He will be, rather, one who can justly call himself the Son of God, because he comes to men in their desperate predicament of his own accord, unsought and uncovenanted, preaching the gospel of love; by the example of his life teaching them how they may live in a community of love; and by his death proclaiming his faith in them as the children, not of Satan, who is the author of their pride and all their destructive passions, but of God, the author of their saving tenderness and loving kindness.

Whether or not Jesus of Nazareth was this person is not the question. The question is whether we have an answer to the gospel that Hobbes preaches in *Leviathan* that is not only real but also irrefutable. Since Hobbes gives us the great Leviathan, we are obliged to give him back the Son of God, whether the historical Jesus was or was not that Son of God; and since Hobbes gives us fear and pride as the sole constituents of man's nature, we are obliged to give him back love, which alone has the power to annihilate the anxiety about self-preservation, the desire of 'glory' and the terror of death.

Nor is it arbitrary but, on the contrary, logical to an exemplary degree to give back to Hobbes the gospel of Christ and no other, since Hobbes himself leaves us in no doubt that it is the gospel of Christ he is seeking to subvert by the gospel of *Leviathan*. His powerful gift of irony is directed principally to this end; and one is inclined to agree with his Christian contemporaries that the Devil cannot often have quoted the Scriptures to such devastating effect as does Hobbes in *Leviathan*.[1] The Old Testament and the New, the Epistles of St Paul and St Augustine's *The City of God* are intimately present to Hobbes's mind at every stage of the conception and execution of *Leviathan*. It is indeed part of the book's whole deliberated plan to subvert the Augustinian conception of the Two Cities, the Earthly and the Heavenly,

[1] Hobbes himself practically admits this in a curt passage in the Epistle Dedicatory to *Leviathan*: 'That which perhaps may most offend, are certain texts of Holy Scripture, alleged by me to other purpose than ordinarily they use to be by others. But I have done it with due submission, and also, in order to my subject, necessarily; for they are the outworks of the enemy, from whence they impugn the civil power.'

by reducing the ideal polity to an Earthly City alone—that Earthly City, the realm of Leviathan, which shall have no Heavenly City for its counterpart. It is no doubt with this end in view that the generation of Leviathan himself is, by one of the boldest, most audacious strokes of the Hobbesian imagination, presented in the image of the Mystical Body of Christ. When the covenant has been made, and all men have been incorporated into that one great artificial man Leviathan, the result, says Hobbes, 'is more than consent or concord; it is a real unity of them all in one and the same man'; and what he means us to understand is that this real unity is achieved by a quasi-metaphysical incorporation of the many into the one, exactly analogous to that proclaimed by the Catholic doctrine of the Mystical Body, which declares all Christians by their membership of the Church to be members of the Mystical Body of Christ.[1]

It is little wonder that Hobbes's Christian contemporaries, when they perceived the profane significance of the Leviathan image, should have felt that the gospel of Christ was being subverted at its foundations by the diabolical gospel of

[1] It is worth mentioning that in the sentence 'This is more than consent or concord, it is a real unity of them all in one and the same person', we have another instance (the only other I have been able to discover in *Leviathan*) of Hobbes's willingness at a crucial point in his argument to sacrifice his philosophical doctrine to his political which we previously remarked in his use of the word 'suggesteth' ('reason suggesteth convenient articles of peace') in his treatment of the laws of nature (pp. 106–8 above). Here, however, the sacrifice goes further than an ambiguity; it amounts to a downright contradiction of his nominalist basis. For on the nominalist theory, there can be no question of the covenant being '*more* than consent or concord' and the incorporation of the many into the one 'a *real* unity of them all in one and the same person': the first can be *only—no more* than—consent or concord, and the second only a *nominal*, not a real, unity. It is possible that Hobbes's striking lapse from consistency here is unconscious: perhaps, at this peak-point of his whole argument, he has been carried away by the excitement of the moment, and has for once lost his logical balance. But this seems unlikely in view of all we have seen of Hobbes's power of sustaining his ferocious consequentiality. It seems more probable that the inconsistency is deliberate, and is intended to serve the same purpose as the use of the word 'suggesteth' in relation to the laws of nature—to ensure for Leviathan, the supreme sovereign, a status and an authority derived from nature, not—as Hobbes's nominalism logically demands—established by convention.

Leviathan. This adaptation of some of the principal Christian images and doctrines is sustained throughout *Leviathan*; and, aside from its profanity, its interest is that it accounts for much of that distinctively 'poetic' intensity and coherence that makes *Leviathan* as genuine a product of the artistic as of the philosophic imagination.

I have suggested that what chiefly rouses our admiration in *Leviathan* is the perfect self-completeness and self-consistency of the whole system. These qualities are so rare, especially in English philosophy, that one would be falling gravely short of a proper appreciation of Hobbes's stature as a philosopher if one did not praise them as they deserve. Yet, in another sense (I have also suggested), Hobbes's moral philosophy is desperately incomplete. It leaves out of account too much of what is observably there in man's nature; and what it principally declines to take account of, the transforming and redeeming power of love, is so vital a constituent of man's nature that to restore it is to undermine fatally Hobbes's whole moral and political doctrine.

The question arises whether *Leviathan* itself offers any confirmation of this judgment upon its limitations. It would be very reassuring (and very pleasant) if, somewhere in *Leviathan*, Hobbes were in some way to recognise some part at least of what he has refused to take account of. For there is nothing so reassuring as confirmation received from the guilty party itself; especially when the guilty party happens, like Hobbes, to have constructed a system so seemingly self-consistent as to leave not the smallest gap through which any part of the excluded experience might, after all, slip in.

Such confirmations are to be found in *Leviathan*. They are not many; they are in each instance brief; and they bring Hobbes closer than ever to the Aristotle of the *Rhetoric* and the *Nicomachean Ethics*.

The recognition of any properly disinterested feeling or attitude is not to be expected. All man's passions, we have learnt, are in a strict sense *self-centred*; 'felicity' consists in 'a perpetual and restless desire of power after power that ceaseth only in death', and the passions from which the life of commonwealth springs are self-preservation and the fear of violent death. It is with surprise, therefore, that we read of the mere possibility of an exception to this universal law of Hobbes's world. 'Of all passions', writes Hobbes 'that which inclineth men least to break the laws, is fear. Nay, excepting some generous natures, it is the only thing, when there is appearance of profit or pleasure by breaking the law that makes men keep them.'[1] '*Excepting some generous natures*': where and how, one wonders, do these 'generous natures' fit into the Hobbesian scheme? And do they make a real breach in the closed circle of Hobbes's argument for the low view of man?

The answer is to be found in another passage, in which Hobbes is discussing the force of 'oaths':

> The force of words [i.e. oaths] being...too weak to hold men to the performance of their covenants, there are in man's nature but two imaginable helps to strengthen it. And those are either a fear of the consequence of breaking their word; or a glory, or pride, in appearing not to need to break it. *This latter is a generosity too rarely found to be presumed upon, especially in the pursuers of wealth, command, or sensual pleasure; which are the greatest part of mankind.* The passion to be reckoned upon is fear.[2]

This recalls a passage in the last chapter of the last Book of the *Nicomachean Ethics*, in which Aristotle is speaking of the ultimate uselessness of what he calls mere 'discourses on ethics' as distinct from the practice of morals:

> If discourses on ethics were sufficient in themselves to make men virtuous, 'large fees and many..would they win'..., and to provide such discourses would be all that is wanted. But as it is, we see that *although theories have power to stimulate and encourage generous youths, and, given an inborn nobility of character and a genuine love of what is noble, can make them susceptible to the influence of virtue, yet they are powerless to stimulate the mass of mankind to moral*

[1] *Leviathan*, ch. 27, p. 195.

[2] *Ibid.* ch. 15, p. 92.

nobility. For it is the nature of the many to be amenable to fear but not to a sense of honour, and to abstain from evil not because of its baseness but because of the penalties it entails.[1]

The emphasis in the two passages is identical. Hobbes and Aristotle are at one in pitching their expectations of 'the mass of men' as low as possible; but they are at one also in recognising in man's nature this quality that they call 'generosity', which renders those who possess it capable of a relatively disinterested love of truth and virtue. This quality, however, they both decline to take into account in their final analysis of man's nature. For it is *too rare* a quality to be presumed upon, they say; and too rare to be presumed upon, in particular, when one is constructing a civil philosophy and is concerned with men exclusively in their political character as 'pursuers of wealth, command, or sensual pleasure'.

When politics are thus interpreted, as exclusively power politics, the quality of generosity is indeed too rare to be presumed upon. But a different view of man's nature can yield a different political philosophy. We remember Socrates' faith in the capacity of men to be transformed—'made better than they are', in his favourite phrase—by this very quality of generosity, this power to respond to noble ideals and noble examples, that Aristotle and Hobbes repudiate. And in St Paul and St Augustine, this generosity is transformed into the saving power of men to respond to the prevenient grace of their all-wise and all-loving Creator. The quality that Hobbes casts out of his commonwealth ecclesiastical and civil as too rare to be presumed upon is the quality upon which both the Platonic and the Christian polities are erected and by which they are both sustained.

The passage, however, that really does make a breach in Hobbes's low view of man is that bearing on the Gallant Man.[2] Hobbes is here defining justice and the just man, and is as before reducing just conduct to conformity with the law

[1] Aristotle, *Nic. Ethics*, x. ix. 3 (Rackham).

[2] This was cited in the discussion of Aristotle's Magnanimous Man, ch. III, pp. 71–2 above.

from fear of the consequences of transgressing it. Then, unexpectedly, comes this passage:

> That which gives to human actions the relish of justice is a certain nobleness or gallantness of courage, rarely found, by which a man scorns to be beholden for the contentment of his life to fraud, or breach of promise. This justice of the manners is that which is meant where justice is called a virtue, and injustice a vice.[1]

This brings back Hobbes's definition of the quality of magnanimity, 'contempt of unjust or dishonest helps';[2] and one begins to make out at last the single positive quality in man's nature that Hobbes acknowledges to be wholly admirable. This is the quality of 'spirit' in the Platonic sense ('a certain nobleness or gallantness of courage'), which is peculiarly associated with the aristocratic temper, and, like Aristotle's 'magnanimity', achieves virtue, not by its love of the good, nor by its horror of and revulsion from evil, but by a contempt of foul play born of the aristocratic quality of pride. Hobbes's Gallant Man, like Aristotle's Magnanimous Man, is just and temperate, not because he loves justice and temperance as such, nor because he fears and abominates injustice and intemperance, but because he is too proud to be unjust or intemperate. He is too proud to fall into the plebeian condition of sin, not because it is sinful but because it is plebeian. The virtue of Hobbes's Gallant Man, in short, is seen to derive, by the nicest paradox, from the ancient Satanic sin of pride.

The paradox invites a last comment upon Hobbes's low view, which (one likes to think) Hobbes himself might have found chastening since it convicts him of a genuine logical flaw in his moral system. If the virtue of Hobbes's Gallant Man is indeed grounded in the Satanic sin of pride 'by which a man scorns to be beholden for the contentment of his life to fraud or breach of promise', is he then not also in the end one of the children of pride, over whom Leviathan is to have supreme sovereignty? And consequently, though Hobbes puts him outside his moral system in *Leviathan*, as too rare a type

1 *Leviathan*, ch. 15, p. 97.

2 *Ibid.* ch. 8, p. 45.

to be taken account of by the civil philosopher, does not his argument demand that he should put him *inside* his system?

It at once demands it and forbids it; and this dilemma is created by the ultimate contradiction between the two passions, pride and fear, that Hobbes postulates as fundamental to man's nature. For pride, though always wicked, is rarely mean; but fear, especially fear for one's life ('self-preservation'), is always mean rather than wicked. Hobbes, it seems, wanted his men both proud and craven, which is a logical impossibility; and his moral system is accordingly flawed at the point at which this contradiction exposes itself, in the account of the Gallant Man.

Of the two ways open to Hobbes for restoring the self-consistency of his system, that of eliminating fear or that of eliminating pride as a fundamental passion, it is obviously the first that would have saved his Gallant Man for the commonwealth. For if Hobbes had postulated only pride as the fundamental human passion; if he had not debased his Satanic vision of men as the children of pride by reducing them to the self-centred, fear-ridden savages of his state of nature, then he would have found for his Gallant Man a logical place in the commonwealth of Leviathan; and so, besides maintaining a self-consistency absolutely complete and flawless, would have enriched his theory of man with a positive ideal of human perfection.

My main purpose, however, was not to suggest how Hobbes might have improved his system on his own terms; it was rather to expose the limitations of those terms by bringing Hobbes to witness against himself. Perhaps the main charm of this self-exposure, by which Hobbes shows that he implicitly recognises a standard of virtue other than and outside of that which he explicitly recognises within his system, is that it vindicates the old Socratic principle, that a false position must at some point expose itself as self-contradictory; and this is a last encouraging (though circumstantial) proof of the limitations of the Hobbesian low view.

CHAPTER V

CHRIST FOR LOVE

ST PAUL'S FIRST EPISTLE TO THE CORINTHIANS

Of all the Pauline Epistles, First Corinthians is perhaps best designed to exhibit, besides the depth and intensity of Paul's Christianity, the sheer variety of his gifts as a moral and religious teacher, and the range of tone and mood he can command for his various apostolic tasks. It also exhibits at least one of his more striking limitations, that expressed in the famous seventh chapter on the subject of celibacy and marriage, and in particular in the formula Better to marry than to burn, which (as many Christians will readily concede to the non-Christian) is not the most felicitous way of expressing the finer possibilities of the sacrament of marriage.

These, however, are features of this fundamental Christian text familiar enough to need no comment; and my main theme turns rather upon the suggestion I made at the end of my discussion of Plato's *Gorgias*, that in the Epistles of St Paul we should find the most convincing evidence of how it may profit a man of the full religious temper to possess that which Socrates and Plato lacked, namely, a revealed God and a revealed Gospel. For the understanding of this vital difference between the Greek and the Christian visions of human life and destiny, both taken at their furthest reach, First Corinthians is again perhaps the most exemplary of the Epistles; and I have accordingly chosen it as the principal (though not exclusive) Pauline text through which to develop this theme.

At the end of the *Gorgias* Socrates, we remember, was only able to affirm that Gorgias, Polus and Callicles, the wisest of the Greeks, could not prove his doctrine to be false; he had not the authority, and therefore not the power, to affirm more. The same is true of the Socrates of the *Republic*, now fully translated into the apostolic Plato; and in this connexion, the great passage towards the end of Book VI of the *Republic*, in which Plato seeks by means of the image of the sun to explain to Glaucon the nature of the Form of the Good, is of crucial importance.

It is in this passage that Plato makes his grand affirmation about the Good, that it 'transcends even the real in dignity and power'.[1] But the passage itself moves, we observe, with a curiously impeded motion. Plato seems reluctant to discuss the matter at all; he continues only because Glaucon is pressing him to it, hanging back all the time; and when at the end Glaucon makes it plain that he has understood nothing of what has been said, Plato gives up with obvious relief the attempt to explain. The decisive passage follows on Socrates' suggestion that the eye is 'of all the organs of sense...most like the sun', and as the sun is to the bodily eye, so the Form of the Good is to the eye of the mind:

'When the mind's eye rests on objects illuminated by truth and reality, it understands and comprehends them, and functions intelligently; but when it turns to the twilight world of change and decay, it can only form opinions, its vision is confused and its beliefs shifting, and it seems to lack intelligence.'

'That is true' (says Glaucon).

'Then what gives the objects of knowledge their truth and the mind the power of knowing is the Form of the Good. It is the cause of knowledge and truth, and you will be right to think of it as being itself known, and yet as being something other than, and even higher than, knowledge and truth. And just as it was right to think of light and sight as being like the sun, but wrong to think of them as being the sun itself, so here again it is right to think of knowledge and truth as being like the Good, but wrong to think of either of them as being the Good, which must be given a still higher place of honour.'

'You are making it something remarkably exalted, if it is the

[1] *Republic*, VI. 509.

source of knowledge and truth, and yet itself higher than they are....'

'The sun, I think you will agree' (Socrates continues), 'not only makes the things we see visible, but causes the processes of generation, growth and nourishment, without itself being such a process.'

'True.'

'The Good therefore may be said to be *the source not only of the intelligibility of the objects of knowledge, but also of their existence and reality*; *yet it is not itself identical with reality, but is beyond reality, and superior to it in dignity and power.*'

This proves too much for Glaucon:

'It really must be devilish superior', he remarked with a grin.

'Well', I said, 'it is your fault, you compelled me to say what I think about it.'

'Don't stop, please', he said, 'or, at any rate, complete the simile of the sun if you still have anything to say.'

'Yes, I still have many things to say.'

'Well, don't omit the smallest thing', he said.

'I fancy', I said, 'that I shall omit much. But...I shall not, if I can help it, omit anything which can be brought forward now.'

'Please don't', he said.[1]

Plato in fact, however, does at this point drop the image of the sun. He gives up the attempt to render intelligible to Glaucon the direct visionary experience of the Form of the Good, and, instead, takes up the geometrical image of the 'segmented line', which brings down the level of the enquiry from this remotest, most inaccessible peak of the Platonic ontology and metaphysics to the comparatively familiar, accessible ground of the Platonic epistemology.

What this account of the Form of the Good shows is that Plato in the *Republic*, like Socrates in the *Gorgias*, cannot affirm more of the Good than that it transcends even reality in dignity and power. He is able to recognise and acknowledge the existence of a single supreme Source of that order of goodness and power which is greater than any that this world

[1] *Republic*, VI. 508–9. Trans. H. D. P. Lee (Penguin Classics) and A. D. Lindsay (Everyman).

can show;[1] he can recognise its transcendent reality and grandeur; and can even hint that he knows more than he is able to say ('I fancy...that I shall omit much'). But he cannot positively affirm more than he has said; indeed he dare not affirm more, for fear (among other reasons) of exposing his secret knowledge to a ridicule from which he would be helpless to defend it.

The case is different for the brilliant Jewish convert to Christianity, Paul of Tarsus. Paul, having, as he believes, seen God face to face on the road to Damascus, has thereby received the authority and the power to affirm positively what Socrates and Plato could only intimate by hints and guesses. From his direct encounter with God he has received the full knowledge of God, of which the essence is the certainty—to such tempers, the indispensable, the precious, the blessed certainty—that there exists a single Source of the whole created universe, invisible, eternal and indestructible, from which everything visible, temporal and mutable in the created universe derives its existence and intelligibility. And for Paul that Source is not Plato's supreme abstraction, the Form of the Good, which, though it almost vibrates with the quality of life from the infused passion of Plato's yearning, yet remains an abstraction, a 'form', an idea. Nor is it that more arid abstraction of Aristotle, the First Cause or Unmoved Mover of the universe; nor is it the comfortless God of Stoicism, who can command obedience to the moral law but cannot give peace, power and joy. Paul's God is not an inference or a presupposition, but a Person; he is the God of Abraham, Isaac and Jacob, the Heavenly Father of Jesus Christ. In some sense, mysterious and indefinable perhaps, yet also definite and certain and irresistibly compelling, he is a Person, who is as infinitely tender and loving as he is infinitely powerful and wise, and sent his only begotten Son to redeem the world.

This, for Paul, is the most important manifestation of the

[1] See ch. I, p. 9 n. above.

divine love, that God the Father should have sent his only begotten Son to redeem the world by bringing it the promise of eternal life, and the grace of the Holy Spirit to help, comfort and sustain men in their efforts to fulfil the moral law. And what the moral law is, and what it demands of us, has only now, in the coming of the Son, been finally revealed to men. The supreme law, which subsumes the whole of the moral law, is the law of love, without which (Paul tells us in First Corinthians) all other virtue is rendered flat, stale and unprofitable:

> If I speak with the tongues of men and of angels, but have not love, I am become as sounding brass or a clanging cymbal; And if I have the gift of prophecy, and know all mysteries and all knowledge; and if I have all faith so as to remove mountains, but have not love, I am nothing. And if I bestow all my goods to feed the poor, and if I give my body to be burned, but have not love, it profiteth me nothing.[1]

This is Pauls' passionate tribute in First Corinthians to God the Father, the Creator, the First Person of the Trinity, to whom in Christ he owes his final allegiance. But Paul's own personal commerce is always with the Son, with Jesus the Mediator. It was Jesus whom he met on the road to Damascus; Jesus who wrung his heart, melted all his stubbornness, filled him with an anguish of shame and repentance for the injuries he had inflicted upon the children of light, and garnered up Paul's whole heart to his person and his Gospel by the single query, 'Saul, Saul, why dost thou persecute me?'

In this connexion, it is helpful to recall again the tribute that Alcibiades pays to Socrates at the end of the *Symposium*. Socrates, we remember, had the power to make Alcibiades 'ashamed' of his base compliances with the standards of the world. He had the power to subdue Alcibiades into a recognition of that order of goodness and power greater than any that this world can show in which he himself so passionately believed; and he had the power even to draw Alcibiades to himself in love and admiration of the daily beauty in his life which made all others by comparison ugly. But what

[1] I Cor. xiii. 1–3.

Socrates lacked was the power to *sustain* Alcibiades in that exalted condition. 'I know I ought to do the things he tells me,' says Alcibiades, 'yet the moment I'm out of his sight I don't care what I do to keep in with the mob. So I dash off, like a runaway slave, and keep out of his way as long as I can.' That, in one sentence, is the difference. Socrates cannot sustain Alcibiades in his weakness; cannot give him the power to persist, without intermission, in the pursuit of the good; cannot render operative in him his knowledge of the good. And this, which Socrates cannot do for Alcibiades, Jesus can, and does, do for Paul.

This is perhaps the moment to touch briefly on a rather large matter, that of the radically different interpretations put upon the phenomenon I have just been discussing by the Christian on the one hand and what I have called the Humanist, or 'religious' Humanist, on the other. The Christian, we know, argues that it is only the Holy Spirit—the Third Person of the Blessed Trinity, God Himself in the shape of the Paraclete—who can thus strengthen and sustain men in their aspiration after perfect righteousness. It is *because*, and only because, Jesus was God (argues the Christian) that he could do for Paul what Socrates could not do for Alcibiades. The Humanist recognises and acknowledges this difference between the efficacious powers of a Socrates and a Christ, and desires to explain it; and (it should be emphasised) it is precisely because he acknowledges the difference to be real and important, not delusory or trivial, and because he desires to explain it, not to explain it away, that he is a 'religious' Humanist, not an atheist or agnostic. The Humanist, however, while acknowledging the difference and desiring to explain it, reverses the terms of the Christian argument. It was because the man whom Paul met on the road to Damascus *in fact* possessed that efficacious power, argues the Humanist, that he is to be accounted 'God'. That is what the terms 'God', 'Christ' and 'Holy Spirit' mean; that is their real, their operative, meaning; and that is how Jesus comes to be known as the 'Son of God'—by the verifiable and verified fact that he possesses the power to command the devotion of men to his Person and his Gospel, and to sustain them in their effort to live according to the saving truths of that Gospel.

Another way of expressing the difference between the Humanist view and that of the historic Church is to say that the Christian deduces the power from the known divinity of Christ, the Humanist deduces the divinity from the known fact of the power. When the Christian is asked, On what compulsion shall I believe that the man who had the unique power to sustain men in the pursuit of righteousness is 'divine' or the 'Son of God'? he answers, Because this man fulfilled, in his life, mission and death, the prophecies of the divinely inspired prophets of the Old Testament, and performed miracles, of which the greatest were his own Incarnation and Resurrection, that no merely human creature could perform. The Christian, in other words, postulates the divinity of Jesus as given by 'revelation', and from the fact of that divinity made known by supernatural means (the prophecies and the miracles) deduces the saving power as its necessary consequence. The Humanist takes the power as the given or known fact, and from that fact deduces what the Christian must mean by the terms 'Son of God', 'divinity' and 'revelation'. And to such a Humanist, who recognises that this power did, as a matter of verified fact, belong to the historical Jesus, the addition of supernatural sanctions is superfluous. For the possession of that power (he argues) is by itself a marvel, or 'miracle', so impressive and so inspiring that it stands in no need of a supernatural sanction either to establish or to confirm its miraculous character.

Returning to St Paul and First Corinthians and fixing our attention upon the facts of Paul's spiritual history without further reference to problems of ultimate interpretation, we are obliged to take as the central fact his vision on the road to Damascus. Leaving aside differences about the meaning of the terms 'vision' and 'revelation', what is certain is that on the road to Damascus Saul of Tarsus is put in possession of a source of light and life that transcends in reality and efficacious power anything that Socrates or Plato ever knew. The result is that Paul is able to proclaim the gospel of Christ with an assurance of being in possession of the Truth—the absolute, complete and final truth—that neither Socrates nor Plato could aspire to, and against their diffidence is able to set a confidence that none but he, even among Christian writers, can command. This is a confidence born of his direct encounter with God on the road to Damascus, and after that perpetually reinforced and sustained by the fellowship of the community into which he has entered by the sacrament of his baptism, by their common devotion to a single Master, by their common acts of worship, and by his own apostolic services to them.

Nor is this a confidence that can ever be shaken by the fear that it may perhaps be a form of vainglory, of self-aggrandisement. 'I have been crucified with Christ', writes Paul to the Galatians, 'yet I live; and yet no longer I but Christ liveth in me.'[1] When he speaks, he speaks, and yet not he but Christ in him. When he preaches Christ the crucified, when he performs his pastoral duties, when he bestows praise here and blame there upon his brothers in Christ in the scattered churches that he cannot reach in person, it is he who does all those things, and yet not he but Christ in him. This is what his discipleship in Christ means to Paul, this sense of living in and through the life of Another, infinitely greater than himself, infinitely more powerful, more tender and merciful; the sense, indeed, of Christ embedded in his flesh, his bones and his blood; and this is the bond that Socrates and Plato were without, of which Paul speaks so powerfully in a famous passage in the Epistle to the Romans:

> What can ever part us from Christ's love? Can anguish or calamity or persecution or famine or nakedness or danger or the

[1] Gal. ii. 20.

sword?... No, in all this we are more than conquerors through him who loved us. For I am certain that neither death nor life, neither angels not principalities, neither the present nor the future, no powers of the Height or of the Depth, nor anything else in all creation will be able to part us from God's love in Christ Jesus our Lord.[1]

It is this same sense of the bond that has been established between God and man by the blessed mediation of Christ and of their indissoluble unity in Christ the mediator that inspires Paul in his anger when, in the opening chapter of First Corinthians, he sternly expostulates with the Corinthians for what he calls their 'faction-fighting':

Chloe's people inform me, my brothers, that you are quarrelling. By 'quarrelling' I mean that each of you has his party-cry, 'I belong to Paul', 'And I to Apollos', 'And I to Cephas', 'And I to Christ'. Has Christ been parcelled out? Was it Paul who was crucified for you? Was it in Paul's name that you were baptised?... Christ did not send me to baptise but to preach the gospel. And to preach it with no fine rhetoric, lest the cross of Christ should lose its power.[2]

Everything in the name of Christ, nothing in his own name; nothing for his own sake, everything for the sake of him who is the Resurrection and the Life. Paul's submission to the spirit of Christ within him is his strength, his bondage is his liberty.

This is for Paul the ultimate source of his liberty and power; its immediate source, however, is the Passion of Christ. Against Socrates' earnest deprecation of the wisdom of the world—'the morality of worldly success' of the *Gorgias*—Paul can proclaim that the wisdom of the world has been annihilated by the Crucifixion and the Resurrection:

Has not God stultified the wisdom of the world? For when the world with all its wisdom failed to know God in his wisdom, God resolved to save believers by the 'sheer folly' of the Christian message. Jews demand miracles and Greeks want wisdom, but our message is Christ the crucified—a stumbling-block to Jews, 'sheer

[1] Rom. viii. 35–9.

[2] I Cor. i. 11–17.

folly' to Gentiles, but for those who are called, whether Jews or Greeks, a Christ who is the power of God and the wisdom of God. For the 'foolishness' of God is wiser than men; and the 'weakness' of God is stronger than men.[1]

And what has supplanted the wisdom of the world? Why, answers Paul, the eternal, immutable, unfathomable wisdom of God, which is a wisdom or knowledge accessible only to 'the spirit'. It is not accessible (he means) to mere sense-perception, which can look but cannot see, and can listen but cannot hear; nor to the mere ratiocinative intellect, which can draw long chains of argument out of given premises, but has no means of knowing whether the premises are true or false; but only to the senses and the mind illuminated by *the spirit*, which gives direct access to the source of life and truth itself and thereby to the wisdom that transcends in dignity and power the wisdom of the world.

And indeed, of all the first Apostles, Paul was perhaps best qualified to know intimately the difference between the activity of the mind unilluminated by the spirit and the same mind exercising its powers by the light of the Gospel revelation. For Paul, the Jew, brought up in the rabbinical schools of Tarsus, liberally endowed with the intellectual gifts that so often distinguish the members of his race, and thoroughly accomplished, one may suppose, in the intellectual skills of rabbinical scholasticism, no small part of the peace, power and joy of his conversion must have been this liberation of his mind from the scholastic learning of the old faith and its emergence into the light of a generality—a comprehensiveness, a universality—of truth such as he could not have dreamt of when he sat at the feet of Gamaliel. Paul's conversion, in short, was for him as much a philosophical liberation as a circumcision of the heart; and this is part of the meaning of the famous passage in First Corinthians,

When I was a child, I talked like a child, I thought like a child, I argued like a child; now that I am a man, I am done with childish

[1] I Cor. i. 21–5.

ways. At present we only see the baffling reflections in a mirror, but then it will be face to face; at present I am learning bit by bit, but then I shall understand, as all along I have myself been understood.[1]

The link between the Pauline metaphysic and the Platonic in this same famous passage hardly needs to be stressed. For Paul, as for Plato, the visible, mutable world of the senses stands in permanent contrast to the invisible, immutable world of the spirit, and in the same relation, that of the reflection to the thing reflected, the shadow to the substance, the appearance to the reality: 'The slight trouble of the passing hour results in a solid glory past all comparison, for those of us whose eyes are on the unseen, not on the seen; for the seen is transient, the unseen eternal.'[2]

And this sense of the transcendent glory of the invisible world—the world of pure spirit, bathed in the noontide light of pure realities, of which the supreme reality is God himself—fills Paul, like Plato, with a passionate yearning to know it face to face. He yearns to step for ever out of the tabernacle of the flesh, to be led into the Promised Land, and be made one in spirit with that which is at once the Source and Substance of all perfection. This is the central experience of the fully metaphysical, or mystical, temper; and it is nowhere more movingly expressed than in the fifth chapter of Second Corinthians:

I know that if this earthly tent of mine is taken down, I get a home from God, made by no human hands, eternal in the heavens. It makes me sigh indeed, this yearning to be under cover of my heavenly habitation, since I am sure that once so covered, I shall not be 'naked' at the hour of death. I do sigh within this tent of mine with heavy anxiety—not that I want to be stripped, no; but to be under cover of the other, to have my mortal element absorbed by life.[3]

This ceaseless yearning of the mystical mind for the final consummation of its love is an experience that Plato knows as intimately as Paul. Plato's yearning to know the Good face

[1] I Cor. xiii. 11–12. [2] II Cor. iv. 17–18.
[3] II Cor. v. 1–5.

to face is as strong as Paul's to know God; and Paul's longing to be under cover of his heavenly habitation is not more intense than Plato's to enter and abide in the world of pure forms. But what Paul is able to add to the Platonic yearning for the mystical union with the Good is the experience of *participation* in the Source of all goodness, wisdom and power. Plato, we remember, looked up and beheld the sun, the image of the Good, and saw that it was the source of light and life, and longed to abide with it, in the life after death that he passionately believed in. Paul also yearns to abide with Christ; but, waiting and yearning, he has in the meantime the unspeakable comfort that Plato was without, that of possessing the cause, the will, the strength and the means to a present participation in the divine nature. The cause is the Incarnation, the Crucifixion, and the Resurrection; the means, the several sacraments of the Church, in particular the sacraments of Baptism and the Eucharist; the strength is given by prayer and fasting, assisted constantly by the beneficent operations of the Holy Spirit; and the will in the faithful is assumed as given. Of each of these fundamental matters Paul has something definitive to say in First Corinthians, and in particular about the Incarnation and the Resurrection, those two great miraculous events which took place in time and out of time, and form to the present day the foundation of the historic Church.

In the eleventh Chapter of First Corinthians St Paul speaks of the sacrament by which Christians celebrate at once the Incarnation and the Crucifixion. By eating the sacramental bread and drinking the sacramental wine, 'in memory of me' (as Paul, recalling Jesus' own words, there puts it),[1] Christians at once commemorate the sacrificial death of their Saviour and enjoy, each time afresh, the experience of participation in the eternal Source of spiritual life. They re-live, each time, the most inward meaning of the Incarnation, which is the saving experience of receiving God's Law in the flesh. In the

[1] I Cor. xi. 26.

person of Jesus, the *logos*—the divine Word or Law, which is Love—is made flesh; the infinite *logical* possibility of truth and goodness is rendered actual and concrete; contracted, as it were, into a single human soul and human body at a particular point in time; and thereby rendered accessible to all men for their salvation. And this again, the experience of an intimate, personal participation in the divine nature, is something that Plato had no knowledge of. Plato could conceive of the Form of the Good as that which transcends even pure being in dignity and power; but he could not conceive of it as incarnate. He could not conceive of it as embodied in a Person, who could by the acts of his life and the consummating act of his death affirm the redeeming power of love with an authority so absolute that it would have the power to draw all men to a love of the good through devotion to his Person. The conception of a discipleship of love rather than a discipline of the mind as the means of achieving the perfect wisdom and virtue that is the condition of salvation in Plato's scheme was, it seems, as far beyond the reach of Plato's religious imagination as the conception of the divine nature assuming human form in order to render itself accessible to men for their salvation; and it is to Paul that we have to turn for an understanding of the meaning of such a discipleship of love, and what it can command in sacrifices that are never felt as sacrifices because all sense of loss is consumed in the glory of possessing and being possessed by Christ:

> What things were gain to me, these have I counted loss for Christ. Yea, verily, and I count all things to be loss for the excellency of the knowledge of Christ Jesus my Lord: for whom I suffered the loss of all things, and do count them but dung, that I may gain Christ. . . I would know him in the power of his resurrection and the fellowship of his sufferings, with my nature transformed to die as he died, to see if I too can attain the resurrection from the dead. Not that I have already attained this or am already perfect, but I press forward to appropriate it, because I have been appropriated myself by Christ Jesus.[1]

[1] Phil. iii. 7–12.

It is the Incarnation, then, that makes possible this intimate, inward possession of the law of love. But the consummation of certainty, the final assurance of its continued, its perpetual, possession, is received from the miracle of the Resurrection. Paul's account of the Resurrection in First Corinthians is (with all its theological implications) one of the great doctrinal rocks upon which the historic Church is founded, and as such is important enough to demand attention in any discussion of Paul as a Christian moralist. But it is also of special interest to the modern religious Humanist. For it challenges him, in a peculiarly direct and uncompromising way, to give if he can his own account of the matter; and this is what I propose to do in an effort to bring out the difference between the Christian and the Humanist interpretation of certain vital facts of our spiritual experience at a point at which (I believe) it can be most forcibly exhibited.

Speaking, accordingly, in the manner of men, as a Humanist, and therefore without reference to the supernatural aspect of the matter upon which the historic Church puts all its emphasis, the meaning of the Resurrection may be said to be the immediate, inward experience of the indestructibility of the saving knowledge that the man Jesus Christ brought into the consciousness of men. This was the knowledge of the redemptive power of love; and the Resurrection was the most complete and most glorious affirmation of its indestructible power to redeem. And (the Humanist would go on) what the historic accounts of the Resurrection in the Synoptic Gospels and the Acts may be taken to express is the fact that this saving knowledge that Christ brought into the consciousness of men was not destroyed when Christ died on the Cross because it could not be destroyed, being *in its intrinsic nature* indestructible. It could indeed be eclipsed; but only for the shortest space of time—according to the New Testament story, only for the space of the three terrible days immediately following Christ's death, when the disciples, who had been charged to preach and propagate Christ's gospel, fell into an anguish of despair and doubt, and the gospel of love was threatened with extinction. And if it *had* been possible that the saving knowledge that Jesus Christ brought into the consciousness of men should pass for ever out of their consciousness, if it had been possible to lose for ever the saving power of that knowledge, then, as Paul says, we should have been of all men the most pitiable. But in fact (to complete this interpretation of the Gospel story) the anguished prayers of the disciples for reassurance were answered. Faith and hope were restored to them—faith in the redeeming power of love and hope in its power to save the whole world—and with these their apostolic fervour and energy; and the gospel of Christ was saved for the world from that time to the present day.

The vital point upon which this interpretation of the Resurrection diverges from the Pauline and Christian is not difficult to see. On this interpretation of the Resurrection, it does not matter whether Christ, as a matter of historical and scientific fact, did or did not rise from the dead. It does not matter on this interpretation whether the tomb, as a matter of historical and scientific fact, was or was not empty. On this interpretation, the physical resurrection of Jesus from the dead is neither asserted nor denied; it is affirmed simply to be irrelevant to what is taken, on this view, to be the real, inward, permanently valid meaning of the mystery of the Resurrection—its meaning as the experienced certainty of the indestructibility of Christ's gospel of love. And to this fact of our most inward experience, nothing is added—nothing *could* be added—for the Humanist by the further fact of Christ's physical resurrection from the dead, even if that fact were historically and scientifically true.

This, speaking in human fashion, as a Humanist, is what one might say the Resurrection essentially means. But this, of course, is not what St Paul says it means. Or, rather, he says that it does not mean *only* this, and that this for the Christian is not even the most important part of what it means. For Paul the Resurrection is not merely the supreme symbol of the indestructibility of Christ's gospel. What Paul insists upon is that Christ actually rose from the dead; that the tomb *was* empty, as a matter of scientifically verifiable fact; that the Resurrection as it is reported in the Synoptic Gospels and the Acts of the Apostles was a historical event; that it happened, visibly happened, before the witnesses named in the fifteenth chapter of First Corinthians: 'He rose on the third day, as the Scriptures had said, and...he was seen by Cephas, then by the twelve; after that he was seen by over five hundred brothers all at once, the majority of whom survive to this day, though some have died; after that he was seen by James, then by all the Apostles, and finally he was seen by myself.'[1] And he insists upon it still more explicitly and with the fullest emphasis in a great passage in the same chapter of First Corinthians—a passage that vibrates in every cadence with his passionate conviction of the truth of the miraculous event, with his terror for the world's destruction if it should be denied, and his anguished appeal to the wretched backsliding Corinthians to see their error and repent before it is too late:

> Now if we preach that Christ rose from the dead, how can certain individuals among you assert that 'there is no such thing as a resurrection of the dead'? If 'there is no such thing as a resurrection from the dead', then even Christ did not rise; and if Christ did not rise, then our preaching has gone for nothing, and your faith has gone for nothing too. Besides, we are detected bearing false witness to God by affirming of him that he raised Christ—whom he did not raise, if after all dead men never rise. For if dead men never rise, Christ did not rise either; and if Christ did not rise, your faith is futile, you are still in your sins. More than that: those who have slept the sleep of death in Christ have perished after all. Ah, if in this life we have nothing but a mere hope in Christ, we are of all men the most pitiable.[2]

And again, a few verses on, with the same passionate agitation:

> If there is no such thing as a resurrection, what is the meaning of people getting baptised on behalf of their dead? If dead men do not

[1] I Cor. xv. 4–8.

[2] I Cor. xv. 12–19.

rise at all, why do people get baptised on their behalf? Yes, and why am I myself in danger every hour?... What would it avail me that, speaking in the manner of men, I 'fought with wild beasts' at Ephesus? If dead men do not rise, let us eat and drink for to-morrow we die....[1]

But it is not so! Christ did rise from the dead, he was the first to be reaped of those who sleep in death.

For since death came by man, by man came also resurrection from the dead; as all die in Adam, so shall all be made alive in Christ.[2]

If there is anything in all Christian writing that could turn even the most ferocious, intransigent Humanist into a true historical Christian, it is, I believe, these passages on the Resurrection in First Corinthians. If to a mind as illuminated with all spiritual knowledge as Paul's, and a heart as dedicated as his to the love of whatsoever things are pure and honourable and lovely, this was the most important truth about the Resurrection, it is indeed hard for the Humanist to resist the suggestion that it does after all matter whether Christ did or did not rise from the dead, whether the tomb was or was not empty as a matter of historical and scientific fact.

The Humanist does in the end resist this suggestion. He does in the end remain firm in his conviction that Paul failed in this instance to put first things first. He failed to put first the essential inward meaning of the Resurrection as (the Humanist still maintains) the supreme symbolic affirmation of the profoundly redemptive experience of the indestructible power of love to transform and redeem the world. This, for the Humanist, is the whole meaning of the Resurrection—a meaning, for him, intelligible enough and complete enough for all the ends of salvation; and it is this that Paul fails to put first, choosing instead, as we have seen, to put all his emphasis upon the Resurrection as a historical event, and insisting that it is its historical truth, and this only, that is the basis of its redemptive power.

So the Humanist resists and rejects in the end the Pauline

[1] I Cor. xv. 29–32. [2] I Cor. xv. 20–2.

account of the Resurrection, but, in view of those passages in First Corinthians, not without the greatest difficulty. The reason I stress the difficulty is that I wish to make it plain that it is not easy to be a Humanist—a 'religious' Humanist, that is, as distinct from a scientific or naturalistic Humanist. It is not easy to be a Humanist if one really understands what it is one is rejecting in that central religious tradition of our civilisation to which we owe whatever spiritual light we may possess. And since it is vitally necessary that the Humanist should understand what he is rejecting in historic Christianity, it is necessary that he should take Christ and Paul seriously, as the scientific and naturalistic Humanists on the whole do not. If his Humanism is to have any claim to intellectual respectability, he must really know what he is rejecting; and to know this he must be prepared to expose himself, to the quick of his soul (as D. H. Lawrence would have said), to the full impact of that which he is rejecting. This kind of exposure is growing less and less common nowadays, certainly among non-Christians and even among Christians themselves; and for this reason it seemed desirable in this discussion of Paul as Christian moralist to present him as directly as possible, letting him speak for the most part in his own voice, so that the impact for those who need it might be as complete as possible.

There are at least two further aspects of Paul's representative greatness as a Christian moralist that deserve detailed treatment but can only be briefly discussed here. The first concerns the metaphysical foundations of the Christian faith implicit in the Epistles, the second Paul's prophecy concerning the redemption of the Jews.

The metaphysical foundations of Christianity are nowhere explicitly stated, or even touched upon, in the Epistles. Paul was in the first and last instance a missionary and a preacher, and it was no part of his task to concern himself with, much less attempt a systematic account of, the purely philosophical implications of the faith he was engaged in propagating. But what is implicit in Paul's pronouncements, on certain important doctrinal points in particular, is sufficient to show the basic character of these metaphysical foundations of Christianity, namely, that they are 'realist' through and through—as consistently and uncompromisingly realist as (for instance) Hobbes's are nominalist; and that such a 'realist' metaphysic is the only logically possible metaphysic for a fully religious view of life, as the other, the nominalist, is the only logically possible foundation of a secular—non-religious or irreligious—view.

If it is asked why a Christian must be a metaphysical realist, the short answer is that only a realist metaphysic is compatible with the postulated existence of a God who is the single supreme creator of the world and everything it contains. The moment the existence of such a God is postulated, there can be no question about the real existence of an order of nature prior to and independent of the constructions of the human mind. *Of course* there is such an order of nature (the religious thinker is able to affirm); and of course the conceptual activities of the human mind can be directed only to the task of discovering the order that is there to be discovered, not (as Hobbes believed) to that of creating out of the discrete particulars of sense-experience an order otherwise non-existent. For the Christian thinker all identity and difference, all connexion, coherence, intelligibility, exist prior to the operations of the human mind because God created the world with these identities and differences and mutual connexions. Things are thus and not otherwise because God made them so; true and false, good and bad, right and wrong, beautiful and ugly are real, not merely nominal, categories. They are grounded 'in nature', not created 'by arbitrary institution', and as such are the foundation, indeed the very condition, of every distinction, classification, hypothesis or law discoverable by the conceptual powers of the human mind.

This, in bare outline, is the realist metaphysic implicit in the Pauline view of the world. It stands at the opposite pole to the Hobbesian view; and a simple but striking illustration of the effect of this difference upon a doctrinal point of equal importance to Hobbes and Paul may be discovered by comparing their accounts of the relation of positive law to morality ('sin').

'Where there is no law, there is no transgression either', says Paul in the fourth chapter of the Epistle to the Romans. 'Where [there is] no law', says Hobbes in chapter 13 of *Leviathan*, '[there is] no injustice.' The propositions are almost identical; but their meanings are so different that one is saying practically the opposite of the other. Paul's statement, it will be remembered, occurs in the course of his great discussion (Rom. iii–viii) of the relation of the Old Covenant to the New, of the old Mosaic Law, carved on tables of stone, to the new Law of Love, inscribed in the tables of the heart. Paul is at once passionately repudiating the suggestion that he has declared the Mosaic Law to have been annihilated by Christ's Law, and at the same time affirming that the New Covenant has transcended and superseded the Old. What Paul means is that the New Covenant, the Law of Christ, has not annihilated but *incorporated* the Old Covenant, the Law of Moses, and in this sense, and this sense alone, has 'transcended' and 'superseded' it. That is why (Paul insists), so far from repudiating the Old Law, he upholds it as 'holy, just and for our good'; and then goes on to explain the specific virtue of the Law—that it made men conscious of their sinful state, therefore conscious of their need for redemption, and thus prepared them for the coming of Christ with his saving gospel. In chapter vii of Romans, in a passage so violently paradoxical that it is little wonder it has often been misunderstood, Paul says,

> Had it not been for the Law, I would never have known what sin meant. Thus I would never have known what it is to covet, unless the Law had said, *You must not covet*. . . I lived at one time without law myself, but when the command came home to me, sin sprang to life and I died; the command that meant life proved death to me.

The command gave an impulse to sin, sin beguiled me and used the command to kill me. So the Law at any rate is holy, the command is holy, just and for our good.[1]

The seeming contradictions in this passage arise from Paul's effort to say two things at once about the Mosaic Law, that, on the one hand, it is and remains 'holy, just and for our good' because it makes us conscious of our state of sin and therefore of our need of redemption, and, on the other hand, that it is, in itself and by itself, the law of death ('sin sprang to life and I died') because it *only* makes us conscious of our sin, but has not also the power to save us from that sin.

It is now not difficult to see what Paul means by the sentence 'Where there is no law, there is no transgression either.' He means that the Commandments, which (to press the parallel with *Leviathan*) are the 'positive law' of the supreme sovereign God, render explicit, and thereby make us conscious of, the sin that is already there in us prior to the enunciation of those commandments or positive laws. Our state of sin, in other words, is 'given', as an intrinsic part of our constitution since the Fall; it is not created, not artificially made, by those laws. Even where there is no law, Paul is saying, there *is* transgression; there is only no knowledge or consciousness of transgression, and therefore no knowledge or consciousness of our misery, which for us is the beginning of salvation.

This, however, is not at all what Hobbes means when he says, 'Where there is no law, there is no injustice'. Hobbes, speaking of the positive law of Leviathan, that mortal god 'to which we owe under the immortal God our peace and defence', means exactly what Paul does not mean. 'The desires and other passions of men', he writes, 'are in themselves no sin. No more are the actions, that proceed from those passions, till they know a law that forbids them: which till laws be made they cannot know: nor can any law be made, till they have agreed upon the person that shall make it.'[2]

[1] Rom. vii. 7–12.

[2] *Leviathan*, ch. 13, p. 83.

And for the final emphasis: in the state of nature, which is the condition of man prior to the creation of commonwealth, 'nothing' says Hobbes, 'can be unjust. The notions of right and wrong, justice and injustice, have there no place. Where there is no common power, there is no law: where no law, no injustice.'[1] And what Hobbes means is precisely what Paul did *not* mean, namely, that moral evil (wrong, injustice—all that Paul means by 'sin') has no existence and no reality in nature. It is brought into being *ex nihilo* by the positive decree of the sovereign; it is not in any sense given, but entirely created.

This is an instance of one kind of difference, that relating to doctrine, which may result from the difference between a realist and a nominalist metaphysical basis. But a comparable difference may be traced also in the more strictly literary matter of imagery—in the imagery used, on the one side, by a writer who sees the universe as a universe of disconnected singulars, and, on the other, by one who sees it as organically connected because stemming from a single source which is the unifying principle of the whole universe. When Hobbes wishes to picture the life of men in society in their mutual disconnectedness, the image, we remember, that naturally suggests itself to him is that of stones ('stones brought together for building of an edifice'): this is, as it were, the emblematic image of Hobbes's universe of disconnected singulars. When Paul seeks to express the idea of the fusion of Jew and Gentile in the Church, the image that naturally springs to his mind is drawn, not from the mechanical operations of the builder's art, but from the natural, the 'organic', art of gardening.[2] Mgr Ronald Knox, in a little book called *St Paul's Gospel*, gives a delightful exegesis upon this passage in Romans, which exactly (though, of course, quite unintentionally) points the contrast with Hobbes's image and all its implications. He stresses the point that St Paul conceives of Jew and Gentile, not as two walls meeting at a common angle,

[1] *Ibid.* ch. 13, p. 83. [2] Rom. xi. 23–4.

but as two growths of olive, one wild, one fruit-bearing, of which the wild growth of the Gentiles is grafted into the fruitful Jewish stock; and this image (he adds) is representative of others of the same organic character, of which the most famous are the image of the True Vine, or the Tree of Life (which, however, is not used by Paul himself but by the author of the Fourth Gospel), and the image of the Church as Christ's mystical Body and the community of Christians as the organic parts of the Body, metaphysically incorporated into it by their common faith in and their common service of their Lord, who is its Head.[1] These images are the poetic expression of that conception of an organically connected universe which stands at the centre of the Christian world-view, and is philosophically grounded in a realist metaphysic.

The character of Paul as Jew—which, paradoxically, is a part of his greatness as a Christian moralist and missionary—emerges with a wonderful vividness in the famous prophecy concerning the redemption of the Jews in the Epistle to the Romans. The whole great discourse begins with a passage that is one of the most moving in all the Epistles:

> I say the truth in Christ, I lie not, my conscience bearing witness with me in the Holy Ghost, That I have great sorrow and unceasing pain in my heart. For I could wish that I myself were anathema from Christ for my brethren's sake, my kinsmen according to the flesh: Who are Israelites; whose is the adoption, and the glory, and the covenants, and the giving of the law, and the service of God, and the promises.[2]

This is the cry of anguish that is wrung from Paul at the thought of his people, the Jews, cut off from Christ's saving Gospel; and what makes it so remarkable is that it should be Paul—now indeed Christ's apostle to the Gentiles, but only yesterday, 'an Israelite myself, a descendant of Abraham, a

[1] It is used in, among other places, I Cor. xii, where Paul is speaking of the varieties of spiritual gifts, and how they may be exercised in harmony within the Church.

[2] Rom. ix. 1–5.

member of the tribe of Benjamin',[1] who, having met Christ upon the road to Damascus, was in that same moment 'appropriated' by Christ, his whole soul grappled to his Saviour with hoops of steel and his whole life given over to preaching Christ the crucified for the salvation of the world—that it should be this Paul who for the sake of his brethren, his kinsmen according to the flesh, could wish himself anathema from Christ, cut off for ever from the source of his life and joy, if by that means he might bring his people the Jews to recognise the Saviour of the world and so participate in the fulfilment of the Promise made of old to their father Abraham. Greater love than this, one may surely say, knoweth no man; and it is little wonder that the sorrow and unceasing pain at the heart of this greatest of the Jewish converts to Christianity should have transmitted itself through the generations to other Jewish converts dreaming of the redemption of the Jews to what they had come to see as the true faith.

This opening passage of the ninth chapter of Romans strikes the key and pitch of the whole discussion that follows, which is conducted virtually in the form of a polemic. The Christian community at Rome have, it seems, grown vainglorious. They have been congratulating themselves on their Christianity, on having seen what the benighted Jews have failed to see, that Jesus was the Messiah and that salvation is now through membership of his Church and by no other means. They have been boasting themselves, waxing proud, in the knowledge that it is now they, the Gentiles, and no longer the Jews who have become God's chosen vessels of salvation.

This is the immediate provocation for Paul's great outburst of wrath. But from the tone and tempo of his voice in these chapters, it is clear that the Romans' spiritual pride is not the only, or even the main, cause of his anger. Their boasting has touched him in one of his most tender spots; and all his suppressed grief and anguish, all his bitter disappointment

[1] Rom. xi. 1.

at the continued resistance of his people the Jews to the gospel of light, break out over the Romans in a storm of thunderous denunciation of the kind familiar from the prophetic books of the Old Testament, though perhaps not wholly consistent with Paul's office as Christ's apostle to the Gentiles. Who are they, demands Paul, to boast that they are better than the Jews? Don't they *know* that it is to this very defection of the Jews that they owe their own present ascendancy in the fields of light? Don't they know that God has only allowed salvation to pass to them, the Gentiles, in order to make his Chosen People the Jews 'jealous', and so before long to bring them to their senses?[1] The Chosen People, once chosen, remain the Chosen People:

> If the first handful of dough is consecrated, so is the rest of the lump,
> If the root is consecrated, so are the branches.[2]

And (Paul goes on) even though it may be true that 'some of the branches have been broken off, while you have been grafted in, like a shoot of wild olive to share the rich growth of the olive-stem', yet (he warns them) 'do not pride yourself at the expense of the branches. Remember, in your pride, the stem supports you, not you the stem.'[3]

It is in this context, of his anger at the vaunting pride of the Romans and his grief at the exclusion of his people the Jews from the promised salvation of the world, that Paul makes some of his most famous theological pronouncements, concerning such fundamental matters in Christian theology as 'grace'[4] and 'election',[5] 'justification by faith',[6] and the fathomless, inscrutable 'judgment' of God;[7] and it is from the last ('Nay but, O man, who art thou that repliest against God? Shall the thing formed say to him that formed it, Why didst thou make it thus?') that he is led back to the Jews and their destiny. Because God's ways are finally inscrutable

[1] Rom. xi. 11. [2] Rom. xi. 16. [3] Rom. xi. 17–18.
[4] Rom. xi. 6–8. [5] Rom. ix. 11–12.
[6] Rom. ix. 30–2. [7] Rom. ix. 19–24, xi. 33–4.

(Paul argues), because he will have mercy on whom he chooses, and compassion on whom he chooses,[1] who is to say that he has not predestined the Jews to an ultimate glorious salvation? For the present, it is true, Israel has fallen away from God, because she placed her trust in 'works', in the law of legal righteousness, and as a consequence has been stricken blind to the transcendent truth of the gospel of love. 'I bear them witness', cries Paul, 'that they have a zeal for God, but not according to knowledge.'[2] And the vital knowledge they lack is that salvation is by faith and by faith alone: faith in Christ the crucified, in him who has fulfilled the prophecies of Isaiah, and has perfected and rendered truly efficacious the Law of Moses, not by annihilating it but by incorporating and transcending it. 'For Christ is the end of the law unto righteousness to everyone that believeth...[And] if thou shalt confess with thy mouth Jesus as Lord, and shalt believe in thy heart that God raised him from the dead, thou shalt be saved.'[3]

Israel as a whole, then, has fallen away from its divine mission; and salvation has passed to the Gentiles because Israel has failed, for the time, to be true to itself. But for the time only. God has not cast off his people; they remain his Chosen People, for 'God never goes back upon his gifts and call.' Though the greater part of this Chosen People has betrayed its divine mission by rejecting Jesus, yet (says Paul) there is left 'a remnant selected by grace'; and it is this remnant, the true spiritual seed of Abraham, the children of the Promise, who are finally to lead the Jews to their redemption in Christ, and with them the whole world. Here Paul's mind fills with the vision of this glorious redemption that is to come; and the voice of the Jew who has great sorrow and unceasing pain at the heart for his deprived brethren and kinsmen according to the flesh mingles with, and presently wholly gives way to, the voice of hope

[1] Rom. ix. 15.
[2] Rom. x. 2.
[3] Rom. x. 4–10.

triumphant. Invoking again the image of the grafting of an olive tree:

> If you [the Gentiles] have been cut from an olive which is naturally wild, and grafted, contrary to nature, upon a garden olive, how much more will the natural branches be grafted into their proper olive?[1]

Therefore, finally:

> If their lapse has enriched the world, if their defection is the gain of the Gentiles, what will it mean when they all come in?... For if their exclusion means that the world is reconciled to God, what will their admission mean? Why, it will be life from the dead![2]

This is the prophecy of St Paul concerning the redemption of the Jews, or (if one prefers to see it another way) Paul's analysis of the Jewish genius and destiny; and on either view it shows Paul in a light as characteristic as it is impressive and touching.

There is one last gift belonging to Paul that some may be inclined to put above all the others. This is his gift as the first and perhaps greatest of all Christian pastors, by which he, like every Christian pastor from the greatest prelate of the Church to the humblest parish priest, daily seeks to do the work of the Holy Spirit; and it is a gift that shows in Paul with an incomparable power and beauty.

When one thinks of Paul the great pastor, one thinks of a man consumed with the tenderness of his solicitude for his brothers in Christ; being all things to all men in order that he may by all means save some; his exhortations always directed by his love, and his love perpetually reinforced and sustained by the presence of Christ within him. If we need to be reminded of Paul's voice in this character, there are two passages in the Epistle to the Philippians to fix it in our memories. The first is the whole of the great sermon

[1] Rom. xi. 24. [2] Rom. xi. 12–15.

in the second chapter of Philippians, which begins with the lines:

> If there is any comfort in Christ, if any consolation of love, if any fellowship of the Spirit, if any tender mercies and compassions,
>
> Fulfil ye my joy, that ye be of the same mind, having the same love, being of one accord, of one mind;[1]

and the second is the exhortation, still more famous, in the last chapter of Philippians:

> Finally, brethren, whatsoever things are true, whatsoever things are honourable, whatsoever things are just, whatsoever things are pure, whatsoever things are lovely, whatsoever things are of good report; if there be any virtue, and if there be any praise, think on these things.[2]

These passages express the loveliest, if not the greatest, of Paul's gifts. He is greater no doubt as theologian, as moralist, and as missionary; but most beloved as the Christian pastor who loved his neighbours many times better than himself, and rejoiced to give his life in their service for the sake of his Lord Jesus Christ.

[1] Phil. ii. 1–2.

[2] Phil. iv. 8.

CHAPTER VI

SYMPATHY FOR LOVE

HUME'S 'ENQUIRY INTO THE PRINCIPLES OF MORALS'

HUME'S *Enquiry into the Principles of Morals* has a prominent place in the tradition of moral thought which I have called secular or utilitarian; and it has this importance chiefly because it is in itself so thoroughly representative of this tradition, but also because it has had a powerful influence on the development of moral ideas in the modern period both in England and on the Continent. Before taking up the *Enquiry* itself, however, it is necessary to discuss briefly another of the features common to most, if not all, of the moralists in this tradition, their so-called empiricism or empirical method in respect to morals. Among the writers chosen to represent this tradition, the empirical approach is present in Aristotle, Hume and John Stuart Mill, and is most conscious and explicit in Hume. It is closely linked with their low or realistic view of man's nature, and is accordingly best approached by considering some further aspects of the moral realism that we have already encountered in Aristotle and Hobbes.

EMPIRICISM

The principal claim of this moral realism is that it grounds itself in the observable realities of men's moral behaviour. It avoids the ideal and confines itself to the actual; it derives the principles of morals from man's nature *as it is*, not as it *might be*. And, as a corollary to this, the moralist must concern himself with what Aristotle calls 'attainable goods', meaning by this that he will dismiss as illusory—for the purpose, at any rate, of a practical science such as ethics—any aspiration after such felicities as may appear to transcend them. The Platonic aspiration after the wisdom and virtue to be attained by the visionary experience of the Form of the Good (or, one may suppose, the Christian aspiration to be perfected in love by the imitation of Christ) accordingly ranks for Aristotle among the 'unattainable goods'.[1]

The link between this aspect of moral realism and empiricism is not difficult to see. The empiricist claims to derive the principles of morals from the observed facts of men's moral behaviour, from what men in fact do, and say, in respect to moral matters—what moral choices they make, what moral beliefs or opinions they appeal to, in support of their specific acts of moral choice. Both Aristotle and Hume constantly invoke, as one class of these observable 'facts' of men's actual behaviour, their distribution of praise and blame, approval and disapproval; what men choose to praise or blame, approve or disapprove, is taken to be among the basic 'facts' from which the principles of morals must, somehow, be derived.[2] The empiricist believes, in short, that it is possible to elicit from the observed facts of men's actual moral behaviour and belief a system of ethics of universal and permanent validity: the facts, he maintains, will yield to analysis not merely descriptive generalisations, about the way men do in fact behave, but also prescriptive generalisations, about the way men *ought to* behave.

What validity is to be allowed to this double claim of the Aristotelian moralist, that he possesses at once a superior view of the nature of morality, his moral realism, and a superior method of enquiry, his empirical method? The claim for the superiority of the moral realism turns out, on closer inspection, to be based upon confusion. For to speak of man's nature 'as it is' and of 'attainable goods' as the sole end of

[1] *Nic. Ethics*, I. vi. 13.

[2] Hume, *Enquiry*, sect. 138, p. 174. Compare Aristotle, *Nic. Ethics*, I. xii. 1–7; I. xiii. 18, 20; III. i. 1; III. ii. 12–13; III. v. 15; V. ii. 2.

moral endeavour turns out to be only a begging of the question, the question that is begged being precisely, What *is* man's nature? What *are* the goods 'attainable' by man? Or, to put it another way: What *is* the furthest reach of human possibility; and, Are the so-called transcendent goods really 'unattainable', or only *more difficult* of attainment than the others? To St Paul, we know, men's capacity to be redeemed by the power of love is as much a part of his nature as courage and temperance and liberality and magnanimity are for Aristotle; and to Plato, who valued courage, temperance and all the other traditional Greek virtues no less than Aristotle, the vision of the Form of the Good is nevertheless not only an attainable good but the supreme good by which alone the attainment of the other goods is rendered possible.

These considerations can only lead to the conclusion that what a moralist *means* by 'attainable goods' or by man's nature 'as it is' depends upon his fundamental view of human possibility. If that view is pitched low, the Platonic vision of the Form of the Good and the Pauline vision of men rendered perfect in love will necessarily rank among the unattainable goods; if that vision is pitched high, those transcendent goods will not only have a place but a central place among the attainable goods. The Aristotelian claim to a superior realism is seen accordingly to be a begging of the further, and more fundamental, question: whether this view of man's nature is in fact more realistic or only more one-sided; whether it is more true, or only more pessimistic; whether what it sometimes gains in coherence it does not always lose in comprehensiveness and completeness. And if it can be shown (as I tried to show in my discussions of Aristotle and Hobbes, and will try to show again in Hume) that it is only less comprehensive and less complete, and more one-sided and more pessimistic, than the other, this will establish a further sense in which it may legitimately be called a low or limited view of human possibility.

Turning now to the empiricism with which the Aristotelian

moralists seek to support and reinforce their claim to a superior moral realism, what emerges on analysis is that it is based on a false assumption, and is therefore as untenable as the moral realism. The empiricist believes that the observed facts of men's moral behaviour will yield not only descriptive but also prescriptive generalisations or 'principles'; and this is the belief that determines (and, for him, justifies) his method of enquiry. But the belief is wholly delusory. The vital transition, from what is to what ought to be, can never be effected by the method of merely cataloguing and classifying and analysing the observed behaviour of men.[1] For knowledge of what is will never yield a knowledge of what ought to be so long as 'what is' refers only to the actual and takes no account of the possible. It can only do so when the notion of 'what is' is referred to some view of human possibility, as distinct from mere human actuality. For men 'ought to be' what they are 'ideally' capable of being: this is the only proper meaning of the word 'ought' in this context; and this necessarily implies some ideal of man, some view of human possibility as distinct from actuality. The empiricist, accordingly, who prides himself on being free of any preconceptions about human possibility, who claims to be unimpeded in his enquiries into morals by any ideal of human possibility, any view of what men might be as distinct from what men are, is, on this analysis, fatally deluded.

This delusion springs from a misunderstanding of his own empirical method. His method demands that he *shall* extract from his observations of men some notion of human possibility, of what men might be, since in the absence of some such view he would be completely unable to pass from what men are to what men ought to be. And since he does in fact make pronouncements about what men ought to be (if he did not, he would not be a moralist at all but merely a sociologist, or perhaps an 'analytical' philosopher of the modern type), some view of human possibility is, and must be, implicit in his

[1] Hume, *Enquiry*, sect. 138, p. 174.

system of ethics. The ideal, in other words, is as inescapably present in the ethical system of every empiricist moral philosopher who *is* a moral philosopher and not a sociologist or an 'analyst' as it is in the systems of the so-called anti-empiricists, like Plato and St Paul. And since the empiricist denies that his system contains any such ideal of human possibility, but his system nevertheless does contain it, it must be concluded that the ideal has slipped in surreptitiously, either with his knowledge or without; and if with his knowledge, there is a lack of honesty in denying that it is there, and if without his knowledge, there is a lack of intelligence in not seeing that it is there. Hume's *Enquiry into the Principles of Morals*, we will see, yields some instructive instances of this surreptitious infiltration of ideals that have, on the empiricist's theory, no business to be there.[1]

[1] It may be objected that the empiricist could admit the propriety, and perhaps even the necessity, of framing an ideal ('paradigm case') of the good man by extrapolation from his observations of human behaviour, and that he only denies the propriety of what he would call an '*a priori*' ideal. Now it is certainly true that the empiricist method can yield an ideal of this kind. But the question is whether this is in any valid sense a *moral* ideal—whether it is genuinely prescriptive, or only (again) descriptive. Surely such an ideal is nothing but a descriptive generalisation—a sociologist's generalisation—derived from the observed moral behaviour of men in a particular community existing in a particular place at a particular time; as such, it can only affirm that this is the ideal that men in that particular community in that place and time actually—as a matter of observed fact—acknowledge as the ideal to which they ought to conform their conduct; and if this *is* all it can affirm, the empiricist has no logical ground for claiming that it is is *also* prescriptive—that this is how men *ought* to behave even in this particular community in this place at this time, let alone in all communities in all places and at all times. There is still no way by which he can make the transition from 'what is' to 'what ought to be', except by extrapolating his observations so far as to claim that what he has observed men to be in this community is what men essentially are everywhere and always—that his descriptive ideal (or paradigm case) is also a prescriptive ideal because it represents the furthest reach of human possibility. But this would be to proclaim exactly the kind of *a priori* ideal that he believes himself able to dispense with by virtue of his empirical method, and leaves him no better off than the so-called *a priori* moralists like Plato, St Paul and the rest. The only alternative for the empiricist (which has in fact been chosen by many modern writers on ethics) is to renounce prescription altogether and confine himself to the purely descriptive (this is the ideal of the good man actually prevalent in the Trobriand Islands, or Middletown, or post-World War II London, or fourth-century Athens, or Imperial Rome); and then, as I suggested, he ceases to be a moralist and becomes an anthropologist or sociologist or historian of morals. This,

The difference, then, between the moral systems of an Aristotle, a Hobbes and a Hume on the one hand, and a Plato and a St Paul on the other have nothing to do with the supposed empiricism or anti-empiricism of their method of enquiry. *Both* groups of moralists are empirical in the only proper sense of the word in this connexion, that both equally claim to ground their moral doctrines in what they believe to be the true observable facts of man's moral nature; and to the eye of St Paul, the transforming power of love is as observable, as empirically verifiable, a fact of man's nature as the pursuit of power is for Hobbes or the pursuit of pleasure or happiness for the utilitarian hedonist. And on the other side, both kinds of doctrine are non-empirical (or rationalist or *a priori*) in so far as both necessarily imply some ideal of human nature—some view of the scope and limits of human possibility, some conception of what men are ultimately capable of in the realm of the moral. The real difference between them turns, therefore, upon the nature of the ideal implicit in them. More specifically, for the purposes of this analysis, it turns upon whether the transcendent elements are to be recognised and admitted as a part of what man is, or are to be dismissed as illusory; whether the transforming power of love is to be placed within or without the furthest reach of human possibility; whether, in short, the limits of human possibility are to be pitched high or low. When they are pitched high, we get the doctrine of Plato's *Gorgias* and St Paul's Epistles, when they are pitched low, we get the doctrine of Aristotle's *Nicomachean Ethics*, Hobbes's *Leviathan*, Bentham's *Principles of Morals and Legislation* and Hume's *Enquiry into the Principles of Morals*.

however, was not the course chosen by Hume, though it is no doubt the only one consistent with the empirical method he advocates in the *Enquiry*. Hume does insist that by this method we may 'reach *the foundation of ethics* and find *those universal principles*, from which all censure or approbation is ultimately derived' (*Enquiry*, sect. 138, p. 174); and it is this claim that exposes him to the criticisms I have set out. See also pp. 175–7 below.

UTILITARIANISM

The more obvious utilitarian features of Hume's moral philosophy are not difficult to disengage. For Hume, as for all Utilitarian moralists, from Callicles in the *Gorgias* to John Stuart Mill, the measure of the good is either the pleasant or the useful or, where possible, both. The pleasant (Hume is able to show to his satisfaction) is in all important instances identical with the useful, either the socially useful or the personally useful. Thus one of the two grand social virtues, Justice, is shown to be based on 'utility' ('social' utility, that is);[1] and Benevolence, the other grand social virtue, owes the esteem in which it is held to its pleasantness or agreeableness.[2] All the other virtues are classified as either predominantly useful or predominantly pleasant; and the overriding virtue of 'social sympathy' is shown to reconcile these two seemingly divergent criteria of the good.[3] For by means of social sympathy the useful is happily also rendered agreeable to us; and after this nothing is left to be desired in this most useful and agreeable of all possible worlds.

Similarly (to pass from Hume's moral doctrine to the political implications of that moral doctrine), the institution of civil society itself is, for Hume, based upon utility or enlightened self-interest, that is, upon the needs of self-preservation. This, of course, immediately brings Hume's view of the institution of civil society dangerously close to Hobbes's; and Hume, who is very conscious of the danger, seeks to mitigate this effect by injecting into his political doctrine the social sympathy already mentioned. It is his recognition of this social sympathy as a constituent of man's nature that, according to Hume, marks the vital difference between his system and Hobbes's.

This, on the face of it, seems plausible enough; and Hume's social sympathy, if it were all it is supposed to be, would

[1] *Enquiry*, sect. 145ff., pp. 183ff.
[2] *Ibid.* sect. 139ff., pp. 176 ff.; sect. 207–8, pp. 257–8.
[3] *Ibid.* sect. 210, p. 260; sect. 220–3, pp. 270–4.

indeed set apart Hume's view of man's nature from Hobbes's by as safe a distance as might be desired. But it is not in fact what it appears to be: on closer inspection it turns out to be strictly circumscribed by the primary passion of self-interest. Its ultimate sanction is still 'utility'; and it remains, in the end, as remote as Aristotle's self-sufficiency and Hobbes's pride and fear from that organically binding power of love that St Paul and St Augustine place at the centre of their moral and political doctrines.

There is a passage in the *Enquiry* that shows with particular distinctness, in spite of Hume's efforts to conceal the unpalatable fact by rhetoric, the ultimately utilitarian character of this social sympathy:

> If any man from a cold insensibility, or narrow selfishness of temper, is unaffected with the images of human happiness or misery, he must be equally indifferent to the images of vice and virtue; as, on the other hand, it is always found, that a warm concern for the interests of our species is attended with a delicate feeling of all moral distinctions; a strong resentment of injury done to men; a lively approbation of their welfare.... How, indeed, can we suppose it possible in any one, who wears a human heart, that if there be subjected to his censure, one character or system of conduct, which is beneficial, and another which is pernicious to his species or community, he will not so much as give a cool preference to the former, or ascribe to it the smallest merit or regard? Let us suppose such a person ever so selfish; let private interest have ingrossed ever so much his attention; yet in instances, where that is not concerned, he must unavoidably feel *some* propensity to the good of mankind, and make it an object of choice, if everything else be equal. Would any man, who is walking along, tread as willingly on another's gouty toes, whom he has no quarrel with, as on the hard flint and pavement?... We surely take into consideration the happiness and misery of others, in weighing the several motives of action, and incline to the former, where no private regards draw us to seek our own promotion or advantage by the injury of our fellow-creatures. And if the principles of humanity are capable, in many instances, of influencing our actions, they must, at all times, have *some* authority over our sentiments, and give us a general approbation of what is useful to society, and blame of what is dangerous or pernicious.

The degrees of these sentiments may be the subject of controversy; but the reality of their existence, one should think, must be admitted in every theory or system.[1]

Leaving aside the fatuity of the example that Hume chooses to illustrate the operation of social sympathy, our willingness to refrain from treading on another's gouty toes when we have no quarrel with him (though this is perhaps not as trivial as it seems, since it betrays the basic shallowness and even frivolity of Hume's attitude to what is after all a central point in his doctrine); leaving aside also the rhetorical flourishes by which he seeks to obscure the insufficiency of his argument (whether consciously or unconsciously need not be decided), and fixing our attention only upon the argument itself, we find it indeed insufficient. For what do we learn but that 'the principle of humanity', that is, the principle of social sympathy, will always prevail *where no private regards draw us to seek our promotion or advantage by the injury of our fellow-creatures*. In other words, where any private regards *are* present, they are all too likely to 'draw us to seek our own promotion or advantage by the injury of our fellow-creatures'; and if this is the case, we are surely no better off with Hume's glorious social sympathy than we were without it in Hobbes's state of nature. Hume's 'social sympathy', accordingly, does nothing in the end to mitigate what he himself called the 'Selfish Theory', which postulates selfishness, or self-interest, as the basic element in man's nature; and we are left in the end, and in spite of Hume's pretensions to the contrary, with no real alternative to the Hobbesian view of man's nature.[2]

[1] *Enquiry*, sect. 183, pp. 225–6.

[2] Another important link with Hobbes is to be discovered in Hume's account of the relation of reason and the passions. In his earlier version of his moral doctrine, in the work entitled, *A Treatise of Human Nature*, Hume's position on this vital matter is uncompromisingly Hobbesian. 'Reason', he declares in the *Treatise*, 'is and ought only to be the slave of the passions' (*Treatise*, II. iii. 3); and this is to take Hobbes's position almost in Hobbes's own voice and accent. In the *Enquiry* (for reasons to be discovered in Hume's much-quoted account, in the autobiographical Preface to his *History*, of the cold reception accorded to the *Treatise* on its appearance) the Hobbesian emphasis is, or appears to be, modified. There we are told that 'reason and sentiment [the passions]

RELATIVISM

Besides the fundamental utilitarian doctrines already mentioned, that the pleasant or the useful or both are the measure of the good, and that self-interest, however enlightened, however mitigated by social sympathy, is the fundamental human passion, there are other recognisable features of the Aristotelian and Hobbesian morality present in Hume's *Enquiry*. Among the important links with Aristotle is Hume's insistent suggestion that the final seat of all moral judgments is an undefined *moral sense*.[1] Unlike Aristotle, however, Hume significantly presents this moral sense as a species of *aesthetic* sensibility; it judges, he says, of the amiable and the odious in moral matters as the aesthetic sense proper judges of beauty and deformity in aesthetic matters;[2] and in thus approximating the moral to the aesthetic Hume departs from Aristotle, and advances in the direction of an anti-rationalist, relativist, and, in the end, subjectivist ethic.[3] This advance, momentous for

concur in almost all moral determinations and conclusions' (*Enquiry*, sect. 137). But when we come to examine the details of the operation of reason in this compromise doctrine, we discover that it has not essentially changed in its relation to the passions. Reason still remains subordinate to the passions: it still remains, for Hume, as for Hobbes, purely 'instrumental', a kind of refined animal cunning, which can direct us to the means necessary for attaining a desired end but has no power to determine the ends themselves. The ends are still exclusively determined by the passions; and while this remains Hume's position, the more moderate phrasing of the *Enquiry* can do nothing to sever the important link with Hobbes that his view of the relation of reason and the passions maintains.

[1] *Enquiry*, sects. 134, 137. Cf. Aristotle, *Nic. Ethics*, II. ix. 7–8; IV. v. 13.

[2] *Ibid.* sects. 134, 135, 137.

[3] Aristotle's complete separation of the practical reason and the contemplative or speculative reason, discussed pp. 91–3 above, may, however, be seen as the thin end of the wedge in this connexion. Certainly the exercise of the practical reason, which is the sphere of ethics, still issues in knowledge, not sentiment, and to that extent Aristotle's view stands squarely opposed to Hume's. Yet the knowledge it yields is not apodeictical, like the 'science' issuing from the exercise of the speculative reason; and because the two kinds of reason are totally disconnected in Aristotle's system, the way is left open for the complete removal of morality from the sphere of the rational, and consequently from the sphere of knowledge or science. The mysterious moral sense that Aristotle persistently returns to as the ultimate seat of our moral judgments is the other important anti-rationalist element in the system of the *Nic. Ethics*.

the history of European moral thought, is principally accomplished by removing our moral judgments, as Hume calls them, from the sphere of knowledge, that which can be known to be objectively true or false, into the sphere of sentiment, that which can only be subjectively approved or disapproved—in other words, merely liked or disliked. And it is this relativist and subjectivist emphasis of his moral doctrine (along with much else in his purely philosophical system) that makes Hume the father of modern logical positivism, as may easily be discovered by reading, for instance, the discourse on morals in A. J. Ayer's celebrated book *Language, Truth and Logic*.

This subjectivist tendency of Hume's ethics has also, however, the special interest and importance of being intimately connected with his famous doctrine of causality in the *Enquiry concerning the Human Understanding*; and for this reason, besides those already mentioned, it deserves to be more closely examined.

Hume advances his 'aesthetic' view of moral judgments in the opening section of the *Enquiry* with a disarming tentativeness. He does not wish to affirm anything, he intimates, but only to enquire into the much disputed question,

> whether we attain the knowledge of them [our moral judgments] by a chain of argument and induction, or by an immediate feeling and finer internal sense; whether, like all sound judgement of truth and falsehood, they should be the same to every rational intelligent being; or whether, like the perception of beauty and deformity, they be founded entirely on the particular fabric and constitution of the human species.[1]

To suggest, as Hume does, that moral judgments are 'founded entirely upon the particular fabric and constitution of the human species' is to suggest that they are entirely psychological. They are not (Hume is saying, exactly like Hobbes[2]) grounded in the nature of things, in the fabric and

[1] *Enquiry*, sect. 134, p. 170.

[2] See Hobbes, *Leviathan*, ch. 6, p. 32: 'For these words of *good* and *evil*... are ever used with relation to the person that useth them: *there being nothing*

constitution of the universe itself, as the Christian moralists believed; they are not derived from an order of nature, which is objective in the sense of being external to and independent of the human mind. On the contrary, he implies (and this is the revolutionary import of his doctrine), our moral judgments are grounded only in the psychological make-up of man. And though the psychological make-up of man is, of course, relatively stable, it is not absolutely so; therefore the moral judgments derived from it can only be relatively, never absolutely, invariable; therefore there is no such thing as an absolute moral law, absolutely binding at all times and in all circumstances; therefore the moral law will vary according to time, place and circumstances, and will not be the same to 'every rational intelligent being'. And that was the point of Hume's carefully worded antithesis in the passage quoted, when he innocently enquired whether moral judgments, 'like all sound judgement of truth and falsehood, *should be the same to every rational intelligent being*; or whether, like the perception of beauty and deformity, *they be founded on the particular fabric and constitution of the human species*'.

This is the consequence of reducing moral judgments to purely psychological phenomena; and this aspect of Hume's moral philosophy has its parallel in his philosophical system—indeed, is supported and reinforced by his most important philosophical doctrines, in particular the doctrine of causality. Hume's central contention about the nature of causality seems, again, innocent enough.[1] Our knowledge of causal relations, he says, is not derived from any intrinsic (or necessary) connexion *in nature* between the so-called cause and the so-called effect, but is derived, wholly and exclusively, from the observed fact of their 'constant conjunction', that is, from the mere fact that the so-called cause and the so-called effect are

simply and absolutely so; *nor any common rule of good and evil, to be taken from the nature of the objects themselves*; but from the person of the man, where there is no commonwealth; or, in a commonwealth, from the person that representeth it.'

[1] *Enquiry*, sects. 44, 58, 59, 61.

repeatedly observed to occur together. This is the simple contention; and again its implications are revolutionary. For what Hume is saying is that from the mere experienced fact of the constant conjunction of the so-called cause and the so-called effect, it is not logically possible to infer any intrinsic or necessary connexion between them. There is in fact no such necessary connexion between the so-called cause and the so-called effect in the nature of things, in the fabric and constitution of the universe.

But (Hume goes on), we do in point of fact make just this sort of inference from the observed constant conjunction of phenomena to their supposed necessary connexion. We make it all the time, both in daily life and in the scientific laboratory; for what is the natural scientist claiming when he claims to have discovered this or that law of nature but that there is an intrinsic connexion in nature between phenomena that he has found conjoined in experience? So we constantly make this sort of inference; yet it is not logically valid; therefore it can only be psychologically valid—a matter of belief (to use Hume's own term), not a matter of knowledge at all. And this is the same as to say that the laws of natural science are never logically or 'scientifically' true, but only psychologically true: they tell us, in the end, nothing about the real constitution of the universe, but only about the constitution of our minds—'the fabric and constitution of the human species'.

This is Hume's doctrine of causality, to which (with all its larger metaphysical implications) modern analytical philosophy owes so much, and its most primitive branch, logical positivism, most of all. Nor has modern logical positivism failed to see the parallel between the essential relativism of Hume's psychological doctrine of causality and that of his psychological account of moral judgments, and has accordingly adopted the moral relativism along with the philosophical relativism.

THE LOW VIEW DOMESTICATED

Returning to the moral doctrine of the *Enquiry*, we discover one further, and especially significant, link between the *Enquiry* and the *Nicomachean Ethics*. The ideal of the Magnanimous Man has also a prominent place in Hume's vision of moral perfection. But he appears in a guise suited to the social ideals of Hume's society, and accordingly wears the aspect of the perfect eighteenth-century clubman. Since 'nothing invigorates and exalts the mind equally with pride and vanity, [while] love or tenderness is rather found to weaken and enfeeble it', Hume's ideal man is he who contrives to practise 'a well-regulated pride without breaking out into such indecent expressions of vanity as may offend the vanity of others'.[1] The view that pride exalts while love weakens is one that Aristotle would certainly have approved; Hobbes would have approved it even more; and along with Aristotle and Hobbes, also (alas) Lord Chesterfield.

There, in one word, is the difference between Hume's low view of man's nature on the one hand and Aristotle's and Hobbes's on the other: Lord Chesterfield, and all that Lord Chesterfield stands for. The view of man's nature that emerges from the honey-tongued rhetoric of the *Enquiry* is low indeed; but it is the eighteenth-century version of the classic low view as we find it in Aristotle and in particular, for the purpose of this comparison, in Hobbes. It is the classic low view domesticated, its Whig interpretation, so to speak. And this Whig corruption is accommodated to the special needs of the eighteenth-century mind by stripping it of all the unpleasant uncomfortable elements, all the savagery, ferocity, and ruthlessness of vision, that made Hobbes's low view such a formidable affair—so formidable (we remember) because it challenged us to find the best reasons, and only the best, for rejecting it. There is nothing formidable about Hume's low view in the *Enquiry*. It has been pared and trimmed and

[1] *Treatise*, II. 2. x, p. 391. Compare *Enquiry*, sect. 204, pp. 252–3.

smoothed and patted into as pleasant and comfortable and agreeable a moral philosophy as one clubman could devise for the instruction and delight of his fellows. *Cheerfulness* is the keynote: whatsoever things are cheerful, whatsoever things are comfortable, whatsoever things are of pleasant report, these, and these alone, are the things necessary to salvation in the moral world of the *Enquiry*. Everything painful or unpleasant in human nature and human life is dissolved out of existence in this fine fluid medium of cheerfulness, this universal sweetness and light, this vision of the life of man in the image of the higher clubmanship; and that this is not an unfair account of the prevailing moral atmosphere of the *Enquiry concerning the Principles of Morals* may be confirmed by glancing at the well-known passage in which Hume seeks to recommend to the reader the pleasantness and agreeableness of Virtue by praising what he calls 'her genuine and most engaging charms':

> But what philosophical truths can be more advantageous to society than those here delivered, which represent virtue in all her genuine and most engaging charms, and makes us approach her with ease, familiarity, and affection? The dismal dress falls off, with which many divines, and some philosophers have covered her; and nothing appears but gentleness, humanity, beneficence, affability; nay, even at proper intervals, play, frolic, and gaiety. She talks not of useless austerities and rigours, suffering and self-denial. She declares that her sole purpose is to make her votaries and all mankind, during every instant of their existence, if possible, cheerful and happy; nor does she ever willingly part with any pleasure but in hopes of ample compensation in some other period of their lives. The sole trouble which she demands is that of just calculation, and a steady preference of the greater happiness. And if any austere pretenders approach her, enemies of joy and pleasure, she either rejects them as hypocrites and deceivers; or, if she admit them in her train, they are ranked, however, among the least favoured of her votaries.[1]

One has the sense here of being asphyxiated in an ocean of cotton-wool. There is nothing solid to resist, nothing real to

[1] *Enquiry*, sect. 228, pp. 279–80.

protest against; indeed, it is this sheer unreality of the Humean happiness and cheerfulness that makes it so lethal. And there is also in this passage, as elsewhere in the *Enquiry*, more than a touch of that archness of manner that suggests that Hume was at least partly addressing himself to the woman reader of the day—that ubiquitious 'fair reader' to whom so much of eighteenth-century prose is addressed and who must be held to account for what is so intolerable in (for instance) Addison's style.

DIOGENES AND PASCAL

There is a passage in the *Dialogue* appended to the *Enquiry* which illustrates, even more vividly than the passage on Virtue, the eighteenth-century limitations of Hume's low view, and at the same time exposes the logical flaw that vitiates his method of enquiry. The chief interlocutor, who may be taken to represent Hume himself, is intent upon explaining what he means by 'artificial' or 'unnatural' lives—the sort of life presumably that no sane man would choose to live; and he cites, significantly, as the two extremes of all possible artificial lives, that of Diogenes the Greek philosopher on the one hand and that of Pascal on the other.

Diogenes is offered as the exemplar of what Hume calls 'philosophical enthusiasm', meaning by this the kind of excess into which philosophy when taken too seriously can lead a man; and Pascal is the supreme example of what he calls 'religious superstition'. The analysis of their aberrations is conducted in Hume's best gentleman-philosopher style, which combines the deadliest incisiveness with the easiest pleasantest urbanity, and is a remarkably interesting period-piece.[1] It evokes, however, a pointed query from the other member of the Dialogue: and Hume's answer exposes, in one sentence, the ultimate parochialism of the view of man's

[1] *A Dialogue*, pp. 342–3.

nature set out in the *Enquiry concerning the Principles of Morals.* 'Yet', enquires Hume's interlocutor,

[is it not true that] both of them [Diogenes and Pascal] have met with general admiration in their different ages, and have been proposed as models of imitation. *Where then is the universal standard of morals, which you talk of?* And what rule shall we establish for the many different, nay, contrary sentiments of mankind?

To which Hume replies:

An experiment which succeeds in the air, will not always succeed in a vacuum. *When men depart from the maxims of common reason, and affect these artificial lives, as you call them, no one can answer for what will please or displease them.* They are in a different element from the rest of mankind; and the natural principles of their mind play not with the same regularity, as if left to themselves, free from the illusions of religious superstition or philosophical enthusiasm.[1]

What we have here is a perfectly circular argument. If Hume is asked how he explains the fact that men have at certain periods universally admired or approved of people like Diogenes and Pascal, he answers that this was due to the prevalence respectively of philosophical enthusiasm and religious superstition, causing men to depart from the maxims of common reason, and so presumably to put themselves beyond human help. And if he is asked in what circumstances men may be said to have departed from the maxims of common reason and to be therefore beyond human help, he answers, When they admire men like Diogenes and Pascal, who are exemplars of men who have departed from the maxims of common reason.

This vicious circle cannot be broken, for there is in fact in Hume's system no universal standard of morals to appeal to, and none to be discovered by Hume's method of enquiry. Indeed, the standard actually employed by Hume, so far from being universal, is merely parochial. The 'maxims of common reason', it turns out, are nothing but the maxims observed in Hume's own society, or, rather, that comfortable cheerful

[1] *A Dialogue*, p. 343.

part of his society that he chose to take cognisance of. They are nothing but the sum of the precepts and practices that make up the moral code of the eighteenth-century gentleman; and Hume's 'common reason' is only the reason of Hume and his select circle of friends.

As such, this criterion too evidently excludes and dismisses a great deal more than the philosophical enthusiasm of a Diogenes and the religious superstition of a Pascal. At one end of the scale, it excludes and dismisses all the higher forms of heroism, from the simplest act of renunciation to the martyr's death; and at the other end, it treats as equally non-existent the cruelties, brutalities and bestialities that men at their basest are capable of. And the criterion of common reason also, of course, treats as completely non-existent the poor, the wretched, the deprived and dispossessed; all those who are weary and heavy-laden will find no logical place, let alone a resting-place, anywhere in the cheerful comfortable universe presided over by 'the maxims of common reason'.

These are a few instances drawn from the huge area of moral fact that Hume's picture of man's nature in the *Enquiry concerning the Principles of Morals* fails to take account of. In view of omissions of such a range and magnitude one might well ask at the end of the *Enquiry*, What does it profit a man to pursue the useful or the pleasant or both if it yields nothing more real or sustaining (or even interesting) than the code of conduct that once prevailed in the smoking-rooms of eighteenth-century London?

PART II
HUMANIST

CHAPTER VII
RATIONALIST HUMANISM

J. S. MILL'S 'THREE ESSAYS ON RELIGION'

WITH John Stuart Mill we reach the first representative moralist in the tradition that I have called the Humanist as distinct from the religious tradition on the one side and the secular or 'utilitarian', stemming from Aristotle, on the other. I have chosen to discuss Mill's *Three Essays on Religion* rather than such better known works as *Utilitarianism* or the *Essays on Bentham and Coleridge* because it exhibits more directly and clearly than the others the Humanist aspect of Mill's mind and temper. The *Three Essays* are typical of Mill in being an examination, as carefully considered and scrupulously fair as it is thoroughly argued, of the foundations of the Christian faith; and its theme is that of all serious enquiries into the nature of religion: What shall a man believe in order that he may be saved?

I mentioned briefly in an earlier chapter[1] some of the main features of this third tradition of moral thought, stressing in particular that it was a religious, not a merely naturalistic or scientific, Humanism, and that it was historically derivative from the two parent traditions already discussed. Now one of the important consequences of its being in this sense derivative is that it must seek to discover its own distinctive character by a constructive critique of its two parent traditions, and in particular the Christian. Since the Humanism we are concerned with claims to be a religious Humanism, yet diverges in radical ways from the central religious tradition of our civilisation, it must in the first instance define as precisely as possible these fundamental points of divergence. This for

[1] Ch. I, pp. 3–9 above.

Humanism is a historical necessity; and it is in recognition of this necessity that each of the four representative moralists I have chosen, John Stuart Mill, Matthew Arnold, F. H. Bradley and D. H. Lawrence, does in his own distinctive way undertake such a constructive critique of Christianity.[1] Mill undertakes it most systematically in *Three Essays on Religion*, Matthew Arnold in *Literature and Dogma*, F. H. Bradley in the Concluding Remarks of his *Ethical Studies*, and D. H. Lawrence—not indeed systematically, but cogently enough—in several of his later works, but most definitively in the story *The Man Who Died*. These texts may not be representative of the thought of these moralists as a whole, but they are uniquely representative of the Humanist aspect of their thought; and it is for this reason that they were chosen as representative Humanist texts.[2]

[1] It should perhaps be mentioned that in my use of the term 'Christianity' I have throughout assumed Christianity's intimate dependence upon and unbroken continuity with Judaism—as the discussion of the life and mission of Jesus (p. 260 below) should show plainly enough; it is only the clumsiness of the title 'Judaeo-Christianity' that has prevented me from using it in every instance. There is, however, a larger assumption implicit in the discussions of Christianity in this book, which is nowhere explicitly mentioned. This, stated baldly, is the assumption that the Christian view of the historical Jesus—subject to the 'Humanist' modifications set out in later chapters—is substantially *right*, the Judaic substantially *wrong*. Or, rather, in view of these Humanist modifications, the hypothesis is that the Christians, Jew and Gentile alike, were right in recognising Jesus' gospel of love as uniquely redemptive and therefore in acclaiming him as their Saviour, but wrong in *also* acclaiming him as the Messiah; and the Pharisees on their side were right to reject Jesus as the Messiah, but wrong in *also* rejecting his gospel of love, refusing to recognise it as the most glorious fruit of their religious tradition, and Jesus himself as the greatest of their prophets. This is a position, one has reason to fear, that will commend itself neither to the orthodox Christian nor to the orthodox Jew; for it convicts them both of being right for the wrong reasons; and it is after all upon the rightness of its reasons that each side takes its theological stand. This nevertheless is the hypothesis upon which the religious discussions in this book rest. Though it cannot here be demonstrated or even argued, it can, I hope, be illustrated; and this is what the later chapters are (among other things) intended to do.

[2] The critique of the other parent tradition, the secular or utilitarian, is not, I believe, so important except for the sake of logical symmetry. It so happens, however, that F. H. Bradley's *Ethical Studies* contains a full, cogent, and very brilliant critique of the philosophical foundations of Utilitarianism, and I will accordingly deal with this briefly in its place.

The suggestion that Humanism is derivative from Christianity in a perfectly neutral, historical sense of the word is likely to be challenged by certain modern critics. Indeed it has been challenged, with much seeming cogency, by T. S. Eliot in two famous essays on Humanism called *The Humanism of Irving Babbitt* and *Second Thoughts about Humanism.*[1] Mr Eliot, it will be remembered, uses less flattering language to characterise what he takes to be the Humanist enterprise. For instance, what I have called the 'derivative' character of Humanism, he calls simply 'parasitic':

> Humanism is, I think, merely the state of mind of a few persons in a few places at a few times. To exist at all, it is dependent upon some other attitude, *for it is essentially critical—I would even say parasitical.* It has been, and can still be, of great value; but it will never provide showers of partridges or abundance of manna for the chosen peoples;[2]

and he denies explicitly the claim that Humanism's critique of Christianity is, or can be, 'constructive':

> It is not the business of humanism to refute anything. Its business is to *persuade*, according to its unformulable axioms of culture and good sense. . . .It operates by taste, by sensibility trained by culture. *It is critical rather than constructive. . . . Humanism can have no positive theories about philosophy or theology.* All that it can ask, in the most tolerant spirit, is: Is this particular philosophy or religion civilized or is it not?[3]

The answer to Mr Eliot is that his strictures may be applicable to the kind of Humanism that prevailed at Harvard in the period immediately before and after the First World War under the inspiration of Irving Babbitt and Paul Elmer More, but are quite inapplicable to the Humanism that is being discussed here. The Humanism of Babbitt owed too much to Christian culture and too little to the Christian religion; it leaned heavily upon Arnold's *Culture and Anarchy*, but completely ignored Arnold's *Literature and Dogma*; it explicitly proclaimed itself to be 'unable to take the religious view', and

[1] Both are reprinted in *Selected Essays.*

[2] *Selected Essays*, p. 435.

[3] *Ibid.* pp. 450–1.

explicitly offered itself as 'an alternative to religion'—not as itself a religious doctrine, but as something other than and opposed to a religious doctrine. It was a Humanism, in short, that was as cultural, critical, ethical and edifying as might be desired, but had not the shadow of a claim to be regarded as a redemptive doctrine; and since the Humanism we are considering makes just this claim, the arguments directed against it must at least be different from (though not necessarily more friendly than) those Mr Eliot directs against Babbitt's Humanism.

The same is true of Mr Eliot's other point, that the Humanism he is speaking of is 'essentially critical', 'critical rather than constructive', that its business is not to refute anything, and that it can have 'no positive theories about philosophy or theology'. This, too, is inapplicable to the Humanism we are examining, and especially inapplicable to it in its relation to historic Christianity. In this relation, it is critical *and* constructive; it seeks to refute a great deal; and it stands in this relation to Christianity for the reason already mentioned, that it finds itself obliged to know intimately what it is rejecting in the present religious tradition, in order that it may discover and define its own character.

It proceeds, however, by this critique of historic Christianity also for another reason, even more important and supremely constructive. A properly religious Humanism must necessarily desire to establish its continuity—its internal, organic continuity, as well as its temporal continuity—with the great religious tradition from which it is derived. The image in which that continuity is perhaps best conceived is that proposed by St Paul in the seventh chapter of the Epistle to the Romans when he is conducting his analysis of the relation between the Old Covenant and the New.[1] Paul proclaims the Law of Christ to have superseded the Law of Moses, but superseded it (he repeatedly insists) by incorporation not by annihilation: not by destroying it, but by so transforming it as to render it truly efficacious. And as Paul conceives of the

[1] See ch. v, pp. 151–2 above.

relation between the Old Law and the New, so the Humanist conceives of the relation between the true Humanism and historic Christianity. The true Humanism, he believes, must and will supersede historic Christianity; but it will supersede it also by incorporation, not by annihilation. As St Paul may be supposed to have said to the Jews, Nothing of the Law of Moses will be lost, so the Humanist says to the Christian, Nothing of the Gospel of Christ will be lost, but everything in it will be transformed and transfigured and rendered finally and completely efficacious. And because finally and completely efficacious for yielding the fullest peace, power and joy to all those who believe in it, therefore finally and completely redemptive.

This is how religious Humanism conceives of its relation to historic Christianity, as a relation of continuity by incorporation and transfiguration; and this is the best reason for its undertaking that constructive critique of historic Christianity which is the most important part of the Humanist enterprise in its present emergent phase.

It is not to be supposed, however, that this most comprehensive view of the relation between Humanism and historic Christianity is equally prominent in the four writers I have chosen to discuss. It is least prominent in Mill, who as a Rationalist could hardly be expected to see the relation between his 'religion of humanity' (as he called it) and historic Christianity in quite the strong Pauline light in which I have presented it. On the other hand, it is very prominent in Matthew Arnold; and also, in spite of the rather wild, undisciplined and often grotesque way in which it is expressed, in D. H. Lawrence. But since it is an emergent Humanism, therefore an imperfect and incomplete Humanism, that we are talking about in each of these four moralists, their Humanist vision is bound to be correspondingly imperfect and incomplete; and what I have just said about the ultimate Humanist view of the relation of the true Humanism and historic Christianity is therefore to be seen as the ideal to which each of them only approximates.

John Stuart Mill's *Three Essays on Religion* may stand as the representative Rationalist critique of Christianity. It is representative, however, not in the sense that it represents the average Rationalist view, but rather the *best*—the highest reach of Rationalism in sympathetic insight into the religious tradition that it is rejecting, and in exact analysis of its own divergences from it.

To understand the direction and emphasis of Mill's critique of Christianity in the *Three Essays*, it is necessary first to know something about the immediate cultural context—'the climate of opinion', in Glanvill's well-used phrase—in which it was produced. The differences between Mill's *Three Essays* and Arnold's *Literature and Dogma* as Humanist texts are unquestionably more interesting and important than the similarities. But they have at least this in common, that neither could have been written at any time before (or after) the time they were actually written, namely, in the latter half of the nineteenth century. This is the period when the 'higher criticism' of the Bible and modern science, in the shape chiefly of Darwinism, had together gravely undermined the foundations of the Christian faith; when the 'spirit of the age' (as Arnold was fond of calling it) had put all in doubt, from the authenticity and reliability of the Scriptures to the historical existence of Jesus himself and the historical factuality of the miraculous events connected with Jesus' life and death. Consequently, the common effort of both Mill and Arnold is to discover what intelligible meaning and what validity, if any, might still be left to the truths of religion when these solvents of the traditional foundations of belief had done their worst. The question they are both trying to answer is, Is religious belief still possible and, if so, in what sense, on what grounds, on what authority? The vital difference is that Mill asks these questions about religion in general and only secondarily about Christianity, whereas Arnold from the start concentrates his attention, specifically and exclusively, upon the Christian religion.

This difference explains, among other things, the difference between Mill's general approach and Arnold's. What Arnold's approach is, and in what sense it is a Christian's approach, as Mill's is not, we shall see presently. The chief sign of Mill's Rationalism is that the *Three Essays on Religion* are almost exclusively an examination of the rational arguments advanced by Christians for the purely theistic foundations of the Christian religion. The emphasis is on the word 'arguments': what Mill is intent upon examining in the *Three Essays* is the supposed evidences supplied by 'reason' (as distinct from 'revelation') for the truth of the Christian religion.

There can be no doubt that Mill draws these arguments chiefly from the Deistic writers of the eighteenth century, those several generations of Christian writers who repudiated, almost as violently as any atheist or agnostic, the authority of revelation in religion, and sought to establish the credentials of the Christian faith on the grounds of 'natural reason' alone. These writers, it seems, are Mill's main source of Christian knowledge; and that is how it happens that the enquiry in the *Three Essays* is centred upon some of their most famous arguments for the existence and attributes of God; for instance (to cite Mill's own chapter-heads in the essay entitled *Theism*), the Argument for a First Cause, the Argument from the General Consent of Mankind, the Argument from Consciousness, and—the most famous of them all—the Argument from Marks of Design in Nature. All these were arguments urged repeatedly, and with innumerable variations in the details, by Christian apologists from the middle of the seventeenth century on, but particularly in the eighteenth century, which Mr Eliot has somewhere justly described as the most *unlovely* period in the history of Christianity in England.

It cannot be denied that this rationalistic approach to the problem does from the start impose a serious limitation on Mill's critique of Christianity; and I shall presently draw attention to some of its effects upon Mill's treatment of specific Christian doctrines. Nevertheless, it is on this very point that I would like to register a disagreement with Professor Willey's account of the *Three Essays on Religion* in his chapter on Mill in *Nineteenth Century Studies*. In a witty and unkind passage, Professor Willey describes Mill's quest for God as a fine cautionary instance of misdirected virtue:

> Mill...is here seen in the last contortions of his life-long research, seeking for God with his earnest, exemplary face turned persistently in the wrong direction....All through his life, like some ungifted Moses, he had tried to strike water out of dry rocks—altruism out of self-love, liberty out of bondage—and now here, in culminating frustration, he tries to draw faith out of reason. The rod taps and taps; the rock yields no drop; while—hidden from his short-sighted eyes—the spring bubbles up close at his back. If any proof were needed of St Paul's proposition that by wisdom (reasoning) no man finds God, here is an admirable one.[1]

The wit here is so charming and persuasive that it is hard not to wish that it were also just. But it is not; indeed, it is very unjust to Mill's earnest exemplary effort. It may be true—I think it *is* true—that Mill had got hold of the wrong end of the stick. Though it may be going too far to say that no man ever came to God by 'reasoning', it is certainly true that the Deistic arguments are never *by themselves* enough to bring men to God; for (as Professor Willey intimates) these arguments are helpless to put a man in possession of the gospel of love in the intimate, inalienable way which for the Christian is the meaning of knowing God. Again, though it may be argued that throughout the seventeenth century (which may count as the last of the ages of faith before the eighteenth-century eclipse set in) Christian theologians were fond of giving what they called 'rational explications' of the great mysteries of the Christian faith, in particular the Incarnation, the Resurrection and the Trinity, this was always done on the

[1] Basil Willey, *Nineteenth Century Studies* (1949), pp. 176–7.

assumption that the existence and attributes of God were not, and could not be, in question. The rational explications were offered as up-to-date analyses, so to speak, of particular points of a faith already securely possessed, never as a means of arriving at that faith. And perhaps Mill should have known all this, and not tried to strike the waters of faith out of the dry rocks of eighteenth-century Deism.

Nevertheless, what seems to me unfair in Professor Willey's account is that he nowhere allows that if Mill did have hold of the wrong end of the stick, the same end had been firmly grasped by thoughtful Christians for nearly two hundred years before. If Mill erred, therefore, he erred with some of the best Christian company; and if Mill was totally deluded about the proper way to arrive at the knowledge of God, it was by Christian example that he was thus deluded. Finally, it has to be remembered that, however absurd this may seem to religious tempers of a different cast, it is a fact of the psychology and history of the Christian religion that for many people these 'rational' arguments have always had, and still have, considerable persuasive force, and are for that reason still used by theologians and preachers who may be supposed to know what they are about. What I am urging, in short, is that Mill's error in basing his critique of Christianity on the arguments of the eighteenth-century Deists is not quite as discreditable to him as Professor Willey suggests, and that it is remarkably to his credit (as Professor Willey himself readily grants)[1] that he should have gone as far as he did in his understanding of Christianity in spite of a false start that might so easily have been completely disabling.

Our main task, accordingly, is to consider just how far Mill's understanding of Christianity did go in the *Three Essays on Religion*; and to this end I propose to take up Mill's account of certain vital matters which, in my judgment, show him at his best as a genuinely constructive critic of Christianity, and have also the merit of exhibiting the distinctive quality

[1] *Op. cit.* p. 175.

of his mind and temper. These representative topics are the doctrine of immortality, which Mill discusses in the Second Essay, entitled *The Utility of Religion*, and the doctrine of divine omnipotence, which is treated chiefly in the Third Essay, entitled *Theism*.

Mill's approach to the doctrine of immortality exemplifies admirably the Humanist approach to every important Christian doctrine. Proceeding on the Humanist premise that any religious doctrine that postulates the reality of a supra-natural, supra-human realm of existence as a necessary condition of its truth is to be rejected, not because it is false but because it is irrelevant to whatever redemptive truth the doctrine may contain, Mill is bound, of course, to reject the account of the immortality of the soul and the life after death set out by the historic Church. Then, having rejected the Christian account of the matter, he proceeds to enquire what truth it may nevertheless contain; and it is the form his enquiry takes that is characteristically Humanist. The question he asks is, What is there in the fundamental and perennial experience of men to answer to the Christian doctrine of immortality? Or, conversely: What is there in the doctrine of immortality that answers a fundamental and perennial need of the human spirit?

This is the question that the Humanist asks about every important doctrine of the historic Church, and about its sacraments and its ritual practices. The question is always: What fundamental need of the human spirit is supplied by it, and, how completely, how fully and finally, is it supplied? To discover what he believes to be the true answers to these questions is, for the Humanist, to discover the true meaning of these doctrines, sacraments and practices of the historic Church; and in discovering their true meaning, the Humanist believes himself to have discovered also the true source of their redemptive power. If (runs this central Humanist argument) these doctrines, sacraments and practices, when stripped of the supernatural sanctions that the historic Church insists upon, can still be shown to answer a fundamental and perennial need of the human spirit, they are shown, by this fact alone, to be redemptive; and when their redemptive power has been established on this ground it rests, for the Humanist, on a ground incomparably more secure and more lasting than that offered by the historic Church itself.

We shall find this Humanist method of enquiry into the foundations of historic Christianity, which is the heart of its constructive critique of Christianity, supremely exemplified in Matthew Arnold's *Literature and Dogma*, on a scale and at a level far exceeding the reach of John Stuart Mill. But Mill within his powers does attempt the same kind of Humanist restatement of at least some of the main Christian positions; and his account of the doctrine of immortality is one striking instance.

Proceeding, then, on Humanist premises and by the Humanist method of enquiry, Mill asks, What is the universal human experience, the fundamental and perennial need of the human spirit, in which the Christian doctrine of the immortality of the soul is grounded? The answer happens to be not at all abstruse. The experience is the terror of physical death as the complete and final extinction of personality; and the need is for the strength to meet this greatest of human terrors and for the comfort that may render it supportable. The Holy Spirit, in the Christian scheme, is the Paraclete, the Comforter, he who dwells perpetually in the hearts of men to comfort and sustain them in their efforts to meet the terrors of the human condition; and the doctrine of immortality, on the Humanist analysis, is distinctively a work of God, the Triune God, in that aspect which Christians call the Holy Spirit.

This is the need of the human spirit that the Christian doctrine of immortality answers; and Mill does not minimise its value and efficacy for this end. On the contrary, he extols both with an ardour that is as impressive as it is moving. But, though he grants with all his heart that the doctrine of immortality has, for so long and for so many, rendered supportable this greatest of human terrors, he questions whether it is as permanent and irremovable a human affliction as has always been supposed. In denying (with all the proper qualifications) that the terror of death is permanent and irremovable, Mill takes his stand upon the good and noble side of the Utilitarian philosophy in its most developed form, which consists in its splendid faith in the ultimate removability of the removable evils of life and its splendid energy in seeking to remove these evils. This one may call the 'social' aspect of the Humanist faith; and Mill expresses it here in his firm belief that the terror of death is likely to be diminished almost out of existence in proportion as the life that is about to be ended has been full, complete and worthwhile. As he himself puts it:

> It is not, naturally or generally, the happy who are the most anxious either for a prolongation of the present life, or for a life hereafter: it is those who never have been happy. They who have had their happiness can bear to part with existence: but it is hard to die without ever having lived.[1]

If it is hard to die only when one has not lived, and if the great majority of those who have not lived have failed to live because the unjust arrangements of an unjust society have fatally impaired their capacity for living, then to the Humanist, who believes that just social arrangements have everything to do with the salvation of human souls, it is imperative to diminish, out of existence if possible, the number of those who have never lived. To those accordingly who share Mill's faith that an overwhelmingly large proportion of the sum total of human suffering is not irremediable, and that a large proportion of this avoidable suffering could be diminished almost out of existence by better social arrangements, there is nothing gross in believing that a better world would greatly augment the number of full, complete and worthwhile lives actually lived. And as the number of such lives increased as a

[1] *Three Essays on Religion*, pp. 118–19.

result of better social arrangements, so proportionately the need for survival in another world would, for the majority of men, cease to have the urgency that has for so long been a familiar part of human experience.

This, however, is not the whole of Mill's Humanist account of the doctrine of immortality. It has also a more positive side; and this is his answer to the question, If the Christian doctrine of immortality is denied, can a man still enjoy the blessing of eternal life? And if this is possible, in what sense is it possible? Let us grant that the desire for some kind of survival after death is minimised almost out of existence as (in Mill's phrase) 'the condition of mankind improves'; yet if there is no survival of the soul after death, if there is no life beyond this, and therefore no possibility of being reunited with the dead in another life, how (the Humanist is asked) shall the continuity of the living with the dead be maintained—that vital continuity which is one of the conditions, if not the main condition, of the persistence of the human race as a real, self-identifiable entity? Mill's answer to this question is, I believe, the true Humanist answer. The continuity of the living with the dead, he says, is established and maintained in the loving remembrance of the dead by the living, and in the loving perpetuation of their works. As he himself expresses it, in his rather stiff phraseology: 'To feel their life prolonged in their younger contemporaries and in all who help to carry on the progressive movement of human affairs' should be a sufficient immortality for the truly selfless, whose 'moral cultivation' would enable them 'up to the hour of death to live ideally [in the mind, the imagination, the spirit, he means] in the life of those who are to follow them'.[1] It is by our loves and by our works that we keep perpetually alive, perpetually render immortal in the spirit, the multitudes of the dead; and this for the Humanist is the true immortality, which needs no doctrine of the soul's survival after death to support it.

[1] *Three Essays on Religion*, p. 119.

This is Mill's considered reinterpretation on Humanist premises of the Christian doctrine of immortality; and it would seem to be self-complete and self-coherent enough to satisfy all the requirements of such a reinterpretation. It is characteristic, however, of Mill's scrupulousness and disinterestedness in the pursuit of the truth that he should discern a hiatus in this account; and, having discerned it, that he should urge it, explicitly and forcibly, as a serious gap in the Humanist's conception of immortality. This gap, in Mill's words, is 'the hope of reunion with those dear to him who have ended their earthly life before him'. This hope of reunion, which is a main part of the consolation offered to men by the promise of eternal life in the Christian scheme, this real and precious consolation for the loss in the body of those we love, the Humanist is, of course, deprived of; and Mill acknowledges his irreparable loss in a feeling way:

> That loss indeed is neither to be denied nor extenuated. In many cases it is beyond the reach of comparison or estimate; and will always suffice to keep alive, in the more sensitive natures, the imaginative hope of a futurity which, if there is nothing to prove, there is as little in our knowledge and experience to contradict.[1]

The agnostic bias of Mill's Humanism is evident in this passage. He does not affirm that, scientifically speaking, the doctrine of the soul's survival after physical death is necessarily false, but only that it cannot, by its nature, be proved to be either true or false, and may therefore be believed or disbelieved. And though he himself, as we have seen, is one of the disbelievers, on the Humanist ground that a belief in the soul's survival after physical death is irrelevant to the fundamental spiritual truth that the Christian doctrine of immortality expresses, yet he acknowledges, with a full recognition of what this implies for a suffering humanity, that in at least one vital point the Christian account supplies a perennial need of the human spirit that the Humanist account is helpless to supply.

[1] *Three Essays on Religion*, p. 120.

Mill's treatment in the *Three Essays on Religion* of the other Christian topic I mentioned illustrates again, though with a somewhat different emphasis, his typically Humanist approach to historic Christianity. The problem of God's omnipotence is more narrowly theological than the doctrine of immortality; but since it has played an important part in the history of Christianity (especially Protestant Christianity) and in the formation of the Christian religious consciousness, it must be taken seriously by the Humanist and treated with the fullness with which Mill in fact treats it.

In undertaking a critical examination of the idea of God's omnipotence in Christian thought, Mill is taking issue with that Christian conception of God which puts an overwhelming emphasis upon His *majesty*, and consequently makes infinite power ('omnipotence') the principal divine attribute at the expense, unavoidably, of those other divine attributes, infinite goodness and mercy. The emotional basis of Mill's systematic attack upon the doctrine in the *Three Essays* is the horror and revulsion he feels at the conception; and in this, it should be said, he is not being the mere Rationalist who repudiates what he does not understand. For a similar horror and revulsion at the idea of an omnipotent God has been felt also by many Christians at various periods and for various reasons. Conspicuous among these in the history of English moral thought were the seventeenth-century Cambridge Platonists, and indeed most of the Christian thinkers in the 'Hooker tradition', the central post-Reformation Catholic tradition in English religious thought. The specific object of these Christians' revulsion happened to be the Calvinist doctrine of predestination—the 'Black Doctrine', as Henry More called it; and they found this doctrine reprehensible for the reason that it rested upon just such a conception of an omnipotent God as Mill is at pains to repudiate, namely, a God in whom goodness and mercy had been subordinated to power. Since the power, being God's, was infinite, the God presupposed by the doctrine of predestination was in imminent danger (as one seventeenth-century writer of the Latitudinarian school put it)[1] of being transformed into an Almighty Devil, a God who exercised his power arbitrarily, therefore irrationally, and therefore—conceivably, at least—tyrannically and cruelly; and such a God (argued these writers) being such an Almighty Devil, could not be a fit object of Christian worship.

The larger theological problem implicit in these discussions of predestination is for the Christian a real problem, and one of the many in Christian theology that does not admit of a single solution. It is important, however, at least to understand it, in order that the relevance and force of Mill's criticism may be properly understood. Stated as simply as possible, the problem turns upon the relative weight that is given to the principal divine attributes. These, by universal Christian consent, are infinite goodness and mercy, infinite wisdom and infinite power. Every Christian, as he is a Christian, is obliged to acknowledge infinite—that is, *limitless*—power as one of the principal divine attributes; for it is a necessary part of God's perfection—an intrinsic property, as Descartes would have said, of the idea of God—that he should be all-powerful, as well as all-knowing and all-merciful.

Now, if this is so (argue the Calvinists, in the great seventeenth-century controversies on this problem), those Christians who, like Hooker and the Cambridge Platonists, desire to subordinate God's infinite power to his goodness and mercy are seriously threatening the proper conception of God's perfection. For if they subordinate divine power to divine goodness and mercy, if they insist that the God whom Christians worship is essentially a 'reasonable' God, who acts in accordance with the reasonable laws that he himself created, what are they doing (ask the Calvinists) but limiting God's power? And in limiting God's power, they are, of

[1] Bishop Samuel Parker, in a work entitled *A Discourse of Ecclesiastical Politie* (1670).

course, making him something less than omnipotent, and thereby undermining, or at least seriously threatening, the Christian idea of God's perfection.

On the other side, the Calvinist heresy, as the Latitudinarian sees it, consists in the diminishing of God's perfection as a God of infinite charity and mercy. If God's power is absolute, and unqualified by his infinite love and goodness, then it can be conceived of as arbitrary and even cruel; and this to the Latitudinarian is a thoroughly blasphemous conception of the divine nature. The seventeenth-century Latitudinarians do not indeed accuse their Calvinist opponents of being blasphemers; on the contrary, one of the Cambridge Platonists, Henry More,[1] freely and generously acknowledges that the Calvinist's error on this vital point springs from the best of Christian motives: it is his awe and humility before the majesty of God that leads him to stress the divine omnipotence ('O man who art thou that repliest against God?'). But in stressing the divine omnipotence at the expense of the divine mercy, he over-stresses it; with the result that, as Bishop Parker said, he is in danger of approximating God to an Almighty Devil.

This, historically, is the problem implicit in the idea of God's omnipotence that Mill undertakes to examine in the *Three Essays*; and the point of mentioning it here is to show again that when Mill repudiates this idea of an Omnipotent God, he does so in some of the best Christian company. What particularly fills Mill with horror, however, is the further implication of the doctrine of God's omnipotence. This is the idea that a good and merciful God who was also omnipotent should have created a world as full of evil as the world we know. A God who created such a world (argues Mill) might be omnipotent, but could not be good and merciful; or, alternatively, if he was good and merciful, he could not be responsible for the evil in the world. And if God is not responsible for the evil in the world, it must be there *in spite*

[1] Henry More, *The Mystery of Godliness* (1660).

of God, against his desire and will; and then God cannot be omnipotent.[1]

Mill's argument about the problem of evil too evidently rests upon an incomplete understanding of the Christian position on this point; for he has failed to take account of the Christian answer to the problem supplied by the story of the Fall and the doctrine of Original Sin. It is not necessary, of course, that Mill should accept the story of the Fall as literally true, as the record of an actual historical event; many Christians nowadays, one understands, no longer accept it in that literal way yet still remain Christians. But it *is* necessary that Mill should understand the meaning of the story of the Fall viewed as a profoundly illuminating myth or parable about the fundamental condition of man, and should understand, in particular, the main theological implications of the story, among the most important of which is the solution it offers to the problem of evil. Mill, however, appears not to know, or not to understand, the significance of the story of the Fall in this connexion; and this makes a serious gap in his understanding of the position he is intent upon repudiating, and accounts for the insufficiency and, even, the naïveté of the argument by which he attempts to discredit it.

Nevertheless, it leads him to a conclusion that is bold and un-Christian, but not therefore irreligious: that omnipotence as a divine attribute were perhaps best discarded. For if (says Mill) it were no longer postulated that God was omnipotent, He could be seen as a Being of great but limited power; and the world as we know it could then be accounted for as the product, not of *omnipotent* goodness, but (in Professor Willey's phrase) of 'a struggle between contriving goodness and an intractable material'.

This in turn leads Mill to a further suggestion, which, again, is un-Christian but not therefore irreligious. He is urging at this point in the *Three Essays* the claims of what he has called the Religion of Humanity, which consists in 'cultivating a

[1] *Three Essays on Religion*, pp. 37–41; 112–13.

religious devotion to the welfare of our fellow-creatures as an obligatory limit to every selfish aim, and an end for the promotion of which no sacrifice can be too great'. In pursuing this end, Mill goes on to suggest, we may see ourselves as 'co-operating with the unseen Being to whom we owe all that is enjoyable in life'; for (he explains)

> one elevated feeling that this form of religious idea admits of, which is not open to those who believe in the omnipotence of the good principle in the universe, [is] the feeling of helping God—of requiting the good he has given by a voluntary co-operation which he, not being omnipotent, really needs, and by which a somewhat nearer approach may be made to the fulfilment of his purposes.[1]

This clearly is not a view that the Christian could accept. No Christian, as he is a Christian, could accept the idea that God 'really needs' the co-operation of men in the fulfilment of his purposes. For it is an essential part of the Christian conception of God that he is absolutely self-complete and self-sufficient, that the divine nature knows no penury but only perfect plenitude, and that God cannot therefore need anything that men can give, while men, on the other hand, need everything that God can give. Nevertheless, though Mill's idea of a God who needs the co-operation of men is not a Christian idea, it is not entirely alien to at least one other leading Christian idea—the idea that God's prevenient grace is powerless to save a man unless he responds to that grace. For is not a man who responds to the divine grace co-operating with God in his effort to save him; and is he not to that extent helping God to accomplish his divine purpose towards men?

Mill's idea, though not compatible with the full theological definition of God, is yet, it seems, compatible with the gospel of love preached by Jesus Christ, which does put all its emphasis upon a Heavenly Father who is, before everything, a Father of infinite mercies and compassions. And since the gospel of love preached by Jesus Christ is also the foundation

[1] *Three Essays on Religion*, p. 256.

of the true Humanism, Mill's idea of men 'co-operating' (as he tenderly puts it) 'with the unseen being to whom we owe all that is enjoyable in life' turns out to be thoroughly compatible at least with the Humanist position.

This brief account of Mill's treatment of two cardinal problems in Christian thought has been intended to show in what sense the *Three Essays on Religion* may be regarded as a serious contribution to that constructive critique of historic Christianity which I have urged as the main part of the Humanist enterprise in its emergent phases. But it shows also how the *Three Essays*, no less than *Utilitarianism* and *On Bentham and Coleridge*, exhibit the general quality of Mill's mind and temper, which Dr Leavis has admirably defined as 'an intellectual distinction that is at the same time a distinction of character';[1] and it shows, finally, the limitations of Mill's Humanism. This, I have already suggested, does not go as far or as deep as Arnold's or (even) Bradley's, for several reasons, of which there is room here to mention only one. It is that Mill remained to the end, and in spite of the spiritual revolution that he describes in his *Autobiography*, too closely tied to scientific principles and methods (particularly to the so-called inductive or empirical method). These serve admirably the purposes of the natural sciences, but can, as we now know, be exceedingly restrictive for other purposes and with other kinds of subject-matter; and they were for Mill restrictive in just this way in his larger enterprises, such as that of the *Three Essays on Religion*. He remained to the end too much the scientist, too little the humanist (in the common sense of the term) to be quite flexible or quite imaginative enough in the employment of his spiritual resources. That the spiritual resources were there is sufficiently attested by all that is non-Benthamite and even anti-Benthamite in Mill's moral and political writings. But his scientific habits of mind impeded their full development and prevented him from using them to

[1] F. R. Leavis, Introduction to *Mill on Bentham and Coleridge*, p. 9.

their full capacity; and this excess of the scientific in the disposition and habit of his mind co-operated with a deficiency of what one may call *religious culture* to produce a variety of Humanism that, though remarkable and impressive in itself, is yet a trifle thin by the side of the more literary Humanism to be discussed in the next chapters.

CHAPTER VIII
CHRISTIAN HUMANISM

MATTHEW ARNOLD'S 'LITERATURE AND DOGMA'

THE deficiency of religious culture in John Stuart Mill is most noticeable when the *Three Essays on Religion* are placed beside *Literature and Dogma.* Compared now with the attitude and approach to Christianity, not of the eighteenth-century Deists or of Jeremy Bentham or Herbert Spencer, but of Matthew Arnold, Mill's does give the impression of being somewhat external, lacking what Coleridge would have called 'inwardness', and for that reason rather bleak and even arid. Mill, one now remembers, though he had studied 'the Bible' and it had made a profound impression upon him, and though he had certainly studied it as something more than a document in the history of comparative religion or an anthropological source-book or a text-book in ethics, had none the less never really been exposed to the full impact of Christ's gospel as the foundation of a living faith. The education he had received from his father James Mill and later completed under the tutelage of Jeremy Bentham was not designed to encourage the most inward appropriation of Christ's gospel; and in spite of his strenuous efforts later in life to repair this loss in his spiritual education, he never completely succeeded. It is this, no doubt, along with the scientific bias of his mind and temper already mentioned, that must be taken to account for what is unsatisfactory in Mill's understanding and treatment of the Christian tradition.

The case of Matthew Arnold was in this respect as different as possible from John Stuart Mill's. If Mill, as a consequence of the defects in his religious education, takes hold of, and persistently keeps hold of, the wrong end of the stick, Arnold unmistakably has hold of the right end. He starts his enquiry into the foundations of the Christian faith with an intimate, first-hand knowledge of the redeeming power of Christ's gospel of love, and with a passionate conviction that it is a unique means of salvation. It is because the Bible uniquely among the great religious writings of our culture possesses the power to draw men into the ways of righteousness that (Arnold argues) it is rightly called the Book of God, the true God. It is because the Christian religion possesses a unique power to regulate conduct (that which, in Arnold's much-repeated phrase, makes up 'three-fourths of life'), and to bring peace, power and joy to those that follow it, that it is the true religion. And its truth (says Arnold repeatedly) is 'experimentally verifiable', in our day-to-day experience of the strength and the sweetness that we in fact receive from the Bible in our efforts to follow the ways of righteousness. The power of God and the power of the Bible 'can be verified as the power of fire to burn or of bread to nourish'; and if any man should deny or dispute this, Arnold asks him, simply, boldly and unanswerably, to *try it and see*:

> Try it! You *can* try it. Every case of *conduct*, of that which is more than three-fourths of your own life and the life of all mankind, will prove it to you. Disbelieve it, and you will find out your mistake, as sure as, if you disbelieve that fire burns and put your hand into the fire, you will find out your mistake. Believe it, and you will find the benefit of it....[1]

And again, with the personal accent more marked:

> Take a course of the Bible first and then a course of Benjamin Franklin, Horace Greely, Jeremy Bentham, and Mr Herbert Spencer; see which has most effect, which satisfies you most, which gives you most power. Why, the Bible has such a power for teaching righteousness, that even to those who come to it with all sorts of

[1] *Literature and Dogma*, ch. x, sect. 3, pp. 325–6.

false notions about the God of the Bible, it yet teaches righteousness, and fills them with the love of it; how much more those who come to it with a *true* notion of God and the Bible![1]

That last sentence takes us straight to the heart of Arnold's principal thesis in *Literature and Dogma.* Most Christians, and certainly all Protestants, would agree whole-heartedly to all that Arnold claims for the saving power of the Bible. What they cannot agree to is his further claim that this saving power of the Bible is independent both of the substructure of miracle and the superstructure of theology upon which, together, the historic Church takes its stand. That Christianity is the true religion and the Bible the unique instrument of salvation Arnold insists upon as passionately as the Christian; what he challenges is the supposed historic foundation of its truth and its power. Are the truth and the power of the Christian religion (he asks) in fact grounded in those miraculous events recorded in the New Testament story upon which the Church puts all its emphasis? Are they grounded in those events in the sense that, if their historical authenticity is questioned, the gospel of Christ falls to the ground, is robbed of its power to sustain men in the ways of righteousness? And if this is not (as Arnold believes) the real foundation of the saving power of the gospel, what is?

Analogous questions arise in connexion with the superstructure of theology. If the dogma of the historic Church is shown to be irrelevant to the saving power of Christ's gospel, does this undermine at its foundations that saving power? And if (as Arnold believes) this is not the case, there is still the further question, If the miracles and the theology are both dismissed as irrelevant, what intelligible meaning is to be given to such central concepts of Christian theology as 'revelation' (the Bible as the 'revealed' Word of God), the 'divinity' of Christ, the 'miracles' of the Incarnation and the Resurrection, the 'mystery' of the Trinity, and all the sacraments of the Church?

[1] *Literature and Dogma*, ch. x, sect. 3, pp. 326–7.

These questions, it should be emphasised, are for Arnold not academic. In an earlier period of the history of Christianity, they would no doubt have been so; but in the latter half of the nineteenth century they are real and urgent questions, which *must* be answered if the gospel of Christ is to survive at all. For (this is Arnold's persistent cry) 'the masses' are no longer reading the Bible; they are falling away from Christ's gospel, being deprived of the unique instrument of salvation because they can no longer accept it on the grounds on which it is still being offered to them. And they are right (Arnold maintains) not to accept it on those grounds because they are in fact no longer valid: they have been gravely undermined by modern scientific and historical researches into the 'evidences of Christianity', by what Arnold calls 'the critical spirit'; and no man can any longer be expected to accept the Gospel on those grounds. Yet the Gospel is a unique means of salvation; men *must* believe in it, *must* possess it, or else suffer the loss of the very possibility of moral life.

Literature and Dogma is Arnold's attempt to meet this desperately urgent situation. It is his sense of urgency that accounts for those features of the style of *Literature and Dogma*—the insistence, the fever, the anger and scorn, the scorching irony at the expense of the Bishops of Gloucester and Winchester—that have always tended to alienate a certain kind of reader, in particular, of course, the Christian reader. Doubtless Arnold would have found it easier to speak with the kind of moderation that such people tend to value (perhaps too much for its own sake) if he had felt less strongly. But for those who share Arnold's view of the situation, his vehemence and warmth and freedom of ironic play will seem not only justifiable but wholly appropriate to his undertaking, and will form an intrinsic part of its power to stir and challenge all minds open to its originality, cogency, and profound contemporary significance.

In *Literature and Dogma*, then, Arnold attempts to meet the situation created by the state of the Christian religion in his time. His task, as he sees it, is to discover and articulate those grounds of the Christian faith upon which it may continue to be believed in as true and redemptive even when 'the critical spirit' has done its worst; and these, once discovered and articulated, are to stand as the true grounds upon which it always has rested and must rest if it is to vindicate its claim to be the true religion. The execution of this task may, for convenience, be considered in two parts. The first is the theoretical part, the famous doctrine of 'literature-and-dogma', which turns principally upon Arnold's view that the Bible is literature, not science, and must be studied as literature if it is to yield the saving truths that it contains. The other part is the application of the theory, which takes the form of a re-examination and reinterpretation of some of the most fundamental points of the Christian faith, such as the meaning of God, the divinity of Christ, the miracles of the Incarnation and the Resurrection, indeed the whole miraculous foundation of historic Christianity, and the meaning of 'revealed' and 'revelation' as applied particularly to the Scriptures. It is pre-eminently by this critique of the foundations of Christianity, to which more than three-quarters of the book is devoted, that *Literature and Dogma* earns its distinguished place in what I have called the Humanist tradition of English moral thought.

Arnold's theory of the relation of 'literature' (the Bible) and 'dogma' (theology) is not systematically set out, but is developed as a natural part of his main enterprise in his account of what he believes to be the true foundations of the Christian faith. This problem of the relation of literature and dogma may easily be recognised as a special case of the larger problem that has received much attention in our own day, that of the relation of poetry and science, or (to express it as a problem of linguistic usage) the relation of what I. A. Richards called, not very satisfactorily, 'emotive' and 'referential' language.

The 'language' problem as such was of no interest to Arnold; there is no suggestion anywhere in *Literature and Dogma* that he was concerned about 'the meaning of meaning' as a purely theoretical problem. What does interest him is the further problem implied by any distinction, however informal, between the language of poetry and the language of science. This is the problem of *truth*—the kind of truth belonging to poetry on the one hand, to science on the other. Arnold's thesis is that religious truth, the kind of truth he is especially concerned with, is essentially a form of poetic, not of scientific, truth. The truths of religion are not established by reference to any merely external, empirically verifiable facts or events (like those miraculous facts and events upon which the historic Church grounds itself). Nor are they established by reference to the merely logical validity of the system of theological implications that can be drawn out of the fundamental saving truths contained in the Bible. The truth of religion, like that of poetry, is established by reference to its emotive power, which is its power to command the passions (emotions) of men and therefore their conduct. It is in this sense that its truth is experimental, directly and intimately verifiable in a way that neither the truth of the supposed historic events nor that of the theological superstructure is verifiable. And that is why that great repository of religious truths, the Bible, must (Arnold argues) be read as poetry, not as science; for only by reading it as poetry can we expose ourselves to the power of the Bible utterances to command our passions and therefore our conduct to the end of perfect righteousness.

In order to read the Bible in this way, as poetry in the broadest sense, we have to bring to it the same literary, or literary-critical, skills that we bring to our reading of imaginative literature. Arnold calls these skills 'tact', 'delicacy of perception' and 'delicacy of judgment', and insists that it is only by the exercise of this tact and delicacy that we are able to read the Bible with a discriminating intelligence. For it is only by reading it under the guidance of a developed literary sensibility that we are able to discern the relative weight to be given to one utterance against another; and this, Arnold believes, is the only safeguard against that disastrous kind of literalism in the reading of the Scriptures which Hooker was already inveighing against some three hundred years before Arnold's time.

Mention of Hooker suggests a further point that perhaps needs to be emphasised to prevent misunderstanding of Arnold's literary approach to the Bible. This has nothing in common with the vulgar modern notion of 'the Bible designed to be read as literature': the Bible read, that is, exclusively for its fine images and plangent rhythms, and the emotional luxury of a small safe quantity of uplift that in no way commits one to the Bible's embarrassing doctrinal content. Arnold is not thinking of fine images and plangent rhythms when he speaks of the Bible as poetry. He is thinking precisely of the doctrinal content and how we may best possess ourselves of its saving truths; and his own Biblical exegeses in *Literature and Dogma* are accordingly not to be regarded as exercises in technical literary criticism, but rather as essays in Scriptural interpretation, conducted in the style of Hooker and the great Protestant divines of the seventeenth century rather than that of I. A. Richards or William Empson.

Turning now to the 'dogma' in the literature-and-dogma antithesis—the science, as he calls it, of Christian thought—Arnold takes the view that it is all a logical superstructure, incorrigibly abstract, and so remote from the saving truths of the Bible that any connexion it may have with these is totally inaccessible to the popular mind. Therefore (argues Arnold) it is superfluous for the ends of salvation, and has merely the vicious effect of obscuring the saving truths. Yet the Church (and this is Arnold's quarrel with the Bishops) continues to put all its emphasis upon the dogma, upon this quasi-scientific, quasi-logical superstructure; and because men are finding themselves less and less able to accept these dogmatic teachings, 'the masses' are falling away from the

Church and thereby being deprived of the saving truths of the Gospel. On this crucial issue, Arnold's grief, bitterness and exasperation call forth some of his most characteristic passages of irony directed chiefly against the symbolic Bishops of Gloucester and Winchester.

One can see the difficulties (to put it as moderately as possible) of such a view as Arnold's for the orthodox Christian. One recalls that T. E. Hulme, that much-publicised convert to Catholicism of the last generation, made a point of announcing that, so far from being drawn into the historic Church by the appeal of what he called its 'sentiment', he was willing 'to swallow the sentiment for the sake of the dogma'. The dogma, it seems, counts for something; and one can go back from T. E. Hulme through nearly twenty centuries of the Church's history as far back as St Paul, to learn, again and again, that the dogma has counted for a great deal, for many, indeed, has counted overwhelmingly. But apart from the historic fact of its having counted in this way, a Christian could also justly tax Arnold with his failure to grasp the nature of the connexion that does exist between the fundamental truths of the Gospel and the dogmatic truths derived from these. It is this vital connexion that Christian writers draw attention to when they speak of the dogmas of the faith as a 'progressive revelation' of Christ's gospel, meaning by this that the dogmatic pronouncements of the Church are a progressive discovery of the full implications of the Gospel truths, and as such an intrinsic part of their meaning. As a matter of historical fact, these dogmatic pronouncements have often been made under the stimulus (or provocation) of particular historic heresies, which have obliged the Church at various times to make fully explicit certain implications of the fundamental Gospel truths that prior to the challenge offered by the particular heresy had remained merely implicit; and having made them thus explicit, the Church then laid them down 'dogmatically', as logically implied in the fundamental Gospel truths and therefore points of faith. In view of this claim of the historic Church concerning the real connexion between the basic truths of the Gospel and its own dogmatic pronouncements, one does not have to be a Christian or a theologian to feel that Arnold, if he himself was not persuaded of the validity of the connexion, should yet have taken the claim into account, and at least argued against it instead of simply ignoring it, as he does.

Nevertheless, when all the necessary criticisms and corrections have been made, there does remain this justification for Arnold's attack upon the dogmatic side of the Christian faith. It is no doubt true that a certain kind of mind, generally the more highly developed, can be led by the dogmatic mysteries of the Christian faith—the doctrine of the Trinity, for instance, or (Arnold's favourite example) of God as a Personal First Cause—into a full and intimate possession of the concrete, 'experimental', saving truths of the Gospel. Arnold's point, however, is that the majority of men are not, and cannot be, led in this way. To 'the masses', he insists, the dogmas have always been unintelligible; but while in the ages of faith, and particularly before the Reformation, they were unintelligible but accepted for truth as the chief part of men's obedience to the Church, they are now, in the later nineteenth century, both unintelligible and rejected as false, or at best as irrelevant to the love and practice of righteousness. Yet the Church insists that the dogmas are points of faith, that sincere belief in them is necessary to salvation, that Christianity stands or falls by them. The Church, on its side, by making acceptance of the dogma a necessary condition of salvation in Christ's Church, puts it *before* the practice of righteousness according to the Gospel commandments; Arnold, on his side, insists that the knowledge and the practice of righteousness 'in the spirit' are the whole of men's reasonable service to God, the beginning and end of Christian wisdom, and that to this the dogma of the Church contributes nothing. And this is the irreconcilable difference between Arnold and the Bishops of Winchester and Gloucester on the matter of dogma.

The more radical part of Arnold's undertaking in *Literature and Dogma*, his reinterpretation of some of the most important Christian doctrines on what are in effect Humanist premises, begins with a preliminary critique of the miraculous element in historic Christianity. On this violently controverted subject, Arnold's position is far in advance of Hume's in his famous essay *Of Miracles*. Arnold's claim is not that modern science has proved the miracles to be false, or even highly questionable as historical or scientific facts—though he does speak of various difficulties concerning the New Testament record that the 'higher criticism' of the Bible has brought to light. His main claim is that the miraculous foundation of historic Christianity has been shown to be irrelevant to the internal, experimental truth of Christ's gospel. The miracles would be irrelevant (he argues) even if they were historically and scientifically true; for they have not, by their nature, the power either to confirm or to disconfirm the saving truths of the Gospel. 'To walk on the sea', Arnold remarks, 'cannot really prove a man to proceed from the Eternal that loveth righteousness; although undoubtedly...a man who walks on the sea will be able to make the mass of mankind believe about him nearly anything he chooses to say. But there is, after all, no necessary connexion between walking on the sea and proceeding from the Eternal that loveth righteousness.'[1]

The emphasis falls upon 'no necessary connexion'. Even if it were scientifically and historically true (Arnold is saying) that Jesus walked upon the waters, this by itself would be powerless to prove that he was the Son of God and that his Gospel therefore proceeded from God, the Eternal that loveth righteousness. There is 'no necessary connexion' between the miracles of Jesus and the redemptive power of his Gospel.

The miracles, then, being merely external, are no evidence of the divinity of Jesus or his Gospel. There is only one kind of evidence that can prove that Jesus' Gospel proceeds from

[1] *Literature and Dogma*, ch. VI, sect. 2, p. 158.

God, and that is internal. 'Its grandeur and truth', says Arnold, 'is brought out experimentally, and the thing is to make people see this';[1] and the task he sets himself in the rest of *Literature and Dogma* is 'to make people see' the profoundly intelligible and valid meaning that the fundamental points of the Christian faith may still possess when they are made to rest entirely upon the evidences of our internal experience, without reference to the external evidences, either the miraculous or the theological, of historic Christianity.

I begin with that most controversial point in Arnold's Humanist account of Christianity, his definition of God. God is not, says Arnold, the Personal First Cause of the universe, as the Bishops of Gloucester and Winchester say; nor is he the Absolute Self-Existent, as the more philosophical theologians say; nor is he even the Supreme Father: he is the Eternal-not-ourselves-which-makes-for-righteousness. In what sense 'eternal'? In this sense, and this only, that God is known to us in our most immediate, most intimate experience as the source of all the values that are most permanent and most indestructible, by which alone we can enjoy peace, power and joy most abundantly and most securely. This, and nothing else, says Arnold, is what we mean when we speak of God as 'the Eternal'. And he is the Eternal 'that makes for righteousness' because these most permanent and indestructible values are essentially *moral* values. They direct our conduct, which is three-fourths of life, and, being the ultimately valid and saving moral values, they cannot but make for righteousness. Finally, God is the Eternal 'not-ourselves': the word 'not-ourselves' is intended to draw attention to our experience of the *obligatory force* of those most permanent and indestructible values that make for righteousness. Our most intimate experience of them is that they are not created by ourselves; that they are not merely subjective, not merely private and personal, nor arbitrary, nor relative to time, place and circumstance. They are experienced, says Arnold, as given, not

[1] *Literature and Dogma,* ch. XII, sect. 1, p. 366.

created; as absolute, not relative; as objective, not subjective. They are so experienced because they prove themselves in experience to be the *only* values by which we can enjoy peace, power and joy; and it is for this decisive reason that they oblige our assent and our obedience.

The argument, then, for God as the Eternal-not-ourselves-which-makes-for-righteousness is as follows: it is in experience that we discover that these values are moral, that is, directly relevant to our conduct—and that is what is meant by saying that they 'make for righteousness'; it is in experience that we discover that they are permanent, lasting and indestructible—and that is what is meant by saying that they are 'eternal', or proceed from the Eternal; and it is in experience that we discover their absolute obligatory force—and that is what is meant by saying that they proceed from the Eternal 'not-ourselves'. The meaning of 'God', accordingly, is this immediate inward experience of the permanence and indestructibility of the values that bear most directly upon our conduct and oblige our absolute assent and obedience. That (Arnold claims) is what we mean by God as the Eternal-not-ourselves-that-makes-for-righteousness, that is all we mean, and that is all we need to mean in order to inherit the Kingdom of God, which, like the kingdom of Satan, is wholly within.

Whether this definition of God is a valid reinterpretation of what the Christian means, or can mean, by God is to be considered later.[1] Another instance of the same kind of reinterpretation of Christian fundamentals is Arnold's account of the meaning of the word 'revelation'. Arnold is concerned, at this point in *Literature and Dogma*, to answer an important charge that had apparently been directed against his Humanist reinterpretations of Christianity, that what he was proposing was merely a 'natural' religion, which dispensed altogether with revelation. Arnold's answer takes the form of an outright repudiation of the accepted Christian distinction between

[1] See pp. 256–7 below.

the natural and the revealed on the ground that, in the form in which the Church insists upon it, it implies a radically false antithesis. There is indeed a difference between the natural and the revealed, but it is a difference in degree, not (as the Church wishes us to believe) a difference in kind; and that this is so may be verified by reflecting again upon our immediate, inward experience of what we call the natural and what we call the divine:

> That in us which is really natural is, in truth, *revealed.* We awake to the consciousness of it, we are aware of its coming forth in our mind; but we feel that we did not make it, that it is discovered to us, that it is what it is whether we will or no. If we are little concerned about it, we say it is *natural*; if much, we say it is *revealed.* But the difference between the two is not one of kind, only of degree. The real antithesis, to natural and revealed alike, is *invented, artificial.* Religion springing out of an experience of the power, the grandeur, the necessity of righteousness, is revealed religion, whether we find it in Sophocles or in Isaiah; 'the will of mortal men did not beget it, neither shall oblivion ever put it to sleep'. . . . The religion of the Bible, therefore, is well said to be *revealed*, because the great natural truth, that '*righteousness tendeth to life*', is seized and exhibited there with such incomparable force and efficacy.[1]

The last sentence proclaims the internal, literary test of what men call the 'revealed'. Wherever a fundamental saving truth is seized and exhibited with incomparable force and efficacy, there (Arnold is saying) we have a piece of revealed knowledge, a revelation. That is all that revelation means, that is all that it needs to mean to account for the saving power of the Gospel; and when this is what it means, it stands in no need of the supernatural element insisted upon by the historic Church to establish or confirm its redemptive character.

And what is true of the revealed is equally true (Arnold goes on to argue) of the miraculous. We have already heard Arnold pronouncing upon the irrelevance of the miracles upon which the historic Church grounds its claim to the 'grandeur

[1] *Literature and Dogma*, ch. I, sect. 4, pp. 50–1 (Arnold's emphasis).

and truth' of Christ's gospel;[1] he now suggests that confirmation of this view may be found in what he calls 'The Testimony of Jesus to Himself'. Throughout the New Testament record (Arnold says) Jesus is constantly shown to be 'insisting on a different evidence', indeed, to be positively repudiating the external evidence from miracles and putting all his emphasis on the internal. It is the disciples who (like the Jews in First Corinthians) ask for miracles, and it is they who rest Jesus' teaching on miracles. But Jesus himself (says Arnold) is shown, again and again, correcting their *Aberglaube*, and insisting upon their immediate inward experience as the proof of the saving power of his gospel. The passage in which Arnold argues this point is representative of his Biblical exegesis in *Literature and Dogma*, and suggests the more imaginative results that may proceed from the critical spirit when this is informed and controlled by a developed literary intelligence. For only such an intelligence is capable of making the fine qualitative discriminations between the several parts of a literary text—here the New Testament record—that yield the invaluable distinction between the quality of mind of Jesus himself and that of his disciples, therefore between the quality and kind of his insight and theirs, and therefore between his attitude to miracles and theirs:

When Nicodemus came and would put conversion on this ground ('We know that thou art a teacher come from God, *for no one can do the miracles that thou dost except God be with him*'), Jesus rejoined: 'Verily, verily, I say unto thee, *except a man be born from above*, he cannot see the kingdom of God', thus tacitly changing his disciple's ground and correcting him. Even distress and impatience at this false ground being taken is visible sometimes: 'Jesus *groaned in his spirit* and said, Why does this generation ask for a sign? Verily I say unto you, there shall no sign be given to this generation!' Who does not see what double and treble importance these checks of Jesus to the reliance on miracles gain, from their being reported by those who relied on miracles devoutly? Who does not see what a clue they offer as to the real mind of Jesus? To convey at all to such hearers of him that there was any objection to miracles, his own sense of the

[1] Above, pp. 211–12.

objection must have been profound; and to get them, who neither shared nor understood it to repeat it a few times, he must have repeated it many times.[1]

The same kind of literary intelligence is to be discerned again in Arnold's account of some of the more important sacramental practices of the historic Church, of the Christian doctrine of immortality, and, most particularly, in his beautiful account of the personality of Jesus, turning upon Jesus' 'secret' and 'method', and the meaning of Jesus' mission, death and resurrection.[2] Arnold's treatment of these matters also deserves the closest attention for what it shows of the Humanist direction of his view of Christianity; and it is with the object of establishing his title to the rank of one of the foremost Christian Humanists of the last age that I propose to discuss his account of each of these vital topics.

The first gives us Arnold defending the Catholic doctrine of the Mass against the Protestant charge that it is 'a degrading superstition'. The grounds on which he defends it are not indeed Catholic; but they are not less persuasive than those, and are to the Humanist completely satisfying. The Protestant view is that the Mass is a coarse, materialistic interpretation of Christ's words 'He that eateth me shall live by me'; and Arnold begins by granting this part of the Protestant objection:

It is indeed a rude and blind criticism of Christ's words: *He that eateth me shall live by me.* But once admit the miracle of the 'atoning sacrifice', once move in this order of ideas, and what can be more natural and beautiful than to imagine this miracle every day repeated, Christ offered in thousands of places, everywhere the believer enabled to enact the work of redemption and unite himself with the

[1] *Literature and Dogma*, ch. vi, sect. 2, pp. 154–5 (Arnold's emphasis).

[2] In view of the quality of religious sensibility and insight exhibited in these representative discussions in *Literature and Dogma*, it is instructive to recall T. S. Eliot's remark about Matthew Arnold, that 'in philosophy and theology he was an undergraduate; in religion a Philistine' (*The Use of Poetry and the Use of Criticism*, p. 105). One feels that bigotry can hardly go further than this in impairing true judgment, to the pursuit of which Mr Eliot had once declared himself dedicated.

Body whose sacrifice saves him? And the effect of this belief has been no more degrading than the belief itself.[1]

He then quotes, with obvious tenderness of feeling, a passage from *The Imitation of Christ* which treats of the Sacrament of the Altar:

For this most high and worthy Sacrament is the saving health of soul and body, the medicine of all spiritual languor; *by it my vices are cured, my passions bridled, temptations are conquered or diminished, a larger grace is infused, the beginnings of virtue are made to grow, faith is confirmed, hope strengthened and charity takes fire and dilates into flame.*

Upon this Arnold comments: 'So little is the doctrine of the Mass to be hastily called "a degrading superstition", either in its character or in its working.'[2] A man who can talk in this strain about a doctrine and a ritual in which he himself does not believe cannot, one feels, be fairly described as 'a Philistine in religion'.

What is true of Arnold's treatment of the Catholic doctrine of the Mass is even more true of his treatment of the other vital Christian matters I mentioned, beginning with Christ's divinity. What intelligible meaning (Arnold asks) can still be attached to the word 'divine' as applied to the historic Jesus when its supernatural and theological meaning has been denied? If Jesus is not divine in the sense in which the historic Church has decreed, in what sense, if any, can he still be so called? Arnold's answer is the true Humanist one: Jesus is divine in this sense alone, that he brought into the world a gospel whose power to redeem all men was absolute and unique, and was *therefore* 'divine', therefore proceeding from the Eternal-not-ourselves-that-makes-for-righteousness. And what makes Christ's gospel so uniquely redemptive, what sets it apart from the wise and good teachings of other great religious teachers, in particular from those of the great line of Jewish prophets in the religious tradition in which Jesus himself was nurtured, is what Arnold calls Jesus' secret and Jesus' method. Jesus secret is *self-renunciation*: 'He that loveth his

[1] *Literature and Dogma*, ch. IX, sect. 6, pp. 305–6. [2] *Ibid.* pp. 306–7.

life shall lose it, and he that hateth his life in this world shall keep it unto life eternal'; and Jesus' method is *inwardness*: 'Except a man be born of cleansing and of a new influence, he cannot see the Kingdom of God.'

Self-renunciation and inwardness, these two (says Arnold), are the unique points in Jesus' gospel. By self-renunciation is to be understood that most difficult part of the love and practice of righteousness which consists in learning to love and serve in a completely selfless way, with reference not to one's own advantage but only to the advantage—the gain, the benefit, the 'good'—of the object of one's love. Its more common names are perfect disinterestedness, generosity, unselfishness; and it is grounded in the belief (or faith) that it is by losing one's self in this wholly selfless love and service of others that one most truly—most fully and satisfyingly—finds oneself. This is Jesus' secret, which he made available to all men for their salvation; and this is what Jesus meant by the saying, 'He that loveth his life shall lose it, and he that hateth his life in this world shall keep it unto life eternal.' As to 'inwardness': this is the method by which we may attain to this selfless love which is the goal of our moral aspiration. It is not to be attained by 'legal righteousness', the merely formalistic observance of the commandments which are God's Law, or by good works performed in a mechanical and piecemeal way, on the supposition that these will add up to salvation. The love and practice of righteousness is not, as the Pharisees appeared to think, a matter of keeping a credit account with God. It is a matter of an inner transformation or conversion—'the birth of the new man', as St Paul called it; a matter of 'turning' the whole soul (in that sense a *conversion*) towards God as the sole source of our power to love and serve our fellow-men—and, as a result of this rebirth, receiving the grace of the Holy Spirit by which we are rendered capable of doing the works of God 'in the spirit' of perfect selfless love. This is the inwardness which (Arnold says) is Jesus' method; and this is what Jesus meant by the saying 'Except a man be born of cleansing and of a new influence, he cannot see the Kingdom of God'.

The secret and the method of Jesus, whose unique redemptive power may be experimentally verified, together establish his claim to be the Saviour of mankind, and are the real meaning of what the Church calls the 'divinity' of Jesus. For Arnold, the Humanist, there is no need to postulate an order other than and independent of the human, or a virgin birth, or a miraculous incarnation, or a physical resurrection, to give an intelligible and valid meaning to the term 'divine'. The divinity of Jesus consists in, and is defined by, his power to affirm, with the absolute authority of absolute knowledge, that self-renunciation and inwardness are the secret and the method by which we may be perfected in our love and practice of righteousness. This, for Arnold, is what the term 'divine' as applied to Jesus really means, this is all that it means, and this is all that it needs to mean in order to ensure for Jesus his title of the Saviour of mankind.[1]

[1] The claim for the *unique* redemptive power of Jesus' gospel is perhaps the most controversial point in the Humanist's doctrine, and is the most difficult to demonstrate or even to argue. The historian in particular is likely to dispute it; and when the Humanist considers that a historian of the stature of Arnold Toynbee, whose knowledge and understanding of world religions overtop those of any living man, has explicitly repudiated (in *An Historian's Approach to Religion*) the suggestion that any one of them, the Christian not excepted, has a claim to be considered unique, he may well quail at his own temerity in persisting in the contrary view. Yet he does so persist, in spite of all he does not know about the remaining six higher religions, and about much else that he ought to know. For what Dr Toynbee's own researches seem to him to establish is that there is in fact no other of the known higher religions that preached Jesus' 'secret' and 'method' in the way in which Jesus preached it; and since it is already established for him by his most intimate inward experience that only the appropriation of Jesus' secret and the practice of Jesus' method can yield the peace, power and joy that is the end of moral and religious life, he is bound to persist in his claim that Jesus' gospel is uniquely redemptive. This is not an argument that will satisfy the historian. But it is perhaps a question whether historical arguments alone are appropriate in this connexion; and the religious Humanist will allow himself to take courage (and comfort) from Hobbes's dictum about the final undemonstrability of ultimate truths even in civil philosophy; 'When I shall have set down my own reading orderly and perspicuously, the pains left another will be only to consider if he also find it not the same himself. For this kind of doctrine admitteth no other demonstration.' (*Leviathan*, Introduction.)

From this interpretation on Humanist premises of the divinity of Christ, Arnold is led to what is perhaps the boldest part of the whole enterprise of *Literature and Dogma*, his interpretation of Jesus' life and mission as a whole, and the miracle of his resurrection; and it is here that the non-Christian, the distinctively Humanist, note sounds most strong and clear. The crucial passages occur in the chapter entitled 'The Testimony of Jesus to Himself'; and they turn upon one principal suggestion, derived from the Christian interpretation of Jesus' life and mission but itself profoundly anti-Christian.

One of the great Christian arguments for the divinity of Jesus, that he was in fact the Christ, has always been that in his life, mission, death and resurrection he fulfilled the prophecy concerning the Stricken Servant of God set out in the fifty-third and fifty-fourth chapters of Isaiah. The Stricken Servant of God in Isaiah was, according to the Church, a 'prefiguring' of Christ; and the fact that Jesus' character, life and death corresponded so closely to those of the Stricken Servant of God in Isaiah had always been taken as a proof that Jesus was in fact the Messiah.

Now Arnold joins the Church in attaching the greatest significance to the fifty-third and fifty-fourth chapters of Isaiah, and in interpreting the life and mission of Jesus in the light of Isaiah's prophecy. But Arnold's interpretation differs radically from that of the Church: what he proposes is that Jesus' life and mission are to be viewed as the result of a conscious adoption and elevation of the ideal of the Stricken Servant of God. Jesus, according to Arnold, deliberately chose that ideal as the highest, noblest, most truly spiritual ideal of the Saviour of mankind available to him in his religious tradition; and, having chosen, Jesus consciously conformed his whole life and mission to that ideal. It is not, as Christians say, because Jesus was divine, the Son of God sent to redeem the world, that he fulfilled Isaiah's prophecy. It was, on the contrary, because he adopted and elevated the ideal of Isaiah, one of the most spiritually minded of the great moral teachers in the religious tradition in which Jesus had been brought up, because he had the spiritual insight and genius to adopt Isaiah's prophecy as the true ideal of Israel's Saviour and to conform his own life, mission and death to that ideal, that Jesus is to be accounted the Son of Man, the Saviour of the world.

That is how Arnold the Humanist argues once more the irrelevance of the supernatural sanction for 'the grandeur and truth' of Jesus' gospel and the redeeming power of his life and death. Jesus did not need to be divine in the Christian sense, the God he was according to the Church, to conform his life to the ideal of the Stricken Servant of God in Isaiah and so become the Saviour of mankind; he needed only to be the man he was, a man of supreme spiritual insight and spiritual genius. In the passage in which Arnold sets out this view, he explains also what is to be understood by the terms 'sacrifice', 'redemption' and 'resurrection' as applied to the life and mission of Jesus:

> The clue is given by the ideal of the stricken Servant of God in the fifty-third chapter of Isaiah. This ideal, as we have seen, Jesus had adopted and elevated as the true ideal of Israel's Saviour; he had corrected by it the favourite popular ideals he found regnant.[1] And, in this ideal of the stricken Servant of God, the notion of *sacrifice* is, that this lover of righteousness falls because of a state of iniquity and wickedness which he has had no share in making, and as the only remedy for it. The notion of *redemption* is, that by endurance to the end, and by his death crowning his life, he establishes all seekers after good in their allegiance to good, enables them to follow it, and to reach true life through it. Finally, the notion of *resurrection* is, that his death makes an epoch of victory for him and his cause, which thenceforward live and reign indestructibly. *He had done no violence, neither was any deceit in his mouth*; *he was bruised for our iniquities, the Eternal hath laid on him the iniquity of us all*:—there is

[1] What Arnold is referring to here is the traditional Jewish conception of the Messiah as the King of the Jews, an earthly king who would come riding into Jerusalem with all the pomp and splendour of an Eastern prince, and establish the Kingdom of God on earth. This was the view of the Messiah held even by the Apostles when they first rose and followed Jesus; and this is the view that Jesus 'corrects' and 'elevates' in accordance with Isaiah's prophecy.

the sacrifice. *With his stripes we are healed*:—there is the redemption. But: *When he hath made his life an offering for sin, he shall see his seed, he shall prolong his days, and the pleasure of the Eternal shall prosper in his hand*:—there, at the end of it all, is the resurrection.

And just these stages we find again in Jesus. *Which of you convicteth me of sin?* he asked the Jews; nevertheless: *The Son of Man must suffer many things and be rejected of this generation, the Son of Man must be lifted up*:—there is the sacrifice. *Except a grain of corn fall to the ground and die, it abideth alone*; *the Son of Man came to give his life a ransom for many*:—there is the redemption. But: *If the grain of corn die, it bringeth forth much fruit*; *I, if I be lifted up from the earth, will draw all men unto me*; *if I go not away the Spirit of truth will not come unto you, but if I depart I will send him unto you, and when he is come he will convince the world of sin, of righteousness, and of judgment*;—there, there is the resurrection and triumph.[1]

This is followed by Arnold's further and final statement of what he believes to be the real meaning of the miracle of the Resurrection; and here, again, what he is chiefly intent upon showing is that Jesus' own words bearing upon his resurrection admit of an interpretation quite other than that put upon them by the historic Church. The historic interpretation, following St Paul in First Corinthians, insists upon an external—a visible, material, physical—resurrection; Arnold's, which is the true Humanist interpretation, as the other is the true Christian, puts all its emphasis upon the internal, the non-material, the purely moral and spiritual resurrection. On this interpretation, the real basis of the New Testament story of the Resurrection is the inward experience of a perpetual rebirth or renewal into a fullness of life and joy—*present* life and joy—that Jesus had made possible to men by bringing them his redemptive gospel of love.

This, for Arnold, is the true and the whole meaning of the miracle of the Resurrection; this is what Jesus himself meant when he spoke of his resurrection to his disciples. 'I do cures today and tomorrow, and the third day I shall be perfected'; 'Destroy this temple, and in three days I will raise it up': these and similar sayings of Jesus have been taken by the

[1] *Literature and Dogma*, ch. VII, sect. 9, pp. 243–4.

historic Church to testify to Jesus' own expectation of a physical resurrection. But quite another interpretation is possible; and this Arnold sets out in a passage that again illustrates both the literary and the Humanist emphasis of his approach:

There is no more powerful testimony to Christ's real use of the words *life* and *death* than a famous text, borrowed from Jewish *Aberglaube*, which popular Christianity has wrested in support of its tenet of a physical resurrection at the Messiah's second advent. Whatever we may think of the narrative of the raising of Lazarus, we need have no difficulty in believing that Jesus really did say to the brother or sister of a dead disciple: 'Thy brother shall rise again!' and that the mourner replied: 'I know that he shall rise again at the resurrection of the last day.' For the answer which follows has the certain stamp of Jesus: 'I am the resurrection and the life; he that believeth on me, though he die, shall live, and whosoever liveth and believeth on me shall never die.' Now, Martha believed already in the resurrection of Jewish and Christian *Aberglaube*—the resurrection according to the Book of Daniel and the Book of Enoch, the resurrection of the last day, when 'they that sleep in the dust of the earth shall awake, some to everlasting life, and some to shame and everlasting contempt'. But Jesus corrects her *Aberglaube*, by telling her that her brother is not dead at all; and his words, out of which the story of the miracle very likely grew, do really make the miracle quite unnecessary. 'He that has believed on me and had my secret,' says Jesus, 'though his body die to the life of this world, still lives; for such an one had died to the life of this world already, and found true life, life out of himself, life in the Eternal that loveth righteousness, by doing so.'

Arnold continues:

Just in the same way again, in his promise to see his disciples again after his crucifixion and to take up his abode with them, Jesus corrects, for those who have eyes to read, he corrects in the clearest and most decisive way, those very errors with which our common material conceptions of life and death have made us invest his death and resurrection. 'Yet a little while', he says, 'and the world seeth me no more; but ye see me, because I live, and ye shall live too. He that hath my commandments and keepeth them, he it is that loveth me; and him that loveth me I will love, *and will manifest myself to him.*' Jude naturally objects: '*How* is it that thou wilt manifest thyself to us and not to the world?' And Jesus answers: 'If a man love me, he will keep my word, and my Father will love him, and *we will come unto him and make our abode with him.*' Therefore the manifestation of himself that Jesus speaks of is nothing external and material. It is—like the manifestation of God to him that ordereth his conversation right, the internal life and joy in keeping the commandments—it is the life for the disciples of Christ, in and with Christ, *in keeping the commandments of God*; those commandments which had at last in their true scope been made known to men, but solely through Christ's method and through his secret.[1]

Finally, there is Arnold's Humanist account of immortality. He quotes 'If a man keep my word, he shall never see death' as one of the several sayings of Jesus which have been taken to support the Christian doctrines of the Second Advent, the resurrection of the body and the New Jerusalem. But Arnold asks us instead to take the words to stand for the internal experience of immortality. He calls it 'the sense of life', 'the sense of being truly alive which accompanies righteousness'; and this experience of life perpetually renewed and replenished—extended to infinity, rendered immortal—in and through the love and practice of righteousness, is for him the true, complete and final meaning of immortality, which needs no doctrines of the Second Advent, the resurrection of the body, or the New Jerusalem to confirm or sustain it.

The passage in which Arnold sets out his account of the meaning of immortality emphasises how incomplete and imperfect in most of us is this 'sense of life'. But if it is so, it is so (Arnold suggests) only because our love and practice of righteousness is so defective; therefore the only way to attain to the full experience of immortality is to grow more and more perfect in our love and practice of righteousness in accordance with the gospel preached by Jesus:

If this experimental sense does not rise to be stronger in us, does not rise to the sense of being inextinguishable, that is probably because our experience of righteousness is really so

[1] *Literature and Dogma*, ch. VII, sect. 9, pp. 245–7 (Arnold's emphasis).

very small. Here, therefore, we may well permit ourselves to trust Jesus, whose practice and intuition both of them went, in these matters, so far deeper than ours. At any rate, we have in our experience this strong sense of *life from righteousness* to start with; capable of being developed, apparently, by progress in righteousness, into something immeasurably stronger. Here is the true basis of all religious aspiration after immortality. And it is an experimental basis; and therefore, as to grandeur, it is again, when compared with the popular *Aberglaube*, grand with all the superior grandeur, on a subject of the highest seriousness, of reality over fantasy.

At present, the fantasy hides the grandeur of the reality. But when all the *Aberglaube* of the second advent, with its signs in the sky, sounding trumpets and opening graves, is cleared away, then and not till then, will come out the profound truth and grandeur of words of Jesus like these: 'The hour is coming, when they that are in the graves shall hear the voice of the Son of Man; and they that hear shall *live*.'[1]

These are some of the reinterpretations of Christian doctrine by which Arnold makes his contribution to the Humanism I have been discussing. There is no question of their being acceptable to the Christian; if they were acceptable to him, he would cease to be a Christian. But to the modern religious Humanist, who has to possess his heart in patience, and in the meantime listens intently for what prophetic voices there may be to give him some sign of what that which is to be will be—to such a Humanist Arnold's is one of the great prophetic voices of the last age, his book a prophetic book, and his constructive critique of the religious tradition from which the true Humanism is to emerge an example, an inspiration, and a hope.

Nevertheless, though it is so exemplary and so inspiring, Arnold's critique of Christianity in *Literature and Dogma* is in important respects imperfect and incomplete. There are serious omissions and weaknesses in his account of historic Christianity; and it is in the interest of the emergent Humanism we are concerned with to know what they are and to understand their significance. I will accordingly return to the criticism of Arnold's doctrine in a later chapter.[2]

[1] *Ibid.* ch. XII, sect. 4, pp. 379–80 (Arnold's emphasis).

[2] Ch. X below, pp. 225–60.

CHAPTER IX

PHILOSOPHIC HUMANISM

F. H. BRADLEY'S 'ETHICAL STUDIES'

In view of the fact that *Ethical Studies* owes at least part of its distinction to its annihilating critiques of Mill's *Utilitarianism* and Arnold's *Literature and Dogma*, there is a pleasant irony in discovering that Bradley has a place in the same moral tradition. Bradley himself virtually admits the connexion with Mill when, surveying the ruins of Mill's *Utilitarianism* at the end of the essay 'Pleasure for Pleasure's Sake', he remarks 'Modern Utilitarianism has a good object in view. Though we understand it differently, we have the same object in view, and that is why we are at issue with Utilitarianism.'[1] And for the connexion with Arnold, T. S. Eliot, who has a great admiration for Bradley and none at all (as we saw) for Arnold, nevertheless perceives that the two men are 'on the same side' and draws attention to the similarity in their style of thought, which he locates, very cleverly, in the 'tone and tension and beat' of their literary styles.[2] This is heartening corroboration of the view proposed here that, in spite of the scorn with which Bradley treats *Literature and Dogma*, there are important affinities between him and Arnold, and that it is therefore not arbitrary to place the two in the same Humanist camp.

The affinities, however, between Bradley and Arnold in particular, go even deeper than those Mr Eliot has mentioned. In his famous essay on Academies, Arnold may deplore the absence in his own iron time of a 'fresh current of ideas' such as the Elizabethans enjoyed, from which the creative artist

[1] Bradley, *Ethical Studies*, p. 124.

[2] T. S. Eliot, 'F. H. Bradley' (in *Selected Essays*, p. 409).

might draw inspiration and spiritual sustenance. But to the historian of thought reviewing Arnold's age almost a century later, it is evident that such a current of ideas did exist; that it took the form of a common direction and emphasis in the philosophical speculation of the age, which was as fresh, new and vital an expression of the *Zeitgeist* as might be desired; and that it animated equally the thought of a man of letters like Matthew Arnold and of a professional philosopher like Bradley. The sources of the new philosophy are Kant and the post-Kantians, mediated by Coleridge and powerfully replenished by Hegel, from whom Bradley immediately derives; its presence in the later nineteenth century and after may be recognised in writers as diverse as Walter Pater and William James, Kierkegaard, Rilke and Henry James; and it is in this same current of ideas, with its freshness only a little staled, that Mr Eliot's own creative life has its beginning.

For the limited purpose of the present discussion, what principally distinguishes this common philosophical medium in which Bradley and Arnold conduct their thinking is the central place accorded to the phenomenon of *consciousness.* The data of philosophy are no longer the contents, or facts, of the (external) world, they are now the contents, or facts, of consciousness; the philosophical generalisations are about, the analyses concern, the contents of consciousness. In *Ethical Studies* we accordingly hear nothing about the principles of morals, but only about 'the facts of the moral consciousness'; nothing again about the truths of religion, but only about 'the facts of the religious consciousness'; and the *summum bonum* of the old philosophers is replaced by a quasi-Hegelian Absolute which is a very much more complex and subtle affair than the Platonic Form of the Good or the Aristotelian End of Ends. And what links Bradley with Arnold at this deepest level is their common effort to wrest a saving objectivity out of the seemingly incorrigible subjectivity of the contents of consciousness. Against the traditional philosophical realism of the historic Church, Arnold, as we saw, sets the new realism of the 'experimentally verifiable'—that which may be discovered to be thus and not otherwise in our most intimate, inward *experience*; and against the dualistic Aristotelian realism, which postulates an order of nature to be appropriated and re-created by the human mind, Bradley, following Hegel, sets a monistic realism that allows reality to nothing but the contents of consciousness, and insists that objectivity is to be discovered nowhere but in the most self-coherent (which, on this view, is also the most comprehensive) ordering of the contents of consciousness.

In this effort to transubstantiate the subjective into the objective Arnold and Bradley are, in their respective undertakings, equally successful. The demands it makes, however, would seem to be peculiarly arduous and exhausting. To be immured with (or within) the contents of consciousness is by itself enough to induce a sense of isolation, even of solitude, that the great traditional realists, from Plato and Aristotle to their last heirs in the seventeenth century, apparently had little experience of. But besides this, the modern philosophical realist,[1] as he pursues his analyses of the contents of consciousness, hovers all the time on the edge of the abyss of total solipsism, the moral concomitants of which are, we know, either the scepticism that Hume successfully escaped or the nihilism that many nineteenth-century thinkers did not escape; and it is no doubt the nervous and emotional strain of maintaining a precarious balance on the edge of the abyss, along with the sense of isolation already mentioned, that may be taken to account for certain characteristic features of the personal style of these writers. The chief of these is their commitment to the ironic view of things, tinged—in Bradley particularly—with a passionate, exalted kind of pessimism that

[1] Though Bradley and his followers are more commonly called 'idealist' in contradistinction to the 'realists', or 'neo-realists', of the school of Bertrand Russell and G. E. Moore, the term 'realist' is used here in the sense explained, to denote the objectivist emphasis of their thought, which sets it apart from the subjectivism of the modern nominalist or quasi-nominalist philosophical schools deriving from Locke and Hume.

is always exhilarating and sometimes chilling; and its typical mode of utterance is irony and paradox of a subtlety new in kind, not merely in degree, in the history of English letters. This distinctive note, viewed as a function of the modern growth of self-consciousness, would repay close analysis, for which there is not room here. It can only be mentioned that in Arnold it sounds to magnificent effect in his criticism, but tends to fall into pathos and even sentimentality in his poetry; and in Bradley it is most powerful and impressive in his polemical writing, less impressive in other parts.

Bradley's remarkable style, however, since it intimately expresses the mind and temper of the man, must be briefly considered on its own merits.

In his preface to the first edition of *Ethical Studies* he expresses a regret that so much of it should be polemical; but no receptive reader will readily share this regret, since Bradley's polemical style is one of its most dazzling achievements. The slaughter of the Utilitarians ('Locke and the friends of Locke') is one awe-inspiring instance. The level of generality is pitched so high that breathing in that air is exceedingly difficult, and impossible to sustain for long together; the argument is of a ferocious intricacy, and a coherence as close and tight; yet it is all made as easy as possible by the marvellous lucidity, the swiftness of the pace, and an energy perfectly compatible with the flexibility and grace of a mind in consummate possession of its powers.

Besides this, there is the surpassing grandness of Bradley's grand manner. The key-note, a kind of a high imperiousness, a devastating *hauteur*, may be heard in the sentence with which he begins his recapitulation of the case against Utilitarianism: 'Hedonism *is* bankrupt; with weariness we have pursued it, so far as was necessary, through its various shapes, from the selfish doctrine of the individual to the self-sacrificing spirit of modern Utilitarianism.'[1] The weariness comes with sublime histrionic effect at the end of his exposure of the

[1] *Ethical Studies*, p. 124.

confusions and contradictions in the Utilitarian doctrine, and does not fail to underline (with due decorum) the magnitude of Bradley's undertaking and achievement in that classic essay. Or there is this longer passage from the first essay, on 'The Vulgar Notion of Responsibility', in which the weariness and disdain combine with the satirical bite of the mounting paradoxes to produce a resplendent dismissive rhetoric:

> What is the popular notion of responsibility? The popular notion is certainly to be found in the ordinary consciousness, in the plain or non-theoretical man, the man who lives without having or wishing for opinions of his own, as to what living is or ought to be. And to find this plain man, where are we to go? For nowadays, when all have opinions, and too many also practice of their own; when every man knows better, and does worse, than his father before him; when to be enlightened is to be possessed by some wretched theory, which is our own just so far as it separates us from others; and to be cultivated is to be aware that doctrine means narrowness, that all truths are so true that any truth must be false; when 'young pilgrims', at their outset, are 'spoiled by the sophistry' of shallow moralities, and the fruit of life rots as it ripens—amid all this 'progress of the species', the plain man is by no means so common as he once was, or at least is said to have been. And so, if we want a moral sense that has not yet been adulterated, we must not be afraid to leave enlightenment behind us. We must go to the vulgar for vulgar morality, and there what we lose in refinement we perhaps are likely to gain in integrity.[1]

Bradley's grand manner shows as all the grander for his power to vary it with a familiar conversational manner, which he commands as easily as the other. But the supreme feature of his polemical style is the irony that can annihilate a man or a doctrine in the space of a single paragraph. His attack on the mechanical metaphors habitually used by the deterministic psychologists of the school of Professor Bain is typical:

> When we hear such phrases as 'the mechanism of the human mind', we feel at a loss, if at least we believe that the sphere of mere mechanism has ceased, before that of the mind has even begun; and when, further, we learn the avowed intention to bring nothing

[1] *Ethical Studies*, pp. 2–3.

but physical methods to bear on the interpretation of mind, what confidence we had altogether vanishes. And proceeding to inquire into the determination of the will by 'motives', we find every term and phrase has a meaning not until we import into the consideration of ourselves the coarsest and crassest mechanical metaphors of pulls and pushes, drawings and thrustings, which we believed to exist not anywhere except in the lowest phenomena of the natural world. Just as, in reading Locke and so many of the friends of Locke, we have nothing before our understanding, until, as it were, we call up before our eyes solid things in space, denting, and punching, and printing another thing called a mind, and this other thing in like manner (how heaven knows) making marks and prints on *itself* also—so, in reading our determinists, the one chance of their terms bringing anything at all before the intellect is for us to keep in sight a thing called a will, pushed and pulled by things called motives; or else certain 'forces' called motives, acting within a given space called self, and, by their 'composition', resulting in no movement at all or a movement called 'will'; uncertain whether such movement is a movement of the whole 'collection' in the space called self, or a movement only of part of that collection.[1]

This is the kind of irony that is no easy form of ridicule but makes its point by a searching and subtle analysis of the strictly *logical* weaknesses of the doctrine it is exposing, presenting it in the form of a fine free paraphrase of that doctrine which accentuates, and thereby exposes, its essential incoherence. Another delightful passage of the same kind is that in which Bradley exposes the confusions in the determinist account of the phenomenon of self-consciousness, using the image of a rope of onions to make his point:

We have all seen onions on a rope. Now each of these onions is not any other onion—it may be taken by itself, as a separate individual; and yet each of these onions is a state of the rope of onions. And, further, this rope of onions is aware of itself—it talks about itself and generally comports itself as if it were inseparable, and, no doubt, it really is what it calls self-conscious. But here is the beginning of delusion; for talking about 'self', we (i.e. the onions) fall into the belief that there is something there under the onions and the rope, and on looking we see there is nothing of the kind. But

[1] *Ethical Studies*, p. 34.

on looking we see even more than this; for the rope of onions is a rope of straw, and that is, being interpreted, no rope at all, but the fiction of a rope. The onions keep together because of the laws of association of onions; and because of these laws it is that the mutual juxtaposition of the onions engenders in them the belief in a rope, and the consequent foolish ideas of a self, which we see in all their foolishness when we perceive, first, that there is nothing but a rope, and then that the rope is nothing at all. The only thing which after all is hard to see is this, that we ourselves, who apprehend the illusion are ourselves the illusion which is apprehended by us; and perhaps, on the theory of 'relativity', in order to know a fiction you yourself must *be* the fiction you know; but it is all hard to understand, especially to a mind which is little 'analytical' and, I begin to fear, not at all 'inductive'.[1]

This is Bradley's polemical style, and it is indeed superb. There is, however, also his other style, perhaps best described as declamatory, which is not so successful. This is the style in which he gives voice to one of his most characteristic moods, that of a lofty disenchantment with the world of men, and in particular the world of 'theoretical men', a disdainful bitterness at their incurable vulgarities and stupidities and perversities. This passage, from the essay 'My Station and its Duties', is an instance:

The non-theoretical person, if he be not immoral, is at peace with reality; and the man who in any degree has made this point of view his own, becomes more and more reconciled to the world and to life, and the theories of 'advanced thinkers' come to him more and more as the thinnest and most miserable abstractions. He sees evils which can not discourage him, since they point to the strength of the life which can endure such parasites and flourish in spite of them. If the popularizing of superficial views inclines him to bitterness, he comforts himself when he sees that they live in the head, and but little, if at all, in the heart and life; that still at the push the doctrinaire and the quacksalver go to the wall, and that even that too is as it ought to be. . . . He sees instincts are better and stronger than so-called 'principles'. He sees in the hour of need what are called 'rights' laughed at, 'freedom', the liberty to do what one pleases, trampled on, the claims of the individual trodden under foot, and

[1] *Ethical Studies*, pp. 38–9.

theories burst like cobwebs. And he sees, as of old, the heart of a nation rise high and beat in the breast of each one of her citizens, till her safety and her honour are dearer to each than life, till to those who live her shame and sorrow, if such is allotted, outweigh their loss, and death seems a little thing to those who go for her to their common and nameless grave. And he knows that what is stronger than death is hate or love, hate here for love's sake, and that love does not fear death, because already it is the death into life of what our philosophers tell us is the only life and reality.[1]

In the following passage the declamatory note is pitched still higher:

It is an old story, a theme too worn for the turning of sentences, and yet too living a moral not to find every day a new point and to break a fresh heart, that our lives are wasted in the pursuit of the impalpable, the search for the impossible and the unmeaning. Neither to-day nor yesterday, but throughout the whole life of the race, the complaint has gone forth that all is vanity; that the ends for which we live and we die are 'mere ideas', illusions begotten on the brain by the wish of the heart—poor phrases that stir the blood, until experience or reflection for a little, and death for all time, bring with it disenchantment and quiet. Duty for duty's sake, life for an end beyond sense, honour, and beauty, and love for the invisible—all these are first felt and then seen to be dream and shadow and unreal vision. And our cry and our desire is for something that will satisfy us, something that we know and do not only think, something that is real and solid, that we can lay hold of and be sure of, and that will not change in our hands. We have said good-bye to our transcendent longings, we have bidden a sad but an eternal farewell to the hopes of our own and of the world's too credulous youth; we have parted for ever from our early loves, from our fancies and aspirations beyond the human. We seek for the tangible, and we find it in this world; for the knowledge which can never deceive, and that is the certainty of our own well-being; we seek for the palpable, and we feel it; for the end which will satisfy us as men, and we find it, in a word, in happiness.[2]

In such passages the feeling is, of course, sincere and even passionate. But the style is mannered: the cadence is too obviously patterned, too neatly balanced, therefore rhetorical in the limiting sense of the word; the adjectives and adverbs

[1] *Ethical Studies*, pp. 183–4. [2] *Ibid.* p. 85.

are too many and too obtrusive; the images often tend to the violent and even melodramatic; and the whole effect is artificial, derivative (from the great classical models, no doubt), and in the end hardly better than the purple-patch writing that finds its way into anthologies of prose. This is not Bradley at his best; and there is a significant connexion between the characteristic defects of this writing and the ultimate defects of the moral doctrine of *Ethical Studies* that we are presently to examine.

To determine Bradley's place in the Humanist tradition in English moral thought, it will be necessary first to mention briefly the main points of the philosophical system in which his moral and religious doctrines are grounded. From there I will proceed to the main parts of his positive doctrine in *Ethical Studies*, his analysis of what he calls the moral consciousness and the religious consciousness; and finally I will indicate what I believe to be the main weakness in his account of the relation of the moral and the religious.

Though Bradley's mature philosophical system, set out in *Appearance and Reality* and *Essays on Truth and Reality*, is incipiently present, it had not yet been fully developed at the time he wrote *Ethical Studies* and therefore need not concern us in its more developed form. All that is necessary for our purpose is to have some notion of what he means by his two cardinal philosophical doctrines, the doctrine of 'aspects' and of 'internal relations'; and these are best understood by seeing them as parts of a total view of reality standing at the opposite extreme to that mechanistic or atomistic view represented by 'Locke and the friends of Locke', against whose crude errors and confusions some of Bradley's best polemics (as we have seen) are directed.

Both the doctrine of aspects and that of internal relations rest upon an essentially *organic* view of reality. All reality, on this view, is an organic whole; every part, therefore, of this whole is 'internally' related to and interpenetrated by every other part. 'Every part is in the whole, and determines that whole; [and]...the whole is in every part, and informs each part with the nature of the whole', writes Bradley in one of the few explicit statements of his fundamental philosophical doctrine to be found in *Ethical Studies*.[1] It is clear that such a view is radically opposed to that of Locke and his successors. For to see reality as they saw it, as a collection of 'atomic' units, held together by 'external' relations (like the law of association of the mechanistic psychologists) is, on the Bradleian view, to violate the essential character of reality; it is to 'atomise' the real, to destroy irreparably its organic, indivisible unity. And it is because Bradley saw this (to adopt an image of Plato's) as a fundamental act of outrage upon the fair body of reality that so much of *Ethical Studies* is directed to the exposure of the prevalent atomistic philosophies of his day and, by anticipation, of our own.

The real, then, being an organic whole, is one and indivisible. But though it cannot be divided, it can be distinguished; indeed it must, if it is to be grasped by the human mind at all. But (and this is the other fundamental Bradleian doctrine) it cannot and must not be distinguished into 'parts' or 'elements'. These are the false misleading metaphors of an atomistic view of reality, and for that reason to be eschewed. Reality is distinguishable (Bradley maintains), not into elements, but *aspects*. By the conceptual powers of the mind, reality is grasped in this or that aspect, from this or that point of view, under this or that *category*; and all these terms, 'aspect', 'point of view', 'category', are interchangeable in the Bradleian system.

To grasp the real under this or that aspect or category or point of view is, indeed, necessarily to limit the real; it is to see the real *only* under this or that aspect, category or point of view, and to that extent incompletely and imperfectly. But (this is the grand Bradleian paradox) it is nevertheless to see the whole of reality in this or that aspect, not merely an

[1] Bradley, *op. cit.* p. 23.

arbitrarily dismembered part of it; and this is what establishes the superiority of the doctrine of aspects over the other. When, for instance, we adopt the scientific point of view, we are not looking at one part or element of the real, as the atomistic philosophies suppose; we are viewing the whole of reality in the scientific aspect. And since the scientific approach is essentially quantitative, the characteristic effort of science is to bring the whole of reality under the category of quantity; and the world of science—the world as seen in the light of science—is therefore the whole world *sub specie quantitatis*, reality viewed under the category or aspect of quantity. Similarly, when we adopt the historical point of view, we are again not looking merely at one part or element of the whole, we are viewing the whole of reality in the historical aspect; and since to view reality historically is to view it in the aspect of the past, the historical activity is that of bringing the whole of reality under the category of the past, and history is therefore the whole world *sub specie praeteritorum*. And (to come at last to the subject-matter of *Ethical Studies*), when we adopt the ethical point of view, we are again not concerned merely with a part or element of the whole of life; we are concerned with the whole of life in the ethical or moral aspect. And since, according to Bradley, to view the whole of life in this aspect is to view it as a function of *the will*, ethics is the whole of life *sub specie voluntatis*, under the aspect or category of the will.[1]

There are two conveniently brief passages in *Ethical Studies* which show very clearly that this philosophical doctrine, though not fully developed in *Ethical Studies*, is yet present by implication. The first is Bradley's comment on Matthew

[1] In setting out this summary account of Bradley's philosophical foundations, I have drawn heavily not only upon Bradley's later works (*The Principles of Logic, Appearance and Reality* and *Essays on Truth and Reality*), but also, and even chiefly, on an important post-Bradleian work, Michael Oakeshott's *Experience and its Modes*. Professor Oakeshott's treatise is a brilliant restatement of the Bradleian position, which amplifies and develops it, and corrects many of Bradley's own errors and confusions. It stands as the most distinguished contribution of the present century to this most distinguished of modern philosophical systems.

Arnold's dictum that conduct is nine-tenths of life. With his customary haughtiness, Bradley 'accepts thankfully' the view itself; but (he adds) he has no expectation that the problems of ethics will be solved '*by [such] a coarse and popular method, which divides into parts instead of distinguishing aspects*'.[1] Arnold, in other words, is guilty of viewing the moral life of man as one part or element of the whole ('nine-tenths of human life'), instead of seeing it as the whole life of man viewed in a particular aspect, the moral. The other instance is Bradley's use of the image of 'the sphere within spheres'. This occurs in a passage in which he is speaking, in a markedly Platonic strain, about the moral life of the individual as an organic order or system (of moral values) composed of subordinate orders or systems:

> Most men have a life which they live, and with which they are tolerably satisfied, and that life, when examined, is seen to be fairly systematic; it is seen to be a sphere including spheres, the lower spheres subordinating to themselves and qualifying particular actions, and themselves subordinated to and qualified by the whole.[2]

The image is used here to picture specifically the moral life of man as an organic whole composed of smaller organic wholes, each of which qualifies the larger whole, and is itself qualified by that larger whole. But it serves equally well to picture Bradley's general view of reality, expressed in the doctrine of internal relations and the doctrine of aspects. Reality is the supreme sphere, which includes within itself such subordinate organic wholes as the spheres of science, history, ethics, and so on. Each of these subordinate wholes, being organic, is therefore a sphere; each is an 'aspect' of the supreme sphere, reality; each is therefore 'internally', or organically, related

[1] *Ethical Studies*, p. 215.

[2] *Ibid.* p. 70. By the 'lower' spheres Bradley means, one must suppose, the more limited, less inclusive, and therefore less important 'spheres' of moral values. For instance, the 'sphere' of values that determines one's conduct in one's profession is 'lower' in this sense—more limited in scope, less comprehensive—than, say, the order or sphere of values that determines our relation to our fellow-men, or to God.

to every other subordinate sphere and to the supreme sphere, reality itself. And that is how reality in all its internally related aspects may be seen as 'a sphere including spheres'.

I return to Bradley's crucial definition of ethics, which, as we saw, is philosophically grounded in his doctrine of aspects and internal relations. It proclaims that morality is the whole of life, or experience, viewed *sub specie voluntatis*, under the category or aspect of the will. The moral activity is distinctively an activity of the will; the will is the defining power of man's nature in its moral aspect; the sphere of morality is the sphere of will; whatever is moral is a function of the will.

This is the definition which directs Bradley's whole brilliant analysis of what he calls 'the moral consciousness', meaning by this the contents, or the facts, of the moral consciousness, that which makes up the sum total or our moral experience. What Bradley believes these basic facts to be is incorporated in his positive moral doctrine in *Ethical Studies*, which he calls 'my station and its duties' and expounds, chiefly though not exclusively, in the essay bearing that title. This doctrine is the heart of Bradley's analysis of the moral consciousness; and through it he is presently to exhibit what he believes to be the ultimate imperfection of morality itself, and to argue the need of religion—the 'religious consciousness'—to complete and perfect the moral by transcending it. It is accordingly important to lay hold of the doctrine of my station and its duties in order to see by what process Bradley passes from the moral consciousness to the religious, and how this vital passage is connected with his definition of morality as the life of man viewed under the aspect of the will.

The basic doctrine is itself an answer to the basic question, What is the ultimate end of moral endeavour, of the activity that we call moral? Bradley answers that the life of man in its moral aspect is directed to the single ultimate end of *self-realisation*. This, however, does not mean the realisation of the self as an isolated atomic unit; it means the realisation of the self as an organic part of a larger whole. 'To realize the self', writes Bradley, 'is always to realize a whole, and. . . the question in morals is to find the true whole, realizing which will practically realize the true self.'[1]

It is this quest that leads him to the doctrine of my station and its duties. The true whole in and through which the self realises itself turns out to be the community—what Plato called the republic or commonwealth, what Bradley himself calls 'the social state'. Indeed, Bradley's doctrine of my station and its duties turns out to be essentially similar to that of Plato in *The Republic*, supplemented by some important points of the teaching of the *Nicomachean Ethics*. As in Plato's system the individual, by performing the function that he is best fitted to perform, at once finds his own true happiness (achieves 'self-realisation') and makes his distinctive contribution to the true well-being of the commonwealth (realises the larger whole of which he is a member), so in Bradley's system the individual, by filling his 'station' and fulfilling the duties belonging to it, achieves the self-realisation that is the end of individual moral endeavour in and through the realisation of the larger whole which is the social state. This is how Bradley himself puts it:

> The 'individual' apart from the community is an abstraction. It is not anything real, and hence not anything that we can realize, however much we may wish to do so. . . . I am myself by sharing with others, by including in my essence relations to them, the relations of the social state. If I wish to realize my true being, I must therefore realize something beyond my being as a mere this or that; for my true being has in it a life which is not the life of any mere particular, and so must be called a universal life.[2]

From this metaphysical account of the matter he goes on to state it in more concrete terms:

> What is it then that I am to realize? We have said it in 'my station and its duties'. To know what a man is. . . you must not take him in isolation. He is one of a people, he was born in a family, he

[1] *Ethical Studies*, p. 69. [2] *Ibid.* p. 173.

lives in a certain society, in a certain state. What he has to do depends on what his place is, what his function is, and that all comes from his station in the organism....[1]

And what is that 'organism' in which the individual has his 'station'? It is not single, but multiple; 'organisms' within 'organisms', the 'sphere including spheres' again:

> There are such facts as the family, then in a middle position, a man's own profession and society, and, over all, the larger community of the state. Leaving out of sight the question of a society wider than the state, we must say that a mans' life with its moral duties is in the main filled up by his station in that system of wholes which the state is, and that this, partly by its laws and institutions, and still more by its spirit, gives him the life which he does live and ought to live.... In short, man is a social being; he is real only because he is social, and can realize himself only because it is as social that he realizes himself. The mere individual is a delusion of theory; and the attempt to realize it in practice is the starvation and mutilation of human nature.[2]

Then again, with the Platonic emphasis even more marked:

> 'My station and its duties' teaches us to identify others and ourselves with the station we fill; to consider that as good, and by virtue of that to consider others and ourselves good too. It teaches us that a man who does his work in the world is good, notwithstanding his faults, if his faults do not prevent him from fulfilling his station. It tells us that the heart is an idle abstraction; we are not to think of it, nor must we look at our insides, but at our work and our life, and say to ourselves, Am I fulfilling my appointed function or not? Fulfil it we can, if we will: what we have to do is not so much better than the world that we cannot do it; the world is there waiting for it; my duties are my rights. On the one hand, I am not likely to be much better than the world asks me to be; on the other hand, if I can take my place in the world, I ought not to be discontented. Here we must not be misunderstood...[3]

and at this point Bradley digresses to clear himself of the possible charge that he is giving an unrealistic account of the common man's fulfilment of his station and its duties:

[1] *Ethical Studies*, p. 173. [2] *Ibid.* p. 174.
[3] *Ibid.* pp. 181–2.

We do not say that the false self, the habits and desires opposed to the good will, are extinguished. Though negated, they never are all of them entirely suppressed, and cannot be. Hence we must not say that any man really does fill his station to the full height of his capacity; nor must we say of any man that he cannot perform his function better than he does, for we all can do so, and should try to do so. We do not wish to deny what are plain moral facts, nor in any way to slur them over.[1]

The doctrine of my station and its duties, in other words, expresses an ideal, not an actuality—the condition of perfect felicity towards which men must constantly aspire, but can never perfectly attain.

The Aristotelian influence is less pervasive than the Platonic, but as recognisable where it occurs. It is conspicuous, for instance, in Bradley's emphasis upon habituation as the main part of our moral development. 'To be moral' (Bradley quotes from Hegel) 'is to live in accordance with the moral tradition of one's country; and in respect of education, the one true answer is that which the Pythagorean gave to him who asked what was the best education for his son, If you make him the citizen of a people with good institutions.'[2]

The doctrine of my station and its duties, viewed as a quasi-political doctrine, expresses what one might call a radical conservatism which is characteristic of the whole temper of Bradley's mind; and it is likely at the present time to be especially repugnant to the liberal-democratic outlook. Nor is it to be denied that the doctrine of my station and its duties has its dangerous side. It easily lends itself to the kind of distortion that can degrade it into a totalitarian doctrine of the Hegelian variety; and in this form it is indeed incompatible with the true democratic ideal. In the form, however, in which Bradley presents it, with the Platonic emphasis rather than the Hegelian, it is sound and salutory, in particular as a corrective to the excesses that an uncritical democratic view is prone to, which Matthew Arnold summed up in his famous

[1] *Ethical Studies*, p. 182. [2] *Ibid.* p. 173.

dictum about 'doing as one likes'. The tendency of the uncritical democratic view is to minimise the principle of order, the subordination of the less to the greater, in the spiritual economy of the individual and in the social organism, and to interpret self-realisation as, precisely, a matter of 'doing as one likes'—recognising no law other than the law of development, or 'progress' ('Progress for Progress' Sake', Bradley might have called it), without reference to the value of the end towards which this progress is directed. It is a view which cares nothing for *perfection*—'the study of perfection', as Arnold called it when he tried to show the Philistines what, disastrously, they were leaving out of account in their philosophy. Viewed historically, the doctrine of 'my station and its duties' is perhaps best seen as Bradley's contribution to the literature of radical protest in the later nineteenth century in England, which had already received some of its most distinguished contributions from Matthew Arnold himself and from such writers as Ruskin and Carlyle. In the details Bradley's doctrine is, in my judgment, inferior to the substantially similar doctrines of these more literary social critics in being much more 'abstract' than theirs because more remote from the actualities of contemporary life. Yet it has the compensating virtue of being firmly grounded in a philosophic system of great power and distinction; and this gives it a largeness of reference and a grandeur derived from the presence of the metaphysical dimension which one misses in the writings of the literary men.

Having come so far in *Ethical Studies* we have reached, or are about to reach, the point where the fatal limitations of the moral view as such are to be exhibited, and the transition to the religious view accordingly made. In the last section of 'My Station and Its Duties', and at greater length in the essays entitled 'Ideal Morality' and 'Selfishness and Self-sacrifice', Bradley sets out some of the vital problems of the moral life that morality by itself, the life of man viewed *sub specie voluntatis*, leaves unaccounted for and therefore unsolved. The doctrine of my station and its duties is, on this view, the highest reach of man in his moral character, as embodied will; yet (Bradley now desires to show) it is incomplete in several important respects. For instance, the community in which a man is expected to fulfil the function proper to his station may be 'in a confused or rotten condition',[1] and when this is the case, it will be incapable of sustaining the effort of its individual members to fulfil themselves in the fulfilment of the duties belonging to their stations. Another difficulty is that 'you cannot *confine* a man to his station and his duties';[2] the whole man (Bradley intimates) is always more than his function, than his station and its duties; and this is the very objection that has been urged against Plato's definition of justice in the *Republic*, that the just man is he who, simply and solely, 'minds his own business', and fulfils perfectly his function in the commonwealth.

The larger doctrine of self-realisation which subsumes the doctrine of my station and its duties also, it seems, raises insuperable difficulties. What, for instance (asks Bradley), are we to say about the great artist or man of science who undoubtedly realises himself in producing works of art or making scientific discoveries, yet may not be, in any common meaning of the term, a morally good man? And if such a contradiction is possible, 'the doctrine which unreservedly identifies moral goodness with any desirable realization of the self cannot be maintained'.[3]

The objections to the moral view itself, however, the view of man's life under the aspect of the will, go even deeper; and they are first moral, then metaphysical. The moral turn upon the perpetual struggle of what Bradley calls the 'good self' and the 'bad self', the 'good will' and the 'bad will'. Man's life, while it remains confined to the moral sphere, while the exercise of the will is our only means of salvation, can never be a *perfect* realisation of that good will, or good self, in the

[1] *Ethical Studies*, p. 203. [2] *Ibid.* p. 204. [3] *Ibid.* p. 214.

perfection of which lies our salvation; therefore the peace, power and joy of the good will perfectly realised remains for ever beyond our reach:

> Our self is not a harmony, our desires are not fully identified with the ideal, and the ideal does not always bring peace in its train. In our heart it clashes with itself, and desires we cannot exterminate clash with our good will, and, however much we improve (if we do improve), we never are perfect, we never are a harmony, a system, as our true idea is, and as it calls upon us to be.[1]

And this ceaseless conflict within ourselves between the good will and the bad points to the second fatal limitation of the exclusively moral view. This is that the life of man, while it remains confined to the moral sphere, is a continual process, a continual 'coming-to-be', knowing no ultimate end within itself in which it can reach the perfection of 'being'. And since whatever is by its nature always in process, always in a condition of 'becoming', is in the Bradleian view (as in the Platonic) *ipso facto* incomplete, imperfect, self-contradictory, the moral life as such is incapable of achieving either self-completeness or self-consistency; and this is its ultimate metaphysical defect. 'Morality does involve a contradiction: it does tell you to realize that which never can be realized, and which, if realized, does efface itself as such.'[2]

These, as Bradley sees them, are the irremediable difficulties inherent in an exclusively moral view of the life of man. The question is now, How, if at all, is the moral life, the life of man under the aspect of the will, to be rendered complete and perfect and free of self-contradiction? How are the inherent gaps in the exclusively moral view to be supplied, its defects to be eliminated? The answer has already been anticipated in *Ethical Studies* before we reach the Concluding Remarks; and it is there that Bradley embarks upon his analysis of the religious consciousness in an effort to show that it is the religious view, and this alone, that can supply the defects of the exclusively moral view.

[1] *Ethical Studies*, p. 232.

[2] *Ibid*. p. 234.

It is worth pausing briefly over some of the anticipations of the Concluding Remarks in the earlier parts of *Ethical Studies*, for they point directly to the grand thesis concerning the inescapable necessity of completing the moral view with the religious. One of the most important of these anticipations occurs in the very definition of 'self-realisation'. Though the realisation of the self as such has been postulated as the end of the moral life, yet the loss of self in a larger whole is constantly emphasised as the means of achieving this end. The idea that personal salvation, individual self-realisation, can only be achieved by membership of a whole, by participation in and sharing of the larger life of a larger whole, is repeatedly touched on in the Essays, and is, of course, the central theme of 'My Station and its Duties'. And, in pursuing this idea, Bradley even reaches the crucial point of asking whether this community of which the individual must seek a saving membership can be a *visible* community at all; for if it can only be one that lies outside and beyond the world of sense, then (Bradley claims) we pass immediately out of the moral realm into the religious, since 'morality on its own ground knows nothing of a universal and invisible self, *in which all members are real, which they realize in their own gifts and graces, and in realizing which they realize the other members*'.[1]

The God of Christianity is presently to be named; but it is hardly necessary to have God, Christ and the Church mentioned by name in order to see that what is said here about a universal and invisible self is a restatement, broadly Humanist in character, of the doctrine of the Mystical Body of Christ, into which those who have received the sacrament of baptism are metaphysically incorporated to 'realise' themselves by losing themselves. The first explicit reference to Christianity and God is made in the discussion of the good will and the bad when Bradley intimates that the perfect realisation of the good will, which is the perfection of morality, is, of course, possible 'if religion, and more particularly

[1] *Ethical Studies*, p. 222n.

Christianity be brought in'. It then becomes possible (he argues) because the good will then becomes identified with God's will, which is itself perfect goodness:

> The ideal here is a universal, because it is God's will, and because it therefore is the will of an organic unity, present though unseen, which is the one life of its many members, which is real in them, and in which they are real; and in which, through faith for them, and for God we do not know how, the bad self is unreal. But all this lies beyond morality: my mere moral consciousness knows nothing whatever about it.[1]

From this it is clear that Bradley recognises, as explicitly as may be wished, an order of goodness and power that transcends the merely moral order; and with so much already given, one turns with a special keenness of interest to the Concluding Remarks, in which this transcendent order is to be more fully defined and its relation to the moral explained.

In view of the expectations raised by what has gone before, the Concluding Remarks are more than a trifle disappointing. One must not indeed ask for more than Bradley has promised: he has been careful to say that they are to be merely tentative and suggestive and not to be taken for a full account of the matter. Nevertheless, even for the most tentative and suggestive of conclusions, they seem excessively inconclusive, and in point of tone and emphasis surprisingly indecisive; and since all this is relevant to the kind and quality of Bradley's Humanism, it is necessary to examine it more closely.

First, however, it has to be established that Bradley's position, whatever its Humanist character may be, is at any rate not Christian. The evidences for this are simple and conclusive. First, he does not believe in the supernatural or in revelation. In a passage betraying a quality of impatience unusual in him, he remarks that 'the notion that full-fledged moral ideas fell down from heaven is contrary to all the facts'.[2] Second, with reference specifically to the Christian religion,

[1] *Ethical Studies*, p. 231.

[2] *Ibid.* p. 190.

he shows no interest at all in its Founder and certainly does not believe in him as the Son of God; in the whole of *Ethical Studies* there is only one reference to Christ, and that is not even quite respectful. Third, his discussion of the sacraments of the historic Church is thoroughly un-Christian in spirit, and it is significant that he should refer to them as its *cultus*—an anthropological term that no serious Christian would use, and some serious Humanists would also prefer not to use or to see used. Finally, concerning God himself: though Bradley, as we have seen, uses the term without embarrassment, yet it is always the *idea* of God and the *meaning* of the idea of God that he is speaking about, not God as the Divine Creator, the Heavenly Father, the First Person of the Trinity; not, again, as Christians speak about God. So Bradley's analysis of the religious consciousness in *Ethical Studies* is distinctly not a Christian one; and it now remains to ask how it is Humanist and what is the quality of its Humanism.

The Concluding Remarks start off in Bradley's best polemical style with an unfair but very brilliant attack on Arnold's definition of religion as 'morality touched by emotion', and pass on to deal, still less fairly, with Arnold's definition of the God of the Old Testament as 'the Eternal-not-ourselves-which-makes-for-righteousness'. The energy and skill of the attack raise one's expectations still further; a man who appears to know so well what is wrong must surely, one feels, know also what is right, and must be able to articulate what he knows with the clarity and assurance of knowledge securely possessed.

It is precisely in this, however, that our expectations are disappointed. Bradley's grasp seems to falter as he embarks at last upon his analysis of the religious consciousness. His phraseology becomes unexpectedly awkward, even clumsy; there is a conspicuous drop in the level of discrimination; and a sudden uncharacteristic uncertainty in his sense of the relative importance of problems, his sense of relevance, and even of mere propriety.

This is not to say that the Concluding Remarks do not contain much that is true, even profoundly true, about religion. For instance, Bradley is at pains to affirm the central importance of 'practice' in the truly religious life, meaning the active living, or living out, of one's faith as the vital test of the reality of one's possession of that faith.[1] No one would deny the importance of practice in this sense for the religious consciousness; it is indeed important, and it no doubt needs to be affirmed with emphasis. Yet (one asks oneself) does it need to be affirmed with quite so *much* emphasis as in the Concluding Remarks? Bradley keeps on coming back to this point about the practice of one's faith as the vital test of its reality; and one feels presently that it is perhaps a trifle obvious to receive quite so much attention from a mind of the order of Bradley's conducting a discussion at this level.

Again, he takes issue at some length with the aesthetic religiosity of the type made fashionable by Walter Pater and his disciples, which Bradley very properly deplores, and dismisses as not religious at all. Such a worship, he says, (as Marius the Epicurean's, one must suppose) 'loses the character of religion, and is often even positively sinful, a hollow mockery of the divine, which takes the enjoyment without giving the activity, and degenerates into what may be well enough as aesthetic and contemplative, but, for all that, is both irreligious and immoral'.[2] This, again, is true; it is thoroughly worth saying; and it has besides a special relevance to the state of religion at the time when *Ethical Studies* was written. But it is *not* one of the central problems for the religious consciousness, and as such does not, one feels again, merit all the attention that Bradley gives it.

These are instances of what one may call Bradley's errors in proportion in the Concluding Remarks, which already diminish their value as a Humanist critique of historic Christianity. But they are trifling compared to the main weakness in Bradley's treatment of the religious consciousness, in his dis-

[1] *Ethical Studies*, pp. 329–30. [2] *Ibid.* p. 338.

cussion of the cultus of religion, that is, the sacramental offices and practices of the Church. Bradley appears indeed to attach the highest value and importance to this cultus; and though his analysis is conducted on Humanist premises, no Christian, one feels, could object (for instance) to the suggestion that 'the cultus is a means to the strengthening of faith, and is an end in itself by subserving that end'.[1] There are other general statements of this kind, equally accurate and acceptable. But it is precisely the generality that is the trouble. There can be no doubt that Bradley has in mind a specific religion, the Christian, when he is setting out his analysis—or *rationale*, as he calls it—of the religious cultus. Yet his analysis is so general, so abstract, that it succeeds only in draining away the specifically Christian character of the institutions and practices he is analysing; and the result is significantly different from Matthew Arnold's reinterpretations of the Christian sacraments in *Literature and Dogma*. Arnold's were as concrete and specific as Bradley's are general and abstract; and the difference is decisive for the relative value of Arnold's Humanist critique of Christianity and Bradley's.

This no doubt is the difference between a distinguished professional philosopher like Bradley and a vulgar literary man like Matthew Arnold (who, Mr Eliot has said, was so lamentably deficient in the right kind of philosophical training): the first can offer nothing beyond a *rationale*, which gives a generalised approval to religious cultuses as such but leaves the plain Humanist without an answer to his plain question, What specifically must he believe and what specifically must he do in order that he may be saved? For (he may well feel) if he cannot be a member of the historic Church and cannot participate in the specific cultus of that historic Church, it profits him nothing to know its *rationale*.[2]

[1] *Ibid.* p. 339.

[2] It is not irrelevant, or unfair, to add that there is a chilly remoteness about Bradley's treatment of this vital matter, a certain detachment of the wrong kind, that leaves one wondering whether he understood, in a really inward way, the central importance of sacramental practice in the religious life.

All these weaknesses of Bradley's account of religious experience in the Concluding Remarks can, I believe, be referred back to a single fundamental error, which vitiates Bradley's whole moral doctrine in *Ethical Studies*, and particularly in its Humanist aspect. His very definition of morality as the life of man viewed *sub specie voluntatis*, under the aspect of the will, is (I want to suggest) a fatally limited and limiting definition of the moral life, the source of all that is unsatisfactory in Bradley's analysis of the moral consciousness and the religious consciousness and therefore in his whole ethical system.

Is this not (one asks oneself) a strangely arbitrary definition of morality? Why *sub specie voluntatis*? Why this emphasis upon the will as the source of the moral activity and the defining feature of the moral life? Why not instead love? May not, indeed *ought* not, the moral life of man to be defined, not as the life of man *sub specie voluntatis* but as the life of man *sub specie amoris*, under the aspect of love?

It may justly be asked whether there are any legitimate grounds for urging this view upon Bradley other than the bare claim for its truth. The answer is that there are the best grounds in the interests of his own doctrine; for that doctrine would be seen to gain everything in self-completeness and self-coherence if love were substituted for the will as the spring of all vital moral activity and the defining feature of the moral life. To begin with, the awkward doctrine of self-realisation would immediately be eliminated, and with it all the insuperable difficulties that Bradley himself had seen to be inherent in it. If love is substituted for the will, the end of moral activity can no longer be defined as self-realisation, not even the realisation of the 'good self' or the 'good will', but becomes, simply, the fulfilment of the law of love. Self-realisation or the perfection of the good will may indeed follow *as a consequence* of the fulfilment of the law of love; but it is no longer the defining end of the moral activity. Similarly, Bradley's lengthy analysis of the pleasure principle, valuable though it is, becomes superfluous; and all the false doctrines that he is at such pains to discredit—duty for duty's sake, pleasure for pleasure's sake, the antithesis between selfishness and self-sacrifice, the errors of the determinist account of moral responsibility—can be dismissed very much more rapidly and economically when love and not the will is postulated as the ultimate source of the moral activity.

But, above all, what is eliminated is the discontinuity between the moral realm and the religious, which—in spite of his effort to bridge the gap by the Pauline doctrine of transcendence by incorporation—Bradley does in the end have to postulate. This discontinuity is annihilated when the moral life is seen to be the life of man under the aspect of love. For then, having from the start taken the most comprehensive view of morality that is possible, there can be no question of having to supersede it by something more comprehensive. The question of supersession and transcendence arises only when the moral life is viewed under the limited and limiting aspect of the will; enlarge our definition, and by the same stroke we remove the limitation that made the transcendence necessary. On the view I am recommending, there need be, indeed there *can* be, no discontinuity; for both morality and religion—what Bradley has to distinguish as morality on the one hand and religion on the other—have been brought under the single aspect or category of love.

But here the question arises again, and more insistently than before: On what grounds do I urge a view that abolishes the very discontinuity between the moral realm and the religious that most of the great religions (and the Christian in particular) have always postulated as inescapably necessary? And on what grounds do I urge that Bradley could, might, or should have held this view?

The answer to the first part of the question is that the Christian, in so far as he is a Christian, must of course affirm the discontinuity of the moral realm with the religious, because he believes that the gospel of love was given to men by supernatural means: brought by God Himself in the shape of a man, inscribed in the tables of men's hearts by the preaching of Jesus and his final sacrificial death, and sustained in the hearts of men ever since by the grace of God in the shape of the Holy Spirit. And because love came by supernatural means, because its source (as Christians say) is divine, not natural, *therefore* there is a discontinuity.

The degree of this acknowledged discontinuity will not indeed be the same for all Christians. The break will be very sharp for those who believe in the total depravity of human nature since the Fall, and insist therefore that salvation depends wholly upon grace and not at all upon 'nature'; whereas it will be less sharp for the Latitudinarian whose tendency is to see the revealed as a divine confirmation of what is already there in nature. But the Christian, as he is a Christian, must acknowledge a discontinuity, which may be more or less sharp but is always absolute, between the human realm and the divine—between reason and faith, nature and grace, the moral life of man and the religious.

The Humanist need acknowledge no such discontinuity. Indeed, if he has understood deeply enough the foundations of his own positive faith, he will discover that he positively may not acknowledge it. For although he believes absolutely in an order of values transcending in permanence, dignity and power the inferior, perishable values of the world, he does not believe that it lies beyond, but only within, the human or natural realm. Therefore love, the supreme value of this transcendent order of values, also lies only within the human realm; therefore it has not (in the Christian sense) a divine, but only a human, source. And since love is the supreme redeeming power in the life of man, and since the life of man is, on this view, confined wholly to the human realm, therefore love redeems man at once and without break in his moral *and* religious nature.

This is how the Humanist position abolishes the discontinuity postulated by historic Christianity. And (to answer our second question) Bradley's position is tending to just such a Humanist position as I have described. He does believe in the redemptive power of love (the last passage of *Ethical Studies* declares this with the fullest emphasis), and he does not believe in revelation or in Christ as the Son of God. Therefore he cannot believe that the knowledge of love was brought into the consciousness of men by supernatural means; therefore it must be there in man by nature. And if it is there in man by nature, and is also the supreme redemptive power in human life, its claim to be the defining power of the moral life (which is now also the religious life) is established; and all that remains is to see this—that neither pleasure nor duty, nor self-sacrifice, nor the will, but only love is the defining power of the moral life. But this is what Bradley does not see; and for this reason his doctrine, besides being not at all Christian, is also incompletely and imperfectly Humanist.

The reason for this last defection in Bradley would be interesting to enquire into. His personal temper no doubt had something to do with it. In *Appearance and Reality* he tells us that he abhorred the thought of appearing in the role of 'a teacher or preacher'; and since nothing could have forced him to assume this embarrassing role so much as the recognition and proclamation of the central place of love in the moral life, one may suppose that this was one reason for consigning it to the religious realm where it could be taken care of by the preachers. Yet, as I have tried to show, it was logically necessary that Bradley should affirm what his whole Humanist system was inviting, urging and pressing him to affirm, that the exercise of love and not the exercise of the will was the defining power of the moral life. It was necessary that he should affirm it even if he did it clumsily and imperfectly, and made a fool of himself by appearing in the role of a teacher and a preacher. For it goes without saying that one will do it clumsily and imperfectly; one is not oneself the Son of God and therefore has not the power to speak the Word in the way in which only the Son of God can speak it. But speak the

Word one must when one knows what the Word is that must be spoken; and because Bradley, knowing and partly knowing, did not speak it, he remains an imperfect Humanist, and his ethical system a Humanist system radically flawed.

In D. H. Lawrence, the last of the writers I have chosen to represent the Humanist tradition, we reach a modern moralist who did attempt to speak the Word. He spoke it clumsily and imperfectly, often indeed vulgarly and grossly; but he did attempt to declare what he knew, that the Word is love and the moral life of man the whole of man's life viewed *sub specie amoris*.

CHAPTER X

MESSIANIC HUMANISM

D. H. LAWRENCE'S 'THE MAN WHO DIED'

At the end of my discussion of *Literature and Dogma*, Matthew Arnold's contribution to the modern Humanist enterprise, I suggested that there were omissions and weaknesses in Arnold's attempt at a constructive critique of historic Christianity that it was important not to ignore or minimise. These may be most conveniently considered in the light of what Arnold believed himself to have achieved in *Literature and Dogma*. Arnold believed that in *Literature and Dogma* he had restated the Christian position in such a way as to involve no loss of any essential part of the Christian faith as the Christian himself professes and practises it; and it seemed to him therefore that there could be no serious obstacle to the Christian's accepting it, whether he was as theologically minded a Christian as the Bishops of Winchester and Gloucester or as innocent of theological preconceptions as 'the masses'. But in this Arnold was doubly mistaken: first, in supposing that the Christian could accept such an account of Christianity and still remain a Christian in the proper historic sense of the word; second, in assuming that he had in fact restated the whole in such a way as to involve no serious loss of any part of a practising Christian's faith. We are here concerned only with the second error; for Arnold's account of Christianity on Humanist premises is in fact incomplete; and the first of his serious omissions concerns the place of the Church in the religious life.

In *Culture and Anarchy* and elsewhere Arnold has much to say about 'the beauty and power of the historic Church'; but in *Literature and Dogma* he does not, one feels, allow to the

Church the importance it has in the religious life. For the Christian, the Church as the Mystical Body of Christ of which he becomes a living member by the sacrament of his baptism is, of course, of central importance. But taking it even on Arnold's premises, as representing the communal aspect of the religious life, it has all the importance of being the material expression of a profound spiritual truth: that our salvation, as St Paul said, is in the *fellowship* of the spirit, not to be sought by the individual, singly and separately, through his individual relationship with the Eternal-not-ourselves-that-makes-for-righteousness, but in community—in an organic membership of an institution which is the visible symbol of the invisible Source of all righteousness. This is, or ought to be, the proper Christian-Humanist view of the institution called the Church; and Arnold's failure to give due prominence to it was perhaps a Protestant lapse which is not consistent with his more Catholic recognition of 'the beauty and power of the historic Church'.

Another important omission in the doctrine of *Literature and Dogma*, closely linked with this, bears upon the question of prayer and worship, in particular worship. Arnold, it will be remembered, singled out as a special object of the anger and scorn he directed against the 'dogma' of the Bishops of Gloucester and Winchester their definition of God as a 'Personal First Cause'. Now it is very likely that what the Bishops meant by a Personal First Cause was something very abstract and remote and deistical, and as different as possible from the God who spoke to Moses out of the burning bush and sent his only begotten Son to redeem the world; and if the Personal God of Judaism and Christianity had in fact been reduced in this way to a more or less empty formula, Arnold had cause, in his time and place, to speak as he did with ridicule and impatience.

Nevertheless, the corrupt or debilitated form of an idea is, we know, never an argument against the idea itself; and a Personal God is more than a central idea of the Christian faith. The experience of a God who is a Person, in a sense not easily defined yet not for that reason less certainly known, with whom an intimate personal communion is possible to those who believe in Him, is essential to the whole Christian experience; and to those Christians who have known it, it is the most precious part of their faith, without which all the rest would be meaningless and worthless. It is this experience which for the Christian makes worship possible; for him worship simply does not make sense *unless* it is the worship of a Supreme Person. The same is true of prayer: this, too, makes no sense for the Christian if it is not addressed to a God who is, in a sense however mysterious and elusive, a Person. Accordingly, when such a Christian learns from Arnold that God is not a Person but an Eternal-not-ourselves-that-makes-for-righteousness, he has a right to feel that such a God, whatever else he may be, cannot be a proper object of his worship and prayer. An Eternal-not-ourselves (he may well argue) is no more conceivable as an object of worship and prayer than Plato's Form of the Good; and since the Christian must be supposed to know what he can and cannot conceive of as an object of his worship and prayer, Arnold's definition of God cannot be acceptable to him.

This is not to say that worship and prayer have no place in the Humanist scheme of salvation. Arnold's own account of prayer may not be complete, but—like almost everything else in *Literature and Dogma*—it is a splendid approximation to a complete Humanist definition. 'All good and beneficial prayer', he says, 'is in truth, however men may describe it, at bottom nothing else than an energy of aspiration towards the Eternal-*not-ourselves*-that-makes-for-righteousness—of aspiration towards it, and co-operation with it. Nothing, therefore, can be more efficacious, more right, and more real.'[1] As for Christian worship, that which for the Humanist is most closely akin to this is what may be called the experience of *rejoicing*. To be capable of rejoicing, with the passion and

[1] Arnold, *Literature and Dogma*, ch. I, sect. 4, p. 43n.

freedom of the author of the Psalms, in the beauty of the world and the greatness of the human spirit, in the power of men to give love and to receive it, in their power to serve one another in this fellowship of love, and in the redemptive power of love itself, may prove to be as real and full a *religious* experience to the Humanist as worship of a Supreme Person is to the Christian. But precisely because it does not postulate a Supreme Person, it would no more be the same as the Christian's experience of worship than Arnold's conception of prayer is the same as the Christian's; and this is another important point in which Arnold, in view of the claim he wishes to make for the doctrine of *Literature and Dogma*, appears to have minimised the difficulties of substituting an Eternal-not-ourselves-which-makes-for-righteousness for the Personal God of historic Christianity.

The point, however, in which Arnold's doctrine is most seriously incomplete (though not, in this instance, culpably so) is that in which modern Humanism has still most to do: in its interpretation of the life and character of Jesus himself. I mentioned earlier that a Humanism that is to have any claim to be called religious must take Christ very seriously; and I would now add that it is the main task of the true Humanism in its present phase to fix its attention upon Christ, and seek to give a complete and cogent account on Humanist premises of the life, character and mission of this man who called himself the Son of God, who possessed a unique knowledge of the saving power of love, proclaimed it with a unique authority, and by a unique act affirmed its imperishable truth.

For the religious Humanist shares with the Christian this certainty of the uniqueness of Christ's gospel. This is what sets him apart from those scientific, naturalistic, anthropological and sociological Humanists who never exactly deny the uniqueness of Christ's gospel and certainly never affirm it, but choose instead to take refuge in that twilight region between affirmation and denial whose contemporary name is comparative religion, where the talk is only about fertility rites and moon-goddesses and the influence of this cult upon that and the parallels between one thing and another, until the need to affirm or deny anything at all about the saving power of Christ's gospel is made, by this competent method, to appear gratuitous and foolish. But what is gratuitous and foolish to the scientific and anthropological Humanist is not so to the religious Humanist; who, believing with the Christian that Christ's gospel of love is a unique instrument of salvation, finds himself obliged to answer the question, What was Jesus of Nazareth if he was not the Son of God?

There is a splendid passage in one of Professor C. S. Lewis's works, *The Problem of Pain*, which the Humanist might well take as a direct challenge:

> There was a man born among [the] Jews who claimed to be, or to be the son of, or to be 'one with', the Something which is at once the awful haunter of nature and the giver of the moral law. The claim is so shocking—a paradox, and even a horror, which we may easily be lulled into taking too lightly—that only two views of this man are possible. Either he was a raving lunatic of an unusually abominable type, or else He was, and is, precisely what He said. There is no middle way. If the records make the first hypothesis unacceptable, you must submit to the second. And if you do that, all else that is claimed by Christians becomes credible—that this Man, having been killed, was yet alive, and that His death, in some manner incomprehensible to human thought, has effected a real change in our relations to the 'awful' and 'righteous' Lord, and a change in our favour.[1]

The crux of the challenge is in the alternatives that Professor Lewis sets before us; and (he adds) 'there is no middle way', to make it quite plain that he believes these alternatives to be exhaustive. But this is what logicians call a false disjunction, meaning by this the postulating of two alternatives as exhaustive when they are not so at all. There *may* be another way (whether it is a 'middle way' between Professor Lewis's alternatives need not be decided); the

[1] C. S. Lewis, *The Problem of Pain* (1940), pp. 11–12.

Humanist believes that there *is* such another way of interpreting the life and mission of the man Jesus—namely, that suggested but not completed by Matthew Arnold in *Literature and Dogma*.

On this view, Jesus was neither a raving lunatic nor the Son of God in the sense in which the Church interprets this claim, but the greatest of the Jewish prophets. He was the greatest moral and religious teacher in the greatest religious tradition that the human race has yet produced; and he was so *much* the greatest of its teachers, transcending by so much his predecessors, as to be, in a proper sense of the word, unique. For it was he alone who discovered the law of love that lay hidden in the old Mosaic Law of his fathers; it was he alone who discerned that this was the law by which the world was to be redeemed; who discerned also, with a unique insight, that the gospel of love was to be preached for the salvation of the world by the man who could fulfil the Messianic vision of Isaiah, the ideal of the Stricken Servant of God, as Arnold calls it; and who, following this insight, uniquely conformed his life and death to that ideal, with results unprecedented in the spiritual history of the human race.

This, in outline, is the third alternative between Professor Lewis's extremes; this is what the 'divinity' of Christ means to the Humanist—the power to know, with unique certainty, the redemptive power of love, to proclaim it with unique authority, and to accept a terrible sacrificial death as the price to be paid for giving it into the possession of the world to the end of time; and this, to the Humanist, is all that it *needs* to mean to explain the greatness of the man Jesus Christ without loss of any vital element of that greatness. It is not indeed the whole Humanist account of the life and mission of Christ: its completion remains the main task of the Humanist critique of historic Christianity, and the only thing certain about it is that it will not be the work of one man or of one generation of men. But even as far as it goes, it goes further than Matthew Arnold took it in *Literature and Dogma*; and it was my first purpose in speaking about it here to suggest the lines upon which this particular reinterpretation might be developed and completed.

Arnold's, however, is only one direction in which this great task is to be pursued. Another, totally different and much more radical, is taken by D. H. Lawrence in his story, *The Man Who Died.* Lawrence's interpretation of the life and mission of Jesus Christ turns upon a bold and startling suggestion, which is either profoundly true or wildly and blasphemously false: that the gospel of love preached by the man who died was in a certain vital respect defective; that this was so because his own most intimate experience of the redeeming power of love was in that same respect defective: that his gospel, therefore, was not and could not be fully redemptive; and that the man who died was therefore not the true Saviour of mankind. Taking this hypothesis as his starting-point, Lawrence pursues its implications in his extraordinary fable, which deals specifically with the resurrection of the man who died. It is, in its bare outline, very simple. The man who died rises from the tomb and returns to the world; there possesses himself of the one piece of saving knowledge he was previously without; and by this means completes his gospel of love and renders it at last wholly redemptive.

Before proceeding to a fuller discussion of Lawrence's fable, it is necessary to correct a common misconception about its main intention. It is not intended to be, as some readers have thought, a rewriting of the Gospel story of the Resurrection using the materials and methods of modern anthropology—the kind of enterprise that has become familiar in this century since the appearance of *The Golden Bough,* and of which a recent and especially ambitious instance was *The Nazarene Gospel Restored* by Robert Graves and Joshua Podro. Lawrence's story, though it does draw upon some of the less abstruse discoveries of modern comparative religion, does not belong with this kind of reinterpretation. It is a strictly imaginative statement of an imaginative possibility: what the resurrection of the man who died *might* have been, what it *might* have meant, if the imaginative possibility set out in the fable had been realised, if the man who died had in fact received that extension of his vital experience which is the story's crux. *The Man Who Died*, accordingly, is not to be taken as a literary exercise in applied anthropology, but as a product of the imagination of a man who, despite his many spots of commonness, possessed a developed moral and religious sensibility and the true prophetic temper, caring passionately about the salvation of the world and being in the highest degree serious in his treatment of moral and religious matters; and possessed also in an unusual degree the poet's gift, by which he could render his moral and religious ideas in the form of a fable exhibiting all the concreteness and immediacy distinctive of the poetic mode of apprehension.

The story tells first of the painful rising from the tomb; and Lawrence figures that agony of the body and the spirit as a form of nausea—a deep bitter nausea of disillusion, from the memory of the blood and nails on the Cross, from the stale, acrid flavours of the tomb:

> His face was banded with cold bands, his legs were bandaged together. Only his hands were loose.... He could move if he wanted: he knew that. But he had no want. Who would want to come back from the dead? A deep nausea stirred in him, at the premonition of movement:...the moving back into consciousness. He had not wished it. He had wanted to stay outside, in the place where even memory is stone dead.
> ...Yet suddenly his hands moved. They lifted up, cold, heavy and sore. Yet they lifted up, to drag away the cloth from his face, and push at the shoulder bands. Then they fell again, cold, heavy, numb, and sick with having moved even so much, unspeakably unwilling to move further.

But presently:

> With a wave of strength that came from revulsion, he leaned forward, in that narrow well of rock, and leaned frail hands on the

rock near the chinks of light.... Strength came from somewhere, from revulsion; there was a crash and a wave of light, and the dead man was crouching in his lair, facing the animal onrush of light.

Slowly, slowly, he crept down from the cell of rock, with the caution of the bitterly wounded. Bandages and linen and perfume fell away, and he crouched on the ground against the wall of rock, to recover oblivion.

To be back! To be back, after all that! He saw the linen swathing-bands fallen round his dead feet, and stooping, he picked them up, folded them, and laid them back in the rocky cavity from which he had emerged. Then he took the perfumed linen sheet wrapped it round him as a mantle, and turned away, to the wanness of the chill dawn.

He was alone; and having died, was even beyond loneliness.[1]

He meets a peasant on the road, who is pursuing an escaped cockerel. The peasant recognises him and is terrified. But the man who died reassures him, and the peasant offers to hide him in his house. The man says he will rest there, and goes with him.

He wakes at dawn, and watches for a while the peasant's young cockerel, asserting (in Lawrence's characteristic phrase) 'the everlasting resoluteness of life'; and as he watches, 'the destiny of life seemed more fierce and compulsive to him even than the destiny of death. The doom of death was a shadow compared to the raging destiny of life.' This is for him the first faint beginning of his resurrection from the dead.

Presently he goes forth to the tomb from which he had risen, and there he meets Mary Magdalene, weeping. He speaks to her, she recognises him, and falls at his feet to kiss them. But he stops her: 'Don't touch me, Madeleine.... Not yet! I am not yet healed and in touch with men.' They go aside among the bushes to speak unseen. She begs him to come back to them, but he refuses; and it is in the conversation with Magdalene that follows that we are made to understand why it is that the man who died is full of the bitter nausea of disillusion. 'My mission is over,' he says, 'and my teaching

[1] *The Man Who Died*, pp. 1099–1101.

is finished, and death has saved me from my own salvation.... Judas and the high priests saved me from my own salvation.' Magdalene asks him: 'Do you want to be alone henceforward? And was your mission nothing? Was it all untrue?'

> 'Nay!' he said. 'Neither were your lovers in the past nothing. They were much to you, but you took more than you gave. Then you came to me for salvation from your own excess. And I, in my mission, I too ran to excess. I gave more than I took, and that also is woe and vanity.'[1]

'I gave more than I took': that, we are to understand, was the falsehood at the heart of the gospel that the man who died had preached. And as he watches Magdalene, aching in all her being now to give more than she takes, the horror of that falsehood comes home to him, filling him with a fresh nausea of revulsion:

> [He] looked at her beautiful face which still was dense with excessive need for salvation from the woman she had been, the female who had caught men at her will. The cloud of necessity was on her, to be saved from the old, wilful Eve, who had embraced many men and taken more than she gave. Now the other doom was on her. She wanted to give without taking. And that too is hard and cruel to the warm body.[2]

And as this knowledge engulfs him, 'a revulsion from all the life he had known came over him again, the great nausea of disillusion, and the spear-thrust through his bowels. He crouched under the myrtle bushes, without strength.'[3]

What is it that is draining his strength? It is the sudden bitter knowledge that to give more than one takes is as destructive of life as to take more than one gives. There is a 'greed of giving' as there is a 'greed of taking'; and when giving becomes a greed for the total sacrifice or annihilation of the self, it is (Lawrence is saying) as thoroughly *erotic* as the greed of taking. The total sacrifice of self is always a sacrifice to Eros; and because in its essence erotic, therefore destruc-

[1] *The Man Who Died*, pp. 1107–8. [2] *Ibid.* p. 1108.
[3] *Ibid.* p. 1109.

tive. For compared with love (and this is the implicit ground of Lawrence's criticism), this giving without taking is too one-sided, too easy and too safe, involving none of the risks of a relationship of love. Love is in its essence reciprocal, a relationship of giving *and* taking, in the particular sense which Socrates appears to have understood so well in the *Symposium*. It is reciprocal in that it is based equally on penury and plenitude: on the need, the dependence, of each upon the other, which is their common penury; and upon that fullness of the loving heart that expresses itself in the adoration and the service of the other, which is the plenitude of love.

For this reason love is not easy, not safe, but full of risks. Its terror is as great as its glory: the crude mortal terror of loss, of total deprivation; and the subtler terrors of coldness, unkindness, misunderstanding—all the kinds and degrees of the last dreadful act of rejection by which the vital connexion that sustains the glory is broken. And the terror, like the glory, is intrinsic to the true relationship of love because love is based, equally and on both sides, on penury and plenitude, and subsists, equally and on both sides, by giving and taking.

If this, or something like this, is the true love, then the other, the self-sacrificial kind, that which (according to Lawrence) gives and gives without taking, does indeed stand exposed as false. Compared with the true love, it is indeed easy, safe and without risk. And when it becomes a greed from being 'carried to excess', it becomes a form of self-indulgence, an emotional luxury, which is not selfless at all but essentially self-centred, and as such a form of the power of darkness.

This—to return to the man who died speaking with Mary Magdalene in the myrtle bushes by the tomb—is what fills him with his bitter nausea of revulsion. If this is what it really is, this self-sacrificial love, this 'greed of giving without taking', it is indeed appalling to think what it makes of the gospel preached by the man who died. It makes his gospel a falsehood, and the man who died a false God. This is the knowledge that makes him crouch under the myrtle bushes without strength.

There is more to say about Lawrence's account of the gospel of selfless love preached by Jesus, and it will be taken up again in its place. For the present, the object is merely to present it with Lawrence's own emphasis, and to suggest that the conception of the true love implicit in his critique is essentially Humanist. How it differs from the Christian is not difficult to see. The Christian would readily acknowledge that Lawrence's account is a true, or at least a sufficient, account of human love, the love of one human being for another. For human beings, being human, are limited, weak, always in need, never self-sufficient; and so their love must necessarily subsist equally and on both sides upon penury and plenitude, upon the mutual need to take *and* to give. But this is not true of men's relationship of love with God. This is unique in that it subsists upon complete penury on one side and complete plenitude on the other. Man owes everything to God, but God owes nothing to man. God knows no penury, but only plenitude. God gives and gives but never takes, having no need to take; and man takes and takes, having nothing to give that God needs. And this, for the Christian, is the highest form of love that men can know. But for the Humanist who knows no God of this kind, the Christian relationship of love to God is intelligible, but not real. The Humanist can conceive it, but he cannot conceive it as real. For him, it is only a logical projection or idealisation of the human relationship of love, which is the only real form of love; and even as a projection or idealisation it is false. For it falsifies the human experience of love by postulating—to the Humanist, arbitrarily—a Supreme Person who knows no penury but only plenitude, who can give and give without taking, who can therefore demand of men that they shall take and take without giving, having nothing to give that this Supreme Person needs. Such a love (says the Humanist) bears no recognisable relation to the love that we do know to be real, the love between one human being and another. Indeed it violates that reality, is therefore false, and because so liable to become erotic in the sense already explained, dangerously and destructively false.

These are the grounds on which Lawrence repudiates the gospel of love of the man who died. The rest of the story is meant to supply what Christ's gospel lacked.

The man who died leaves Magdalene and goes back to the cottage of the peasants. There he remains some little while until his wounds have healed and he has begun to enjoy 'his immortality of being alive without fret'. He sets forth to wander the earth as a physician, 'because the power was still within him to heal any man or child who touched his compassion':

> I will wander the earth, and say nothing. For nothing is so marvellous as to be alone in the phenomenal world, which is raging, and yet apart. And I have not seen it, I was too much blinded by my confusion within it. Now I will wander among the stirrings of the phenomenal world, for it is the stirring of all things among themselves which leaves me purely alone.[1]

And there is another seminal thought stirring in the recesses of his mind: 'And perhaps one evening, I shall meet a woman who can lure my risen body, yet leave me my aloneness. For the body of my desire has died, and I am not in touch anywhere.'[2] Not being in touch anywhere, he is not yet risen.

His wanderings lead him, somewhere on the coast of Lebanon, to a grove of Mediterranean pine-trees and evergreen oaks, in which stands a temple. The temple is consecrated to the goddess Isis, Isis Bereaved, Isis in Search:

> The goddess, in painted marble, lifted her face and strode, one thigh forward through the frail fluting of her robe, in the anguish of bereavement and of search. She was looking for the fragments of the dead Osiris, dead and scattered asunder, dead, torn apart, and thrown in fragments over the wide world. And she must find his hands and his feet, his heart, his thighs, his head, his belly, she must

[1] *The Man Who Died*, p. 1113.

[2] *Ibid.* p. 1114.

gather him together and fold her arms round the re-assembled body till it became warm again, and roused to life, and could embrace her, and fecundate her womb. And the strange rapture and anguish of search went on through the years, as she lifted her throat, and her hollowed eyes looked inward, in the tormented ecstasy of seeking. . . . And through the years she found him bit by bit, heart and head and limbs and body. And yet she had not found the last reality, the final clue to him, that alone could bring him really back to her. For she was Isis of the subtle lotus, the womb which waits submerged and in the bud, waits for the touch of that other inward sun that streams its rays from the loins of the male Osiris.[1]

The temple of Isis Bereaved, Isis in Search, is tended by a young priestess. She had had the temple built when she was twenty years old, and had now for seven years been dedicated to the service of the goddess. Before she became the woman who served Isis, she had lived in the world, 'in Rome, in Ephesus, in Egypt'. Her father had been one of Antony's captains, and the young girl had known the great world governed by power and pleasure, by Caesar and Antony, and had been sought by these men. But she had found them wanting; they had left her alone, unroused. She had wondered why this should be so, and an old man, a philosopher, had one day explained it to her. 'Rare women', he had said, 'wait for the re-born man':

For the lotus. . . will not answer to all the bright heat of the sun. But she curves her dark hidden head in the depths, and stirs not. Till, in the night, one of these rare invisible suns that have been killed and shine no more, rises among the stars in unseen purple, and like the violet, sends its rare purple rays out into the night. To these the lotus stirs as to a caress, and rises upwards through the flood, and lifts up her bent head, and opens with an expansion such as no other flower knows, and spreads her sharp rays of bliss, and offers her soft, gold depths such as no other flower possesses, to the penetration of the flooding, violet-dark sun that has died and risen and makes no show. But for the golden brief day-suns of show such as Antony, and for the hard winter suns of power, such as Caesar, the lotus stirs not, nor will ever stir. Those will only tear open the bud. Ah, I tell you, wait for the re-born and wait for the bud to stir.[2]

[1] *The Man Who Died*, pp. 1118–19.

[2] *Ibid.* p. 1120.

So she has waited, and is still waiting when the man who died appears in her grove.

They first encounter each other watching, from opposite sides of the promontory upon which the temple stands, the act of sex of a slave boy upon a slave girl. It is performed quickly, furtively, in terror—'the blind frightened frenzy of a boy's first passion'. They turn away from it with indifference; this is not what either is seeking. The priestess goes to her temple to perform her rites, the man follows, and she finds him there on the steps of the temple. He asks for shelter, she says that she will send a slave to lead him to it, and goes away:

> Beautiful were her ivory feet, beneath the white tunic, and above the saffron mantle her dusky-blonde head bent as with endless musings. A woman entangled in her own dream.[1]

The slave presently comes to tell her that the stranger is a malefactor; he has seen the scars in the pale skin of his feet and in the palms of his hands as he lay asleep in his shelter. The priestess goes to look, gazes at the sleeping face, 'worn, hollow, and rather ugly', and, being a true priestess, discerns 'the other kind of beauty in it, the sheer stillness of the deeper life'. As she gazes, she finds that, for the first time, she is 'touched on the quick at the sight of a man, as if the tip of a fine flame of living had touched her'.[2] Then it comes to her that this was the lost Osiris: 'She felt it in the tip of her soul. And her agitation was intense.'

Towards sundown she goes to him and sits by him, watching the westering sun. She asks him directly, Is he not Osiris? And he replies, flushing suddenly: 'Yes, if thou wilt heal me. For the death aloofness is still upon me, and I cannot escape it.'[3] To himself he says when she is gone: 'I have risen naked and branded. But if I am naked enough for this contact, I have not died in vain.'[4] That night he goes with her into the temple, and there she heals him.

[1] *The Man Who Died*, p. 1121.
[2] *Ibid.* p. 1123.
[3] *Ibid.* p. 1126.
[4] *Ibid.* p. 1130.

The consummation in the temple is the climactic scene of the story, and is rendered in every detail with an extraordinary power, delicacy and beauty. The story ends within three pages of it. He stays with her a while longer; she conceives by him; and then he has to leave her because her mother is plotting to hand him over to the Roman soldiery.

> So he knew the time was come again for him to depart. He would go alone, with his destiny. Yet not alone, for her touch would be upon him, even as he left his touch on her. And invisible suns would go with him. . . . The man who died rowed slowly on with the current, and laughed to himself: 'I have sowed the seed of my life and my resurrection.'[1]

This is Lawrence's fable of the true Resurrection. It is profoundly stirring to the imagination of the modern Humanist, who feels himself obliged to grapple with the questions it raises. Is this a valid conception of the true Resurrection and the Second Coming, and therefore by implication a valid conception of the true Saviour of mankind? Or is it merely a fantasy, wildly extravagant and profane, springing from Lawrence's well-known doctrinal belief in the restorative powers of sexual love? And if it is valid, what are the grounds of that validity; and what is its importance for the emergent Humanism that I have been discussing?

These questions need to be answered if the place of Lawrence's story in the moral tradition I have called Humanist is to be established; and I propose to take them as a starting-point for the further discussion of the story. This will be ranged under three main heads. First, I want to consider what it is in the Christian attitude to sexual love that makes Lawrence's enterprise at least intelligible; and this will lead me to discuss certain passages in St Augustine's *The City of God* in illustration of the Christian attitude. Second, I want to indicate what seems to me to be the main weakness in Lawrence's understanding of the gospel preached by the man who died, and the effect of this gap in his understanding on

[1] *The Man Who Died*, pp. 1137–8.

the value of his story as a Humanist text. Third, I want to suggest in outline the way in which Lawrence's story would have to be corrected and amplified in order that it might express, more fully and completely, the Humanist conception of the Son of God, the true Saviour of mankind.

For my first topic, the Christian attitude to sexual love, I have taken St Augustine's account of *concupiscence* in the Fourteenth Book of *The City of God* as my main text because, being at once a peculiarly representative and peculiarly definitive statement of the Christian view, it seemed to me to satisfy better than any other text I know the special conditions of this enquiry. It is representative, first, in an *a priori* sense, in that it is the work of a writer who is universally recognised to have had a profound influence upon Christian thought and attitudes in the great formative period of the Church's history. But it is representative also in the sense that the Church's attitude to sexual love has, as a matter of empirical fact, always been, and remains to the present day, essentially Augustinian, as certain of its authoritative pronouncements clearly show. As for the definitiveness of Augustine's account: its great virtue is that its treatment of the subject is in the highest degree specific. It is a direct statement of the experience itself, based upon direct, first-hand knowledge; and it exhibits equally the poetic gift of rendering the 'felt' quality of the experience with the utmost particularity and the philosophic power to analyse the experience with precision and incisiveness. As such, it is probably unique in the whole range of Christian writing on this vital topic; and though the analysis is not complete (for reasons of 'modesty', as Augustine himself explains in the passage), it is vivid, powerful and subtle enough to serve admirably the purpose of this discussion.

The chapter in which the crucial passage occurs is entitled 'Of the evil of lust: how the name is general to many vices, but proper unto sexual concupiscence.' This is the passage:

Although...there be many lusts, yet when we read the word 'lust' alone, without mention of the object, we commonly take it for the unclean motion of the generative parts. For this holds sway in the whole body, moving the whole man, without and within, with such a mixture of mental emotion and carnal appetite that hence is the highest bodily pleasure of all produced: so that in the very moment of consummation, it overwhelms almost all the light and power of cogitation. And what wise and godly man is there who being married, and knowing, as the apostle says, 'how to possess his vessel in holiness and honour, and not in the lust of concupiscence, as the Gentiles do, which know not God', had not rather (if he could) beget his children without this lust, that his members might obey his mind in this act of propagation, as his other members in fulfilling their particular functions, and be ruled by his will, not compelled by concupiscence? But the lovers of these carnal delights themselves cannot have this emotion at their will, either in nuptial conjunctions, or wicked impurities. The motion will be sometimes importunate against the will, and sometimes immovable when it is desired, and being fervent in the mind, yet will be frozen in the body. Thus wondrously does this lust fail man, both in honest desire of generation, and in lascivious concupiscence; sometimes resisting the restraint of the whole mind, and sometimes opposing itself by being wholly in the mind and in no way in the body at the same time.[1] Justly [therefore] is man ashamed of this lust, and justly are those members (which lust moves or suppresses against our wills, as it lusts) called shameful.[2]

Augustine goes on to explain that man's subjection to this lust of concupiscence has been the direct result of the Fall; the disobedience of the flesh (as he puts it) was made a testimony to the disobedience of man: 'Without doubt therefore man's nature is justly ashamed of this act: for that disobedience, whereby the genital members are taken from the will's rule and given to lust's, is a plain demonstration of the reward that our first father had for his sin, and that ought to be most apparent in those parts, because thence is our nature derived which was so depraved by that his first offence.'[3] In two later chapters,[4] Augustine allows himself to speculate on the nature

[1] St Augustine, *The City of God*, bk. XIV, ch. 16 (Everyman ed., p. 47).
[2] *Ibid.* XIV. 17 (p. 47).
[3] *Ibid.* XIV. 20 (p. 51).
[4] *Ibid.* XIV. 24, XIV. 26 (pp. 54–5, 56–7).

of the act of generation before the Fall—how 'our first parents might have produced mankind without any shameful appetite', without 'concupiscential desire'. He dilates a little on the details of this prelapsarian kind of generation, and then stops because 'This theme is immodest,... [and] needs must our discourse hereupon rather yield to shamefacedness than trust to eloquence'.[1]

The details of Augustine's analysis of the act of sex in the passage on concupiscence are worth the closest attention; and perhaps the first thing to remark is that it is a marvellously accurate and vivid description of the act of sex when it *is* merely concupiscential. When there is not what Shakespeare called a marriage of true minds between a man and a woman, and therefore no bond of the heart and the mind to sustain the intimacy of the physical union; when the physical act is not the consummation of that union of hearts and minds but the bare biological act of sex, then it is exactly as Augustine says: 'The motion will be sometimes importunate against the will, and sometimes immovable when it is desired, and being fervent in the mind, yet will be frozen in the body.' As an analysis of the physical impotence actually experienced by the concupiscent man this is as brilliant as it is brief. For it is indeed often the case that the sexual passion when it is uninformed by love becomes purely mental or conceptual, and therefore incapable of being translated into act—'fervent in the mind yet frozen in the body'; and as such it is a form of that eroticism which is self-defeating and self-destructive.

If more extended confirmation of the accuracy of Augustine's analysis should be desired, it is to be discovered ready to hand in almost any modern Existentialist novel. *The Age of Reason* by Jean-Paul Sartre is an instance. There, exhibited in detail, in a succession of nightmare episodes, is the horror of bare concupiscence uninformed by love; there the act, each time, turns to dust and ashes in the very moment of consummation; and the wages of sin are paid in the form of a

[1] *Ibid.* xiv. 26 (p. 57).

spiritual death more terrible than any Augustine could conceive. On the other side, the best works of D. H. Lawrence are intent upon exposing the very concupiscence that Augustine speaks of—the falsity and corruptness of a sexual relation that is purely mental, self-conscious in the most opprobrious sense of the word, 'fervent *in the mind*', as Augustine says, and therefore 'frozen in the body'.

Lawrence's main effort, however, was to expose the false, corrupt forms of sexual love by celebrating it in its true and pure forms; and this, which is Lawrence's triumph, is Augustine's failure. Augustine in his account of concupiscence nowhere distinguishes between the moral quality of the sexual act when it is and when it is not informed by love. Indeed it is plain that, for Augustine, the sexual act is never anything but concupiscential. Love has no power to transform it in any significant way; there is no essential difference between the bare biological act of sex and the act of sex which is the physical consummation of a union of hearts and minds.

This is the fatal flaw in Augustine's analysis. But what is perhaps even more significant is that the failure to distinguish between one kind of sexual passion and another springs from a still more fundamental error, also to be discovered in the passage on concupiscence. This is Augustine's emphasis upon *the will* in his analysis of the act of sex. It is because in the sexual act the generative organs are 'compelled by concupiscence, not ruled by the will' that it is unclean; it is because 'in the very moment of consummation... [it] overwhelms all the light and power of cogitation' that it is to be accounted lust. But the emphasis is false: it is not the absence of control by 'the will' but the absence of love that turns the act of sex into something unclean. When the bond of love, the sanctifying tenderness of each for the other, is absent and there is present only a ravening appetite for possession, then indeed the act is unclean. But when the sense of a bond, intimate and indestructible, is present, generating the tenderness that draws them to their consummating union in the body, the act of consummation is thereby blessed and sanctified and has nothing of the unclean in it.

Then also that other aspect of the sexual act that Augustine finds so disturbing, that oblivion which the poets called the 'little death', the overwhelming of the will and the reason, need have no terror in it. The act of sex does indeed 'in the very moment of consummation overwhelm almost all the light and power of cogitation'. But when love is present, this is no cause for either fear or shame. For it is as certainly the mark of love completely and perfectly consummated between a man and a woman as is the oblivion of self that the religious mystic experiences in his consummating union with God. As in that so in this, the oblivion marks the loss of the self in something outside of and other than itself. Nor is it a losing of each self *in the other*: there is here no loss of identity, of essential selfhood; no 'merging' of the kind that Lawrence especially (and rightly) feared and hated. It is rather a losing of both selves in the sanctifying medium of their tenderness; and because this tenderness, though created and sustained by their love, is yet something outside of and other than themselves, to lose themselves in it is at once to find themselves and each other. The consummating oblivion in the act of sexual love is therefore thoughtless and wordless not because they have fallen away from 'reason', but because they have transcended it. It is as thoughtless and wordless as the oblivion that (according to the mystical writers) descends upon the soul in its final blessed union with God; and this is the true analogy of the act of sex when it is informed by perfect love: the light and power of cogitation are indeed put out, but by the greater light and power of love—not, as Augustine thought, by the darkness of the bestial appetite of concupiscence.

The transition from St Augustine's view of sexual love to that of the historic Church bristles with difficulties. To begin with, it is perhaps historically meaningless to speak of the Church's possessing a single view of sexual love; for its view in this (as in other matters) has not remained static but has changed a great deal since the patristic period, even more since the Reformation, and most of all since the beginning of this century. We have it on the authority, for instance, of a French canon of the Roman Catholic Church, Canon Jacques Leclercq, that even 'the sacramental quality of marriage' is a modern discovery. 'The full realization of the sacramental quality of marriage is certainly one of the achievements of the Church in the twentieth century', writes Canon Leclercq. '...Right down from the apostolic age it has been known that marriage is a sacrament, but this has been, as it were, buried in the consciousness of the Church; it has only been able to emerge gradually and it is only in our own days that it is opening out and fully blossoming in the light.'[1]

What is true of the institution of marriage may be equally true of sexual love itself, which the Church has always recognised as the natural foundation of the sacrament of marriage. It may well be the case that the nature of sexual love is at present receiving from the Church an attention more close and careful than at any other time in its history, and that its sacramental character too is about to receive the kind of recognition that would effectively nullify the Augustinian view. In that case, it would be no surprise if there existed at the present day wide differences of attitude in respect to sexual love between the various Christian Churches and between the various sections or 'parties' of a single communion such as, for instance, the Anglican. There is, besides, the usual margin of difference between the official view of a particular Church and the views of its individual members; and on this topic in particular the margin can be so wide that at least some of the pronouncements of 'liberal' Christians would seem to express an attitude scarcely distinguishable from that of the Humanist. The question of the Church's attitude to sexual love is thus full of difficulties, and not to be lightly embarked upon; indeed not to be embarked upon at all if, as

[1] Leclercq, *Marriage: A Great Sacrament* (1951), p. 11.

in the present instance, one's subject does not demand a full treatment.

What my subject demands is only that I should draw attention to the most fundamental and indisputable differences between the Humanist attitude and the Christian, in order to render intelligible the grounds of Lawrence's rejection of the Christian attitude in his story *The Man Who Died*; and for this purpose, the Christian attitude is sufficiently defined by certain authoritative documents of the historic Church, which continue to the present day to guide its doctrinal pronouncements and pastoral practices. The largest and most indisputable of these differences shows itself, I believe, the moment the Humanist affirms with Lawrence the *intrinsically* redemptive power of sexual love. When carnal love (as Christians call it) is not merely concupiscential in Augustine's sense, but springs from the tenderness that is antecedent to love and always presupposed by love, and is sustained by the true union of hearts and minds, then, says the Humanist, it is in itself redemptive.

This is what the Church denies. For the Church, sexual love is redemptive only under certain conditions; and these are set out in that portion of the Christian marriage-service which defines the three ends for which the sacrament of marriage was ordained, first, 'for procreation', second, 'as a remedy against concupiscence', third, 'for mutual society, help and comfort'.

To the Humanist none of these is a necessary condition of the redemptive power of sexual love. The first, procreation, being a natural and desirable consummation of the marriage of true minds and bodies, is always a natural and desirable *consequence* of the kind of sexual love that is truly redemptive. But it is never, for the Humanist, more than a consequence, never more than strictly extrinsic to that which, being already fully redemptive, cannot require procreation to render it redemptive—or, as Christians say, to sanctify it.

The second end of marriage, that it shall be a remedy against concupiscence, shows very clearly that the Church in its very marriage service endorses St Augustine's account of the physical side of sexual love. Whatever the views of individual Christians may be on this matter, and whatever the reservations with which particular communions may treat this clause of the marriage service,[1] the fact that the clause is there, firmly entrenched in the marriage service of the historic Churches, is enough to establish its official status. And what it expresses, very plainly, is the view that the physical side of sexual love is intrinsically bad—corrupt and corrupting, and for that reason (like some unpleasant disease) requiring a 'remedy', which is happily supplied by the institution of marriage. It is not necessary to pursue the full implications of this item in the Church's definition of the ends of marriage to see that it expresses an astonishingly low view of the physical basis of the marriage union; and because low, therefore false, and therefore to be repudiated as Lawrence repudiates it in the fable of *The Man Who Died.*[2]

As to the third end of marriage laid down by the Church, that it shall be for mutual society, help and comfort: this to the Humanist expresses again a strangely inadequate and unimaginative view of the finer possibilities of the marriage of true minds. To say this is neither to deny that such a marriage would indeed entail (among so much else) the giving of this mutual society, help and comfort, nor to minimise its value and

[1] I understand that the Church of England, for instance, will allow this clause to be omitted where there is a positive objection to it by communicants wishing to be married within the Church.

[2] If it should be argued (as Christians have argued) that this is not a low but a 'realistic' view of sexual passion, the Humanist will deny the realism both in the light of his own view of its redemptive power and by bringing the Church to witness against itself. For in respect to those forms of love which the Church does believe to be redemptive, like the *caritas* that Jesus preached, it takes a conspicuously unrealistic view. Indeed, it takes such an exalted view of the love it knows and understands as to have seemed to the irreligious in the past two thousand years hopelessly 'idealistic' or Utopian. In this the irreligious are wrong and the Church is right; and for that very reason the Church cannot consistently use the plea of 'realism' to defend its low view of sexual love as expressed in the definition of the second end of marriage. What the Humanist has to infer from the Church's false 'realism' in this connexion is that, as Lawrence's fable intimates, its *knowledge* of this kind of love is in a radical way defective.

importance. But, in the absence of any explicit recognition of the physical bond in which in marriage the desire to give and receive mutual society, help and comfort is grounded,[1] or any suggestion either that sexual passion is the pillar and ground of the sacrament of marriage or that this sexual passion, when it is love and not lust or mere concupiscence, is in itself redemptive, the formula remains desperately insufficient to express the more exalted possibilities of the marriage relationship.

For the Humanist, accordingly, sexual love is not and cannot be redemptive under the conditions laid down by the Church in its definition of the ends of marriage.[2] And for the Humanist of Lawrence's temper, one may imagine how his sense of the difference between his view of the redemptive power of sexual love and the Christian is intensified when he reads, for instance, the late Pope Pius XII's Encyclical on Holy Virginity, in which the virgin state is reaffirmed to be the highest and best state for the service of God. His Holiness, while praising and magnifying the state of marriage as equally blessed, nevertheless endorses St Augustine's view of the virgin state as a state of '*physical integrity*'; and it is this phrase that betrays the persistent Augustinian bias of the Church's attitude to the physical side of sexual love. For the Church, now as always, the act of sexual union necessarily involves a *loss* of 'integrity'; it is a form of dis-integration or corruption; concupiscential, after all, as St Augustine said, and for this reason to be eschewed by those who would wish to devote themselves to the service of God. And this view of the

[1] It is true that the carnal bond is mentioned later in the marriage-service, when the bridegroom says to the bride, 'With this ring I thee wed, *with my body I thee worship*, with all my worldly goods I thee endow.' But it is not unfair to suggest that this is the part of the marriage-bond that the Church takes least seriously, as its views on divorce and the remarriage of divorced persons, to be mentioned presently, clearly show.

[2] Since this was written, the report of the proceedings of the Lambeth Conference held in 1958 has been published, including its resolutions on 'The Family in Contemporary Society'. This contains a section entitled 'Theology of Sexuality and the Family' which, besides commanding attention on its own merits, has also the closest bearing on the subject of the preceding pages. I have accordingly set down some comments on this important document in Appendix C below.

superiority of the virgin state is confirmed by the full definition of the second end of marriage in the marriage service, which declares the sacrament of marriage to be ordained as 'a remedy against concupiscence and to avoid fornication, *that such persons as have not the gift of continency might marry and keep themselves undefiled members of Christ's body*'; which shows that the Church's understanding of the redemptive power of sexual love has not advanced a step beyond St Paul's in that least inspired part of First Corinthians where he grants with all his heart that it is better to marry than to burn, but urges those who have the gift of continency to be continent because that is the 'best state' for the service of God.[1]

Finally, to complete the evidence for the irreconcilable difference between the Christian and the Humanist views on sexual love, there is the attitude of the Church to divorce and remarriage. The Church not only countenances but positively insists on maintaining and preserving the kind of marriage which, for the Humanist, has ceased to be a marriage in any but a nominal, legalistic sense of the word; the kind of marriage from which the sanctifying medium of tenderness has perished, as it can and often does perish, irrecoverably; the kind of marriage-union, therefore, in which to the Humanist physical relations between a man and a woman are not only undesirable or inappropriate but grossly and indefensibly immoral. When the Humanist finds the Church nevertheless proclaiming the indestructible sacramental nature of such marriages, and insisting upon this with all the force of its marriage laws, by which such persons are forbidden to redeem their loss, to re-create the sanctifying medium of tenderness in a second union,

[1] It should perhaps be added that the Humanist's rejection of the Catholic view of the virgin state is not a rejection of sexual abstinence as such. Voluntary abstinence as a purely practical expedient in special circumstances, for the accomplishment of special tasks and for special types of people, may be necessary (though never desirable); and there would be no objection to the celibacy of the religious orders if this were the Church's ground for insisting upon it. The Church's ground, however, is not practical expediency, but (as we learn from the Papal Encyclical quoted above), the exaltation of virginity as the 'best state', and the explicit suggestion that sexual life is a falling-away from this most perfect of states; and it is this dogma that the Humanist takes issue with.

from which it need never perish, or, as in some communions, refused readmission to the Church when they have sought to redeem their loss by a second union; when by either expedient the Church makes it clear that it will not only countenance but positively insist upon maintaining and preserving a marriage-union that to the Humanist has fallen into squalor and deformity, it is evident that we have here still another way of measuring the distance between the Humanist conception of the redemptive power of sexual love and the Christian.[1]

[1] Christ's own pronouncements on marriage and divorce, upon which the historic Church claims to base its attitude, admit of an interpretation very different from that put upon them by the Church. The crucial statement, 'What God hath joined together, let no man put asunder' (Matt. xix. 6), made in reply to the question of the Pharisees, 'Is it lawful for a man to put away his wife for every cause?' (Matt. xix. 3), has been taken to express the view that a marriage sanctified by the Church is literally a bond (or bondage) that may in no circumstances be dissolved. But this, the Humanist suggests (following Matthew Arnold's example), may be altogether too literal a way of interpreting Christ's words. Having before him in his time the spectacle of a general laxity in sexual morals among Jews and Gentiles alike, and, among the Jews in particular, what would be called today a high incidence of divorce owing to the easy divorce law of the Pharisees (referred to in this very passage, Matt. xix. 7), what Christ is much more likely to have intended than an absolute prohibition of divorce is the injunction *to take the marriage bond and its responsibilities with the utmost seriousness*—to treat it as a solemn and sacred bond ('For this cause shall a man leave his father and mother, and shall cleave to his wife; and the twain shall become one flesh. So that they are no more twain, but one flesh', Matt. xix. 5–6), which is on no account to be dissolved on frivolous or arbitrary grounds, as the Pharisees were accustomed to do. This interpretation would seem to be confirmed by that other famous statement, bearing directly on divorce, 'Whosoever shall put away his wife, except for fornication, and shall marry another, committeth adultery: and he that marrieth her when she is put away committeth adultery' (Matt. xix. 9). The single legitimate ground for divorce is fornication, in the modern idiom, sexual promiscuity; and this shows again that the emphasis is on the immorality of a frivolous, irresponsible attitude to the sexual relation. It is not, as the modern divorce law has laid down, adultery—the isolated or sporadic lapse from sexual continence in marriage—that is sin; but fornication or sexual promiscuity, which degrades the marriage bond to the point of nullifying it, by degrading the sexual relation in which the sacrament of marriage is grounded.

To the Humanist, at any rate, there are only two possible views. If Christ did mean what the Church supposes him to have meant—if he could insist upon the literal indissolubility of a marriage in which the sexual relation, the 'natural' foundation of the sacrament of marriage, could no longer be sustained because the bond of love had perished from it—he was not the Son of an infinitely tender and merciful God; and if he was the Son of God, he could not have meant what the Church supposes him to have meant. The Humanist prefers to take the second view.

It is not my purpose to pursue these matters further than is necessary. My concern has been only to make it clear just how wide and irreconcilable is the difference between the Humanist and Christian conceptions of the nature and importance of sexual love, and to suggest how this makes intelligible the rejection of the Christian attitude by such a Humanist as D. H. Lawrence.

It can still be asked why Lawrence should have chosen to express his rejection of the Church's attitude to sexual love by means of a fable about the man who died. Why not, for instance, by a fable about the Church itself, as fabulists in the past have never hesitated to do? Why so deliberately about the historical Jesus? The reason is twofold: first, that Jesus, being the Founder of the Church, is the ultimate source of all Christian knowledge and experience; second, that the Church explicitly claims to derive its views on sexual love and marriage from its Founder. Consequently there is a logical and dramatic propriety both in holding Jesus responsible for the attitude of the historic Church and in referring this attitude back to Jesus' personal, individual experience and knowledge. And, from there, the main dramatic argument of Lawrence's story can be developed with the strictest consequentiality: if there is anywhere a gap in the Church's understanding of sexual love, it is there because there was the same gap in Jesus' understanding of it; if the loss is to be repaired for all men, it must first be repaired in the Redeemer himself.

To recognise this as the central argument of *The Man Who Died* is to recognise another profound (and very poignant) aspect of its religious meaning. It would seem that Lawrence had come to understand only at the end of his life[1] how strange and revolutionary his doctrine of the redemptive power of sexual love really was, how inaccessible to men (who always saw only as in a glass darkly, but could not be brought to see

[1] *The Man Who Died* was the last work he wrote, and was published posthumously.

face to face), and how it could therefore not be preached by a man born of woman but only by the man who died, who was God himself. It needed the true Redeemer, the true Son of God, to make the Word flesh, and to declare it in the unique accents and with the unique authority of God himself, in order that it might be made accessible to men for their salvation. And this is the last and perhaps most important reason why Lawrence's fable about the redemptive power of sexual love had to be centred upon The Man Who Died.

The main weakness of Lawrence's story is in his misunderstanding of certain vital aspects of the historic Jesus' character, personality and doctrine, in particular of the gospel of selfless love that Jesus preached. Lawrence reduces it, we remember, to 'the greed of giving without taking', and presents it as one of the subtler forms of eroticism. But in this he is guilty of the same kind of mis-analysis as we observed in St Augustine's treatment of concupiscence. As Augustine failed to distinguish between the sexual passion that is merely concupiscential and that which is informed and sustained by love, so Lawrence fails to distinguish between the selfless love that Jesus preached and its erotic corruption or perversion. This debased form of Christian love has always been recognised by Christians and non-Christians alike, and it hardly needed Lawrence's savage portrayals of the type exemplifying it, from the unfortunate Miriam in *Sons and Lovers* to Donna Carlota, the Christian wife in *The Plumed Serpent*, to convince us of its existence. But Lawrence cannot, or will not, see that this is the corruption of the real thing; and the reason is, one must suppose, that he did not believe in the reality of the real thing—the selfless love that has its whole soul fixed upon the object of its love, is concerned only to adore and serve the beloved (whether that beloved is God or another human being), and is so completely absorbed in its acts of worship and service that it is wholly unconscious of itself as performing those acts. This is what Jesus meant when he spoke about the loss of self ('he that loveth his life shall lose it, and he that hateth his life in this world shall keep it unto life eternal'), the total unconsciousness of self in the perfect exercise of love, by which the lover most completely finds at once his self and his truest happiness. Such a conception of selfless love excludes by definition that erotic satisfaction, that greed of giving, which Lawrence sees as the fatal taint in the love Jesus preached. How can it be a form of greed, of *self-centred* love, when its defining feature is its total unconsciousness of itself? Lawrence's insistence on its being tainted by greed or self-love is, I suggest, the most serious failure in his understanding of the doctrine of the man who died.

It is not perhaps surprising that Lawrence's understanding of the love Jesus preached should be so imperfect, since his own experience of it was so patently limited; and the main interest of this limitation is that it invades his understanding of the very sexual love that he does believe in as truly redemptive. *The Man Who Died* (along with *Lady Chatterley's Lover* and perhaps *The Woman Who Rode Away*) is most nearly free of that element of violent, destructive conflict, springing from the clash of incorrigibly self-centred natures, which in most of Lawrence's previous works, from *Sons and Lovers* to *The Plumed Serpent*, is treated as an essential and natural part of the sexual relation. It is there exalted in the name of various Lawrencian dogmas—the mystery of the difference of the sexes, the inviolate selfhood of the self, the passion for aloofness of the male self on the one side, for 'merging' and loss of self of the female on the other; but the religious mind will have no difficulty in recognising in these dogmas the features of fear, pride and self-love, but chiefly fear. For when, as in Lawrence, an extraordinary capacity for love (and need of love) is combined with as extraordinary a capacity to resist and resent the necessary condition of love, that to find one's self one must lose it, it is indeed inevitable that he should suffer perpetually from the fear of a total loss of identity in the act of loving, which seems to have haunted Lawrence all his life and is one of the central experiences repeatedly enacted in his novels and stories. There are signs in his later works of a gradual weakening of this obsessive fear, resulting in a corresponding weakening of the destructive element in the sexual relation and a strengthening of the kind of tenderness that drives out all fear, pride and self-love (Mellors, we remember, was the man 'who had the courage of his tenderness'); and *The Man Who Died* represents the most advanced point in Lawrence's development in this direction. But, even there, we still hear too much about the aloofness and aloneness of the man who died; too much also about the self-sufficiency, marked by her 'indifference', of the priestess of Isis (the guarantee, presumably, that she will not wish to cling to or merge with the risen Osiris); too much about his need, too little about hers; and, most particularly, we perceive that the man who died leaves at the end to enjoy the fruits of his resurrection alone. There, in that last seemingly trivial act, may be seen the ultimate imperfection of Lawrence's understanding of his own gospel of sexual love. He knows intimately its redemptive glory; but he does not, to the end, know how that glory is to be *sustained*. To put it in Christian terms: he knows the infinite, immutable, eternal Love in its creative power, in the aspect of God the Father; he knows it in its power to free us from the evils of our fallen condition (fear, greed, vanity and the rest), which is God in the aspect of the Son; but he does not know it in its power to sustain and perpetuate its sweetness and strength in those who have faith in it, which is God in the aspect of the Holy Spirit. And while there is this gap in Lawrence's understanding, his gospel remains powerless to annihilate the fatal defect in the very love he is preaching—the *transitoriness* of the glory belonging to it, which for many will remain the last unanswerable argument against its claim to be the supremely redemptive form of love. This argument, one must presume, can only be answered by demonstrating that the transitoriness is no part of sexual love perfected but only of our imperfect, unredeemed experience of it; and such a demonstration is perhaps reserved to be the decisive miracle of the unborn Saviour.

There are other flaws in Lawrence's portrayal of the man who died, which bear more directly on the character and personality of the historical Jesus. In one of the passages quoted earlier in this chapter,[1] Lawrence tells us how the man who died sets out to wander the earth and enjoy for the first time the phenomenal world. He is made to say to himself: '[Before this] *I have not seen it, I was too much blinded by my confusion within it.* Now I will wander among the stirrings of the phenomenal world, for it is the stirring of all things among themselves which leaves me purely alone.' The suggestion that the historic Jesus was blind to the phenomenal world, because he was too busy preaching his gospel to give himself a chance to see it, is flatly contradicted by the evidence of the Synoptic Gospels. If ever a man was in touch with the phenomenal world and never lost touch with it, that man was Jesus. If ever a man with a saving mission, preaching strange, revolutionary doctrines, felt himself intimately at one with the natural world, and constantly affirmed, in the natural imagery in which his parables abound, his sense of the organic continuity of the human world with the natural, such a man again was Jesus. If Lawrence missed these literary evidences, he missed them no doubt because he was blinded by the preconceived notion that a man with a saving mission *must* be so tied up in his preaching as to be bound not to see the phenomenal world. But since this is not true of the historical Jesus, Lawrence by insisting on it falsifies Jesus' character and personality, and correspondingly damages the truth of his dramatic rendering.

The persuasiveness of Lawrence's fable is further reduced by certain familiar features of his style. The jargon is much less insistently and obtrusively present in the *The Man Who Died* than in his other works of the same kind (*The Plumed*

[1] P. 267 above.

Serpent, for instance). But there is enough left to cause distress: the tiresome recurrence, for instance, of the pet epithets ('subtle', 'strange', 'soft', 'sensitive' and the rest); the insistent repetitiveness, intended for rhetorical emphasis but giving the effect of emotional bludgeoning; the fine sensuous perceptions too often ruined by cadences intolerably clumsy or banal; and the occasional turns of phrase as intrinsically vulgar as they are dramatically inappropriate. When, for instance, the man who died is made to say to himself 'And perhaps one evening I shall meet a woman who can lure my risen body, yet leave me my aloneness', one feels that the biological phrasing may be in harmony with Lawrence's personal style and that of the Lawrencians of the nineteen-twenties but is distinctly out of harmony with the personal style of the man who died.

If one takes the exalted view of Lawrence's story that I have proposed, that it ranks as a prophetic or quasi-scriptural work in the emergent Humanist tradition, these defects in his rendering of the gospel and personality of the man who died are clearly important. If, as I suggested, the most important part of Humanism's constructive critique of historic Christianity is the interpretation on Humanist premises of the character and mission of the man Jesus Christ, it is imperative that the interpretation set forth under the laws of poetic truth and poetic beauty in such a representative text as *The Man Who Died* should be valid. For if it is not valid, the story is impaired in its prophetic aspect and its value correspondingly diminished. The serious flaws in Lawrence's understanding of the gospel of the man who died have just this effect: they betray in Lawrence a failure of vision, a falling away from the objective reality of the thing he is seeking to render in his story; and it is this that leads him to falsify the object by cheapening and degrading it.

It would be possible to show that the doctrinal weakness of the first half of Lawrence's story intimately affects its artistic integrity. Where the conception is defective, there the execution is correspondingly flawed. A work of art that falsifies reality in the particularly disabling way of cheapening and degrading it is (it could be argued) inferior as a work of art in just the degree in which it is doctrinally false. And its inferiority as a work of art reflects back in turn upon its value as a text for the true Humanism.

I propose, however, to confine myself to a critique of the story in its purely doctrinal aspect; and the argument (which is directed only against the first half of the story) is as follows. It is Lawrence's defective understanding that leads him to see the gospel of love that Jesus preached before his death and resurrection as a false gospel; it is this in turn that leads him to hang the whole of the first half of his story upon the nausea of disillusion with which the man who died rises from the tomb and returns to the world; and it is this nausea of disillusion—as we learn from the conversation with Mary Magdalene by the myrtle bush—that leads the man who died to repudiate the gospel that once he preached. These, the nausea of disillusion and the violent repudiation, are a logical consequence of Lawrence's erotic interpretation of Jesus' gospel. But if (as I have argued) the erotic interpretation is false, then the nausea of disillusion ceases to be necessary; and then the violent repudiation of the gospel of selfless love is likewise not necessary; and if this reasoning is correct, the doctrinal argument of the whole of the first half of the fable is seriously flawed. The way would then seem to be open for a 'revised version' that would remedy the defect in Lawrence's vision and so in the conception and execution of his remarkable story.

This is what I now propose to do: to suggest what I believe to be a finer because more truly and consistently Humanist fable about the resurrection of the man who died; and I will proceed on the same assumptions as those implicit in Lawrence's story. The first (which was touched on in an earlier chapter[1]) is that the true Humanism will supersede the true Christianity not by annihilating it but by incorporating and

[1] Ch. VII, pp. 184–5 above.

transforming it. Nothing of the Gospel of Christ will be lost, but everything in it will be transformed, transfigured and rendered finally and completely efficacious—and therefore finally and completely redemptive.

The second assumption is that the true Humanism, like the true Christianity, must be, in some sense, Messianic. It must believe that the complete and final Word, the Word that will redeem the world, must be made flesh in order to be made accessible to men for their salvation. It must believe that the love which will finally and completely redeem the world can be known in its perfection only by a single Man, can be proclaimed with the absolute authority of perfect knowledge only by a single Man, and can be imprinted upon the hearts and minds of men, to the end of time, only by that same Man. This is what is meant by saying that the true Humanism must be Messianic; it is for this reason that the Humanist is still in the grave, awaiting the true Annunciation. But this is the most obscure and mysterious part of the religious Humanism I have been discussing, and it is impossible to say more about it here. It had to be mentioned only because some such view is implicit in Lawrence's story.

Proceeding on these two assumptions, the revised version will begin by eliminating the bitter nausea of disillusion upon which Lawrence bases the first half of his story. It will suppose that the man who died does not return disillusioned but, on the contrary, with all his divine energy and all his faith, hope and charity unimpaired. And when he speaks to Mary Magdalene by the myrtle bushes, he does not repudiate the gospel of selfless love that he preached before his death and resurrection, but reaffirms it. As the man who died reaffirmed the Law of Moses ('Think not that I came to destroy the law or the prophets: I came not to destroy but to fulfil'[1]), so the reborn Saviour reaffirms the Law of Christ, the gospel of selfless love, saying 'Without this nothing'. Whatever may have to be added to it, drawn out of it, done to transform

[1] Matt. v. 17.

it in order to make it fully and finally redemptive, without this nothing.

So it is the same Jesus whom Mary Magdalene and the others had known and adored who now rises from the tomb and comes back to them, with no bitter nausea of disillusion but, as before, full of tenderness and sweetness and strength; and he comes back (we are to suppose) to give them fresh hope and courage, and to serve them again by imparting to them his divine knowledge of God's mind. But though it is the same beloved Jesus who returns, it is yet not the same Jesus. For this Jesus, the reborn Saviour, they discover, is preparing to go once more into the wilderness in search of something. It is mysterious, elusive, a something-he-knows-not-what; but whatever it is he knows he must seek it out. For he has come to sense within himself a flaw that he must mend in order that he may complete his divine mission. He does not know what it is; he only knows that it is there, and that he is under the old compulsion again to go and seek that which will supply this defect in himself, by which he will complete his redemptive knowledge and make himself the true Saviour of mankind.

And where does this mysterious compulsion come from? Perhaps from within—from the 'everlasting resoluteness of life', the 'determined surge of life' that Lawrence speaks of. But how much better if it should come from without, from the Heavenly Father himself ('I and my Father are one', said Jesus), as a further intimation of what the Son was to do for the redemption of the world. And because coming from the Father, therefore compelling him to leave his disciples and friends (but tenderly and sweetly, not cruelly and brutally, as he leaves Mary Magdalene in Lawrence's story), and to go forth into the wilderness again to seek this further and last piece of redemptive knowledge that God the Father wishes him to possess for the final salvation of the world.

This is the scheme of the revised version of the first half of Lawrence's story. From there, the story would continue exactly as Lawrence wrote it: telling how the man who died, in obedience to the command of his Heavenly Father, finds the woman of Isis in the temple on the Mediterranean coast, and there discovers what it was he had been sent to find. And there, in that temple, the complete and final Word is made flesh; and the man who died returns to the world to preach the final, perfected gospel of the redemptive power of love.

This, I suggest, would have been a better story than Lawrence's, for reasons at once artistically and doctrinally sound. For it would possess two vital elements that Lawrence's story lacks. In the first place, it would preserve a continuity, in character and temper, between the man who died and the man who rose, between the man who preached a gospel of love which was not false but only incomplete and imperfect and the man who preached the final, complete and perfect gospel of love. In the second place, it would leave unimpaired his link with God the Father, which Lawrence has so violently severed in his own treatment of the fable. Because it is one of the *données* of the situation that the Son believes himself to derive all his power and authority from the Father, that he does nothing in his own name but everything in the name of the Father, it is doctrinally and artistically necessary that the bond between the Son and the Father should be retained inviolate. And with these two conditions satisfied, the principal object of Lawrence's fable would be perfectly accomplished—that the Son of God should go forth to complete his saving knowledge, that he should possess himself of this knowledge in his own divine body, and, having possessed himself of it, should thereby render his gospel of love wholly and finally redemptive.

This would have made a fable to body forth the true Humanist conception of the Son of God, the Saviour of mankind. But such a fable, one feels, being outside of the compass of Lawrence's vision, was probably also outside of the compass of his powers as an artist. It is a conception better adapted perhaps to the genius of the angelic novelist Henry James, whose vision of human possibility was so much larger and more generous than Lawrence's, whose understanding of the true Humanism went so much deeper, and who affirmed as authoritatively as Lawrence, only less obtrusively and less stridently, the redeeming power of human love. But there is always Sir Philip Sidney's dictum to remember, that the good is not the less good because the better is better; and though the hypothetical fable that Henry James might have written is, I believe, better than Lawrence's, Lawrence's is nevertheless remarkable enough as a prophetic text for the Humanist conception of the true Messiah.

CHAPTER XI

CONCLUSION

IT must now be left to the reader to judge whether the twofold object of the book, mentioned in the opening chapter,[1] has been successfully accomplished. Nevertheless it may be of some use to indicate, in respect to the principal object, what I take to be the main points of the doctrine that has emerged from the discussion of the selected authors and texts, and, in respect to the second, subsidiary object, to draw attention to a few salient instances of the way in which the principles and methods of literary criticism have been applied in the treatment of the philosophical material.

The second may be taken first. In examining the argument of a typical Platonic dialogue such as the *Gorgias*, we found ourselves obliged to distinguish at a certain point between two kinds of proof—the poetic, operating by the primarily emotional and sensuous impact upon the subject of a series of highly charged images, and the ratiocinative, or strictly intellectual, proceeding by a method of argument designed to expose logical confusions and contradictions in the subject's position.[2] Further, in our search for the principles of the Socratic dialectic, the first Appendix shows that its characteristic operations are illuminated by viewing it as a poetic-dramatic convention, which owes its most powerful and subtle effects (the Socratic paradox, for instance) to a simultaneity of statement essentially similar to that of the 'metaphysical' metaphor.[3] In studying Aristotle, the most un-poetic of philosophers and moralists, we found that we had to give close attention to the tone, accent and emphasis of his 'voice'—in the famous character-sketches in the *Rhetoric*, for

[1] Ch. I, p. 1.

[2] Ch. II, pp. 47–9.

[3] Appendix A, pp. 301–27 below.

instance, and in the significant parentheses in the *Nicomachean Ethics*—in order to arrive at a proper estimate of his moral realism.[1] The same was true for Hobbes; and here besides, in our examination of Hobbes's political doctrine, we gained an important insight into the intention and design of *Leviathan* by perceiving the significance of Hobbes's ironic appropriation and exploitation of certain fundamental Christian images.[2] Again, in attempting to appraise F. H. Bradley's Concluding Remarks as a Humanist document, it was necessary to distinguish between the admirable intention and the subtly inadequate execution of his critique of historic Christianity; and this could only be done—as in any work of imaginative literature—on the internal literary evidences.[3] In Matthew Arnold's Humanist reinterpretation of historic Christianity, on the other hand, it was Arnold's developed literary intelligence in the handling of the Bible texts that gave his interpretations their authority and persuasiveness;[4] and in D. H. Lawrence's story *The Man Who Died*, its value and its deficiencies as a prophetic Humanist text were seen to be connected with its virtues and short-comings as a work of art.[5] None of the detailed analysis upon which these judgments were based could in this context be set out as fully as might have been desired; but if the lines upon which such a fuller analysis might be conducted have been clearly enough indicated, and if something has been done to suggest the value of the approach as a whole, this particular object of the book will have been achieved.

The development of the main theme, concerning the three traditions of moral thought, has turned upon an examination of the place and importance accorded to love in the moral systems representative of each. The predominantly religious systems, such as the Platonic and the Pauline, have been

[1] Ch. III, pp. 61–4, 66–7, 76.
[2] Ch. IV, pp. 110–11, 125–7.
[3] Ch. IX, pp. 246–9.
[4] Ch. VIII, pp. 215–25.
[5] Ch. X, pp. 283–8.

shown to be distinguished by their common affirmation of an order of transcendent values, of which love (in the Christian scheme) or virtue (in the Platonic) is the supreme transforming and redeeming power. The predominantly secular systems—Aristotle's, Hobbes's and Hume's—have taken happiness (or pleasure) and utility as the ends of moral endeavour, and self-interest, fear and pride as the springs of moral conduct; and they have denied or minimised the reality and importance of love in the moral life, and *a fortiori* its power to transform and redeem. The Humanist systems, imperfect and incomplete though they all are, have been shown to stand with the religious systems in affirming an order of goodness and power greater than any that the worldly world can show, of which the crown is love, but with the secular in denying either the reality or the necessity of the supernatural sanction upon which the historic religions, in particular Christianity, have based their claim for the transforming and redeeming power of love.

The principal points of the Humanist doctrine that have emerged from the analysis of the chosen authors and texts are the following:

(1) Humanism has sought to discover and define its own character by a constructive critique of historic Christianity. Thus John Stuart Mill in his *Three Essays on Religion* gives an essentially Humanist account of the Christian doctrines of immortality and divine omnipotence; Matthew Arnold in *Literature and Dogma* reinterprets on Humanist premises some of the principal points of Christian faith and practice; F. H. Bradley attempts a Humanist critique of the Christian *cultus* in the Concluding Remarks of *Ethical Studies*; and D. H. Lawrence in *The Man Who Died* suggests a vital defect in the Christian conception of the redemptive love, and intimates that this defect is to be supplied by the reborn Saviour.

(2) The relation between the true Humanism and the Judaeo-Christian religion from which it is derived is con-

ceived to be exactly parallel to that which historic Christianity postulates between the Old Covenant and the New. As the Law of Christ superseded the Law of Moses, not by destroying it but by incorporating it, so the Humanist faith is to supersede the Christian by incorporating and transforming it in such a way as to render it completely and finally efficacious.

(3) The unique contribution of Humanism to the religious knowledge of the world is its affirmation of sexual love as the supremely redemptive form of love.

(4) Humanism, like its predecessors in the central religious tradition of our civilisation, is Messianic in character. It believes that the redemptive power of sexual love can be affirmed only by a single, individual Person, who shall proclaim it with the authority derived from his unique knowledge of its power to redeem, and shall thereby make the complete and perfect Word flesh for the final salvation of the world.

In the exposition of this positive doctrine, the method has been, so far as possible, historical and analytical, and little attempt has been made to draw out its prophetic implications, or to adduce contemporary evidences, either literary or extraliterary, in support of these. The prophetic aspect, however, will not be lost upon the religious mind. For such a mind will long since have come to see the contemporary world as a world in travail, perishing for the lack of a saving faith, and all the destroying evils of the time as symptoms of the universal suffering and signs of the need for a universal redemption. Nothing will be too little or too great to find a place in its encompassing vision of a world hovering on the edge of the abyss. A book-of-the-month called *The Outsider*, testifying to the extinction of human feeling in representative modern men; a film called *The Prisoner*, bearing witness to the systematic bestiality which in so many places has become the norm of the relation of man and man; the plays of Tennessee Williams, recording the convulsive nausea of a man of crude but strong sensibility at the mean, shabby falsities—the incorrigible *phoneyness*—of the values dominating his culture: such phenomena, to the religious mind, will not be less significant as symptoms of a world ripe for destruction than the helplessness of the historic Churches to give either doctrinal or pastoral guidance to the masses of their faithless faithful; the fear and imbecility governing the conduct of international affairs; the shallow scepticism dominating the academies of the Western world; the corruption of independent feeling and judgment by the techniques of modern propaganda; the ever-growing scale and magnitude of the commercial debasement of values in the popular forms of entertainment. And these will not less potently induce a sense of the helplessness and desolation of modern man than will the growing stock-piles of nuclear weapons, by which the rulers of the world may within the life-span of this generation effect the physical annihilation of all life on this planet.

On the other, the positive, side, the air of the modern epoch, for those who have ears to hear, will be full of prophetic voices: generally confused, often ignorant, vain and foolish; yet all according to their capacity divining the need for a new redemptive vision, and seeking according to their lights to supply it. In this quest for the redemptive love, the systematic enquiries of churchmen, philosophers and poets will again not be more significant (though they may be more helpful) than the wild romances of an Elinor Glyn; the Kinsey Reports; the article in a popular journal documenting the sexual problems of modern American wives and husbands; the heart-throb columns of the women's magazines; the sad bad love-poem in the odd corner of the daily newspaper. These for the prophetic mind are the fumblings, often unendurably pitiful, of the unilluminated towards the same light that directs the profounder explorations of a George Eliot, a Rilke, a Kafka, a D. H. Lawrence, and shines with such splendour in the writings of Henry James.

So the grounds for hope are not absent, though never equal

with the grounds for despair. Together they may lead the prophetic mind to picture the modern world as poised either for a new Flood or a new Annunciation; and when the prophetic passion burns most strong in him, he may well feel his life consumed by the unceasing struggle between terror of one and hope of the other, his sense of the urgency of the universal need, and his helplessness by his own effort to bring the longed-for redemption a step nearer. Then St Paul's cry beats in his head day and night,

> Who shall deliver me out of the body of this death?

and the prayer of the stricken,

> God have mercy upon us
> Christ have mercy upon us.

I have said, however, that it has been no part of the intention of this book to pursue these prophetical implications. Its method is historical and analytical; at its furthest reach, it has not gone beyond the analysis of logical possibility; and this would not serve the prophetic mind for so much as a starting-point.

Nevertheless, if (as the religious everywhere believe) ultimate reality is rational; and if the analysis of logical possibility set out in the last chapters possesses the rationality proper to itself, namely, self-coherence, and consistency both with known religious premises and with the relevant facts of the condition of modern man, such an analysis may have the limited value of preparing the mind (and perhaps the heart, too) for the reality which, when it breaks upon the world, will vindicate the logic by consuming it in its redeeming fire.

APPENDICES

APPENDIX A

SOME PRINCIPLES OF SOCRATES' DIALECTICAL METHOD

It is not uncommon for the reader coming fresh to Plato to find himself puzzled or exasperated (or, generally, both) by certain weaknesses, as they seem to him, of the Socratic dialectic. These weaknesses may appear serious enough to undermine the validity of the whole method as a method of argument or logical persuasion; and they reduce themselves to two in number. The first turns upon the seeming simple-mindedness of Socrates' adversaries; the second, upon the seemingly sophistical arguments by which Socrates so often brings down his adversary. The two points are closely connected. It is precisely because the adversaries appear to be so simple-minded that they are brought down by these sophistical arguments of Socrates: they seem to be so slow and so stupid, so incapable of keeping even one jump ahead in the argument; so ready to say 'Yes, Socrates' where the reader would say 'No, Socrates, by no means'—and would know just how to make things really difficult for him. To this critical reader, accordingly, Socrates' victories in the Platonic Dialogues seem altogether too easy; and a case in point is the celebrated argument in the *Gorgias* by which Gorgias himself is vanquished: when Socrates, having received Gorgias' assent to each of the propositions, 'He who has knowledge of building is a builder; he who has knowledge of medicine is a medical man; he who has knowledge of music is a musical man', then 'traps' him into assent to the proposition 'He who has knowledge of justice is a just man' (*Gorgias*, 460B). In this typical instance of a Socratic argument by analogy, it is held that Gorgias has been trapped into assent to a thoroughly false proposition by a thoroughly sophistical argument.

The answer to these objections is to be sought in a better understanding of the peculiar features of the dialectical method as a method of instruction; and these in turn are best understood by seeing how the dialectical method differs from another and distinct method called the *didactical* method.[1] A simple way of grasping the main difference between the two methods is to see the dialectical as the method of instruction of the market-place, the didactical as the method reserved for the academy, the historical models for the latter being Plato's Academy and later Aristotle's Lyceum. The didactical method, in other words, is specifically designed for *the student*: he who is by definition reflective and analytical, bent upon the acquisition of 'knowledge' in the full Platonic sense of the word, and accordingly comes to the academy with the avowed object of being taught. His relationship to his teacher is that of pupil to master—not that of answerer to questioner, as in the dialectic; *qua* pupil he comes to learn from the master—not, in the first instance, to argue with him; and the method by which he is taught is the systematic method of didactics.

The master of didactics, in any given course of instruction, always starts with an explicit statement of his premises ('primary propositions', Aristotle calls them). He then explains, clearly and unambiguously, the meanings of the key-terms of his premises or primary propositions: for example, 'When I say that all men desire only what is good, I am using the word "good" in this sense, not in that, and I mean by "desire" this not that'; or: 'I say that it is a greater evil to do injustice than to suffer it; and by "injustice" I mean thus

[1] My authority for this distinction, as a historically real distinction in Greek philosophy, is Aristotle himself, who in two of his logical treatises, the *Topics* and the *Prior Analytics*, uses the terms 'dialectical' and 'didactical' to designate two distinct methods of instruction, and throws out some invaluable hints concerning the differences between them. These hints, however, are characteristically brief and obscure, and need to be closely analysed to yield the principles of the two methods that they in fact contain. For a discussion of Plato's own use of the term 'dialectic', see Appendix B, 'Two Meanings of Dialectic'.

and thus, and by "evil" thus and thus.' Then, having defined the key-terms of his premises or primary propositions, he proceeds to draw out, step by step, the logical consequences of these premises or primary propositions, and so reaches the conclusion, the particular affirmation to which he desires the pupil's assent, by a method of argument that is rigorously consequential and therefore genuinely a proof or demonstration.

This is the didactical method of instruction; and the pupil, so long as he has understood the premises or first propositions of the argument and has followed each step in the argument, is logically obliged to give his assent to the conclusion. Moreover (and this is a vital point), the pupil is at every stage allowed to ask for explanations and elucidations: for further elucidation, for instance, of the terms of the premises of the argument, if these have not been made sufficiently clear; and for elucidation of the logical rules by which any given step in the argument is made to follow from the preceding step. But (it should be added) that is all the pupil *is* allowed to ask—only for explanations and elucidations. He is not allowed to dispute the master's definitions or the rules of logic by which he makes his inferences. For (as Hobbes put it in a brilliant comment on the didactical method):

> When a master is instructing his scholar, if the scholar understand all the parts of the thing defined, which are resolved in the definition, and yet will not admit of the definition, there needs no further controversy betwixt them, it being all one as if he refused to be taught.[1]

This, in the briefest outline, is the method of didactics which, first practised in the Academy of Plato and the Lyceum of Aristotle, became the basis of the famous scholastic method of instruction practised in the universities of Europe in the medieval and Renaissance periods, and remains substantially the method of instruction followed in the mathematical sciences at the present day. And what the method chiefly presupposes is (to recapitulate) an interlocutor who is not an adversary but a pupil coming to be instructed and willing to learn; and

[1] Hobbes, *Of Computation or Logic*, vi. 15.

in order to learn, willing to relinquish or suspend all preconceptions (as we would call them) about the given subject-matter. The last is the crucial point which Plato and Aristotle expressed in terms of their famous distinction between knowledge and opinion. The pupil *qua* pupil, when he enters the academy and submits himself to the didactical method of instruction, relinquishes or suspends all 'opinion' concerning the subject-matter: the sort of opinion he would have picked up from the sophists, the politicians, the lawyers—from all the articulate voices of the 'climate of opinion' in that time and that place. And he relinquishes or suspends this opinion in order to receive knowledge from the master—the master being the true philosopher, the true lover of wisdom, who by definition possesses knowledge as distinct from opinion.

The dialectical method differs from the didactical in presupposing an interlocutor of quite a different type. Being the method of instruction designed for the market-place, the dialectical method is addressed to a type of person different in all important respects from the pupil of the academy. It is addressed to what we would call the ordinary man-in-the-street, the ordinary unreflective man, the man whose analytical powers in particular are conspicuously undeveloped, whose mind therefore will be particularly deficient in the qualities of coherence and consequentiality. This does not mean that he is unintelligent. On the contrary, he may have plenty of practical intelligence, like Callicles in the *Gorgias*; or plenty of spirit, like Polus; or even passion, like Thrasymachus in the *Republic*. But he is distinctly not an intellectual —distinctly not what we would call today a 'trained intelligence'. In contemporary terms, the adversaries in a dialectical argument are not to be conceived of as superior undergraduates reading for a stiff honours degree at a superior university, but rather (say) as those younger sons of county families whose intellectual endowments are acknowledged to be modest; who have tended to spend their time with horses and boats and fast motor-cars rather than with books; who have gone into politics or the church or the army or the navy because someone in the family always has—or, alternatively, may have become playboys of the less offensive kind, having enough general intelligence to be interested in current affairs, the arts (especially perhaps the cinema—'the art of the cinema'—and classical jazz), and even to engage from time to time in a little modest journalism for the better Sunday papers.

This is the kind of young man that Socrates, the master of dialectic, is in the habit of buttonholing in the market-place of Athens and engaging in dialectical argument. But the adversary need not, of course, be a young man at all. He may be a more mature man, like Callicles in the *Gorgias* or Gorgias himself, who is already successfully engaged in politics or teaching or big business; and then what Socrates has to contend with, as in the *Gorgias*, is not only his generic ignorance and muddle-headedness but also his specific vested interest in the particular 'art' he happens to be practising.

This, then, is the first point about the adversary in a dialectical exchange: that he is not necessarily stupid but only not reflective; not analytical, not a 'trained intelligence', but not therefore lacking in a certain degree of seriousness about serious matters—for if he were, he would not allow himself to be drawn into argument with Socrates at all. He is not necessarily frivolous or irresponsible, but only desperately misinformed and muddle-headed.

And the reason that the Socratic adversary is so misinformed and so muddled is (to express it again in terms of Plato's great distinction) that he lives wholly in the realm of opinion as distinct from knowledge: all his ideas—on morals, on politics, on the arts—are merely the prevailing notions on these matters that he has picked up in a characteristically haphazard way from all the common sources of popular opinion—from whatever were the equivalents in fourth-century Athens of the popular magazines, leading articles in the daily newspapers, the pronouncements of Brains Trust Committees, desultory conversations in pubs, Espresso cafés, and so on. All his opinions are picked up in this haphazard way, and are, of course, accepted quite uncritically. And since the grand point about opinion as distinct from knowledge is precisely that it is *unexamined*—nothing in the realm of opinion is ever probed to its foundations, nothing is ever considered in its relation to anything else, but everything is fragmentary, mutually disconnected, essentially incoherent—since this is the nature of opinion, it is not surprising that the moral and political ideas of Socrates' adversaries should be riddled with internal contradictions, and should form, in the strict Platonic sense, a *chaos* instead of a *cosmos.*

But (and this is a further important point about the adversary in a dialectical exchange) he is not only steeped in opinion, but, being a passionate rather than a reasonable man—a man governed exclusively, or almost exclusively, by his emotions—he tends to cling to his favourite opinions, resisting, sometimes violently, always vigorously, any attempt to dislodge him from these opinions or beliefs by which he believes himself always to have guided the conduct of his life. And so Socrates has also to contend in his adversary with something very familiar in human nature, that which goes by the name of perversity—the disposition to resist any attempt to dislodge us from our settled opinions, for no other reason than that they happen to be our own.

This in turn discloses to us the last important attribute of the Socratic adversary, that (unlike the superior undergraduate at the superior academy) he does not really want to be instructed at all. He does not, certainly, mind spending an odd hour or so arguing with Socrates in the market-place, hearing his notoriously mad ideas, and trying to understand what he is driving at. But what he really wants, like the ordinary unreflective man in every age, is to be comfortably confirmed in the opinions he already comfortably holds, to be given the best reasons for continuing to hold them, in short, to be 'flattered', in the Socratic sense of the word, rather than instructed—sustained in his good opinion of himself rather than, in Socrates' favourite phrase, 'made better than he is'.

This is the sort of man that Socrates, the great moral teacher and political reformer, the great Christian missionary of the pre-Christian world, passionately desires to make better than he is—desires to lift out of the realm of opinion into the realm of knowledge as the first necessary condition of his salvation. And this missionary work he seeks to accomplish by the method designed specifically for the instruction of this sort of common unreflective man; and it is by reference to the kind of man to which it is addressed, with all the severe limitations that this circumstance imposes on the master of dialectic, that the main features of the dialectical method must be understood.

The first limiting condition, or rule, of the dialectical method has been defined by Aristotle in a rather gnomic utterance in the treatise called the *Prior Analytics.* In a didactical argument, writes Aristotle, 'the demonstrator [that is, the master of didactics] does not ask for his premise, but lays it down, whereas *the dialectical premise depends on the adversary's choice between two contradictories*'.[1]

That is all; but it is enough to make a point of profound importance for the understanding of the dialectical method: the master of dialectic—the 'questioner', Socrates—is not allowed to start the argument with a premise or first proposition *proposed by himself*. In the argument with Polus in the *Gorgias*, for instance, he is not allowed to start by saying 'I affirm that to do injustice is a greater evil than to suffer it; and what I mean by "injustice" is thus and thus, what I mean by "evil" is thus and thus, and by "greater" thus and thus. Do you understand, Polus, what I am affirming; and do you assent to it?' This would be the correct procedure for the master of didactic in the academy. But the master of dialectic

[1] *Prior Analytics*, 24 a 23–6.

has to proceed by asking the adversary *to choose between 'two contradictories'*; so, in this instance, he begins by saying, 'Would you say, Polus, that to do injustice is a greater evil than to suffer it, or, rather, that to suffer injustice is the greater evil?' Polus answers, 'To suffer injustice is of course, Socrates, the greater evil'; and this now becomes the first premise of the whole dialectical argument. But since Polus, the adversary, is steeped in 'opinion', he chooses the *false* alternative: the adversary in a dialectical argument, being what he is, always *by definition* chooses the false alternative; and this means that a dialectical argument invariably proceeds from a false premise or first proposition. This is the crucial point about the dialectical method that Aristotle is making when he says 'The dialectical premise depends upon the adversary's choice between two contradictories'; and to understand its significance is already of the greatest help in understanding some of the otherwise puzzling features of the whole method.

It explains, for a start, why Socrates can never *prove* his own position to be true, but can only prove the adversary's position to be false. If we take a mathematical argument as our model, say a proof in geometry, it is evident that the proof *is* a proof only if the theorem that it is proving is in fact *true*. But the theorem can only be proved true if the starting-point (the postulate or 'hypothesis') from which the proof proceeds is true; so, generalising the model case of a geometrical argument, we are able to say about every argument that it can only prove something—that is, establish a *truth*—if, and only if, the equivalent of the postulate or hypothesis in geometry is in fact *true*. And that, exactly, is the procedure in didactics, which is in fact no more than a generalisation of the procedures of the mathematical sciences. But when an argument must, by definition, start from a false premise, which is the case in the dialectical argument, it is evident that that argument cannot 'prove' anything—cannot, that is, establish any *truth*; it can only expose the falsity of the false premise from which the argument started by showing that it leads to self-contradiction.

This is the first point about the dialectical method which follows from the nature of the adversary—that the questioner, or master of dialectic, can never, *in the strictly argumentative part of the dialectic*, prove his own position to be true, but can only prove the adversary's position to be self-contradictory and therefore false. I emphasise 'in the strictly argumentative part' because—as we may see in the *Gorgias*, the *Republic* and almost all the later Dialogues—Socrates can, and does, at various points affirm his own positive views. But he never affirms them—not explicitly, at any rate—in the argument itself; the affirmative or discursive portions of the *Gorgias*, the *Republic* and so on always lie outside of the strictly dialectical argument; and this is entirely in accordance with the principles of the dialectical method I have been stressing.[1]

The second important feature of the dialectical method that follows directly from the nature of the adversary is contained in the rule that no frontal attack, so to speak, on the false opinion held by the adversary is permissible. When Polus, for instance, chooses the false alternative of the two contradictories offered to him by Socrates, that it is a greater evil to suffer injustice, it is against the rules of the dialectic for Socrates to answer, 'But, Polus, that is quite wrong. Don't you see and don't you know, you foolish boy (or 'you ignorant boy' or 'you depraved boy'), that it is a greater evil to *do* injustice?' For Polus, who does not think he is ignorant or foolish, and does not frankly mind being thought just a little depraved—Polus will answer, No: he doesn't see and he doesn't know. He will simply refuse his assent, the argument will come to a dead stop, and Socrates' efforts to redeem him from his errors will be stultified. Socrates could indeed go on

[1] I have discussed the way in which positive affirmations may be made implicitly *within* the framework of the dialectic in the section on the Socratic paradox (pp. 321–7 below).

to say, 'Ah, but Polus, let me prove to you, foolish (or ignorant or depraved) as you are, that it *is* a greater evil to do injustice'. But the moment he does this he is abandoning the dialectical method for the method of didactics; and this *ex hypothesi* is forbidden to the master of dialectics.

So it is a necessary consequence of the nature of the adversary in a dialectical dispute that a head-on collision between questioner and answerer should at every point of the argument be avoided. And this means, in turn, that the questioner Socrates has to proceed with the utmost circumspection and the utmost circuitousness in the conduct of the argument. Having started—having *had* to start—from the false premise proposed by the adversary, he must, as it were, cast his ratiocinative net as wide as possible. He must proceed first, step by step, to a point seemingly quite remote from and irrelevant to the disputed question, receiving the adversary's assent to each proposition proposed to him for the reason, precisely, that these propositions seem so remote from and unconnected with the disputed proposition that he can see no reason to withhold his assent; and then, step by step again, work back from the remote propositions to the immediate proposition that is the crux of the argument.[1]

A particularly brilliant instance of this wide-flung Socratic argument occurs in the Second Book of the *Republic*,[2] where the whole argument turns upon the rather puzzling proposition that *money-making* (or 'wage-earning', as it is commonly translated) is no intrinsic part of any of the special arts, medicine, music, navigation and so on. Now Socrates' ultimate purpose in this argument is to compel the assent of his adversary, Thrasymachus, to what he believes to be the true

[1] The point about these seemingly remote and irrelevant propositions is, of course, that they are not really remote and irrelevant. They are related to the disputed proposition as the general is to the particular. The disputed proposition is simply a particular case of the more general propositions proposed by Socrates; and it is because the adversary does not recognise the particular in the general that he gives his assent to the more general propositions, and so is forced finally, by the logic of the Socratic method, to give his assent also to the particular proposition entailed by the more general.

[2] *Republic*, 341–7.

definition of the art of government, namely, that it is essentially a service, not a career, and that the true, the good, ruler or politician is he who practises his art in a completely disinterested way, with no thought of personal gain, but with thought only for the welfare of the ruled.

This is the view that Socrates wishes to maintain against Thrasymachus' view that government is 'the rule of the stronger' and that it consists in the most effective exploitation of the ruled by the ruler. He proceeds accordingly, in the strictly dialectical argument, to undermine Thrasymachus' position by the following logical strategy. In order to show that Thrasymachus' view that the ruler rules only for his own benefit and not at all for the benefit of the ruled is false, he will show that the 'benefit' of the ruler—personal gain, that is—is no *intrinsic* part of the art of ruling—no part, that is, of the true definition of the good ruler or good government. But, to show this, he will first seek Thrasymachus' assent to the more general proposition that money-making (or wage-earning) is no intrinsic part of *any* 'art'—medicine, music, navigation, and so on. And in order to gain his assent to this proposition, he will first seek his assent to the proposition that the art of money-making is itself a distinct art; for if it is itself a distinct art, with its own distinct subject-matter, it can be no intrinsic part of any other art.[1] But, finally, this argument itself presupposes an analogy between *all* the arts; and this analogy Socrates, the master of wisdom, knows Thrasymachus will not think of disputing, whatever else he may dispute. For in this, the definition of an art and the analogy of all the arts, Socrates could count upon the universal agreement of all

[1] When Socrates speaks of the art of money-making or wage-earning as a 'distinct art', he must, I think, be supposed to have in mind the ancient art of usury—money-making having for its sole object money-making, and the money-maker (the usurer), in strict accordance with the Socratic definition of an art, concerned with the benefit or improvement or increase of his specific subject-matter, namely, money. If we think of the more complex modern equivalents of the ancient art of usury (the Stock Exchange, banking, brokerage, and so on), the validity of Socrates' view that money-making may be regarded as a distinct art is strikingly confirmed.

the educated Greeks of his time. It formed at once the broadest and the most neutral—morally neutral—common ground between Socrates and his contemporaries; and that is why, here as elsewhere, he takes this for his starting-point in the particular dialectical argument he is engaged upon.

So this is how we reach, at last, the logical starting-point of this whole argument about the nature of government between Socrates and Thrasymachus, from which Socrates begins his attack upon Thrasymachus' position. This, the famous 'analogy of the arts', is the outermost circle of the series of concentric circles of argument that Socrates has constructed around the crucial proposition to which he desires Thrasymachus' assent. It is the outermost circle because the most inclusive; and the most inclusive because the most general; and because so general, therefore so seemingly remote from and irrelevant to the disputed issue at the centre. And so it is from this outermost point, the analogy of the arts, that Socrates works his way inwards, circle by circle, through the successive propositions already mentioned, receiving Thrasymachus' assent to each, until Thrasymachus is forced to concede that the 'benefit' of the ruler is not the end of government. And if Thrasymachus' view is false, Socrates' view must be true (that the ruler rules for the benefit of the ruled, not for his own benefit), since the alternatives proposed at the beginning were agreed to be exhaustive.[1]

This is one of many examples in the *Republic* of what I have called the wide-flung Socratic argument. But the *Gorgias* and all the other Dialogues yield similar instances, some of them almost as elaborate as this, the elaborateness, the circuitousness, being in each instance imposed upon the master of dialectic by the nature of the adversary in a dialectical argument.

The nature of the adverasary explains also that most suspect feature of the dialectical method, the disposition of the

[1] This point, that the alternatives proposed at the beginning of a dialectical argument are always taken to be exhaustive, is further discussed below (pp. 320–1).

master of dialectic to use sophistical arguments. In this connexion again, Aristotle supplies the key to the problem:[1]

> Adverse criticism is not to be passed...upon the argument on its own merits, [or] upon the questioner [the master of dialectic]. *For it may well be that the argument is bad, but that the questioner has argued with the answerer in the best possible way: for when men lose their tempers* [that is, become angry and perverse] it may perhaps be impossible to make one's inferences straightforwardly as one would wish: *we have to do as we can.*

Given an adversary who is by definition perverse, determined to cling to his false opinions, and liable to grow angry ('lose his temper') when he is challenged, and so bring the whole argument to a stop—given such an adversary, *we have to do as we can.* The master of dialectic will always use the best argument possible in the circumstances; but the best argument possible in the circumstances may be—may *have* to be—an inferior argument. This is so for the reason that Aristotle has here indicated; but also for the other reason, already explained, that the dialectical argument has by definition to start from a false premise, and that the master of dialectic is at no point permitted to halt the stream of false consequences by explicitly affirming and proving his own (true) definitions of the disputed matter.

A good instance of this sort of sophistical or near-sophistical argument is the first of the several arguments against Callicles[2] in which Socrates seeks to prove that pleasure and pain are not the same as good and evil, by arguing that in enjoying the pleasure of drinking when we are thirsty, we are 'simultaneously' suffering the pain of thirst and the pleasure of quenching our thirst. In other words, pleasure and pain can co-exist in a given situation; and since Callicles has already granted that good and evil cannot co-exist in the same way (a man cannot in the same moment of time be both good and evil), it follows that good and evil cannot be the same as pleasure and pain.

[1] *Topics*, 161 b 5–10.

[2] *Gorgias*, 496–7.

This may justly be regarded as a sophistical argument. To begin with, the physiological basis of the argument seems of doubtful validity: is it, as a matter of physiological fact, true that the 'pain' of being thirsty and the 'pleasure' of quenching thirst are 'simultaneous'? But, what is more important, this questionable physiological fact is 'proved' by what appears to be merely a pun on the word 'when': 'One enjoys [pleasure], though in pain, *when*...one drinks when one is thirsty....'[1] The sophism, it would seem, is in taking the word 'when' to mean 'at the same moment as' when it really means in this context 'in the condition of'. You enjoy the pleasure of quenching thirst when you are *in the condition of* being thirsty; and to put it that way does not imply the simultaneity *in time* upon which Socrates' argument depends.

So, if this objection is valid, this does appear to be a sophistical or 'verbal' argument. But, remembering the immediate context of this particular dialectical situation (*Gorgias*, 495 A)—that Callicles has already implicitly admitted that the pleasant and the good are not the same, and that he is now only persisting in his hedonist position out of perversity ('for the sake of the argument', as he himself puts it)[2]—it is clear that Socrates is 'doing as he can', that is, meeting Callicles' perversity by an argument as good as the dialectical circumstances allow.

There are further ironies in this situation, to be touched on presently in another connexion.[3] But taking it even so far, it may stand as a fair example of what Aristotle must have had in mind when he defended the 'bad' argument in dialectics on the ground that 'when men lose their tempers [that is, are perverse],...we have to do as we can'.

The inferior or sophistical argument must then, it seems, be accepted as a legitimate because inescapable feature of the dialectical method, imposed by the fundamental conditions of the Socratic dialectic. This concession, however, is subject to

[1] *Gorgias*, 496 E (Lamb's trans.).
[2] See ch. II above, pp. 48–9.
[3] See pp. 316–19 below.

an important reservation. The argument may sometimes appear to be sophistical when it is in fact not so; and in such cases the argument will be seen to be valid, not sophistical, if what I called the 'common ground' between the questioner and the answerer, Socrates and his adversary, is taken fully into account. The famous argument by which Gorgias is vanquished (*Gorgias*, 460 B) is a case in point. Gorgias assents to the proposition 'He who has knowledge of justice is a just man', having been led to this point by what appears to be a false argument by analogy. But what has to be remembered is, first, that Gorgias has already assented to the distinction between knowledge and opinion, this being part of the common ground between him and Socrates; and, second, that he shares also Socrates' conviction that morality, the knowledge of justice and injustice, is an 'art', and *qua* art analogous with the other arts or special sciences (navigation, medicine, music, *etc.*).[1] If this common ground is given full weight, the argument that leads to Gorgias' assent to the proposition 'He who has knowledge of justice is a just man' is seen to be not sophistical but valid.

This will frequently be found to be the case with Socratic arguments that appear to be sophistical but in their total context are not so. And the total context, it must now be explained, includes not only this common ground between questioner and answerer, but something else, equally important. This is the psychological character, which is also the moral character and the dramatic character, of the adversary himself. What kind of man is he? What particular class or type of false opinion does he represent in the Dialogue? What are the main moral and psychological features of a man holding this sort of false opinion? What specific form accordingly will his generic perversity take? Where is he likely to yield and where to resist?

These are some of the questions that the reader of the Platonic Dialogues must attempt to answer in order to grasp

[1] See also ch. II above, pp. 30–3.

the total context of the argument. And to see the moral and psychological character of the adversary as an important part—perhaps the most important part—of the total context of the argument is to receive another light on the apparently sophistical arguments in the Platonic Dialogues. What is an inferior, an unconvincing, an unfair argument to the critical modern reader may not be at all sophistical in this sense when addressed to a particular adversary in a particular dialectical situation.[1] The critical modern reader may justly have reservations about this or that argument; the adversary, being the sort of man he is, holding the views he does, standing for what he does, has no such reservations; and it is psychologically right, and therefore logically permissible by the rules of the dialectical method, that he should so often be convinced by arguments that would not, and would never have been meant to, convince anyone but this particular adversary in this particular dialectical situation.

This being so, it is of the first importance in studying the Platonic Dialogues, but especially the predominantly ethical Dialogues like the *Gorgias*, to determine with the utmost care and exactness the moral and psychological type of each of the principal adversaries. For it is only by relating the arguments, and above all the decisive argument—that by which the adversary is finally vanquished—to the character of the adversary to whom it is addressed that their validity and their force can be properly appreciated.[2]

An interesting, because unusually subtle, instance of the Socratic genius for conforming the dialectical method to the kind of adversary he is dealing with occurs in the *Gorgias* in the contest with Callicles at that point in the argument at

[1] This critical modern reader would not, in any case, as a rule belong to the type of the common unreflective man for whom the dialectical method is intended. He would belong rather to the type of the pupil in the academy, who is 'clever' in the way the Socratic adversary is not, and (what is more important) is not 'perverse'; he is therefore capable of being taught by the method of didactics, which by definition is ruled out for the typical adversary in a dialectical argument.

[2] See ch. II above, pp. 29–30, 34, 37–8, 41–3.

which Socrates introduces the image of the catamite.[1] The objection can be made[2] that, given the view of Callicles' character and personality as the type of the thoroughly sophisticated, thoroughly cynical and corrupt man of the world, was it likely that he would be so profoundly shocked by the catamite image as Plato wishes us to believe? Would he be so shocked as to admit without reservation that the pleasure of the catamite was a 'bad' pleasure, and so give away his whole hedonist position? It was exceedingly unlikely (the objector urges) that a man like Callicles *would* be shocked in this way by such an image; and the more unlikely in view of the well-known historical fact that homosexual relations were generally accepted as normal and natural in educated Greek society at this period. So (the objector concludes), was not Plato in this instance being just a shade too naïve, and in just the way that one would expect an innocent unworldly philosopher to be naïve?

The objection, cogent though it seems, is not difficult to answer. Further reflection on the catamite image in its context discloses that Socrates, so far from being hopelessly naïve about the worldly type that Callicles represents, has, on the contrary, a profound insight into its subtler weaknesses. For what Socrates is here exploiting for his dialectical purpose is one of the last infirmities of the worldly man in all times and places, his disposition (in the common phrase) *to draw the line somewhere*—and to draw it always in the most arbitrary place and on the most irrational grounds.

One need not go further for a parallel than the stock type of hard-headed, hard-boiled, tough-as-nails business man, who will think nothing of driving the hardest bargains in his business dealings and flouting the finer points of morality in his private life, but will *draw the line* (for instance) at his wife's wearing slacks on a Sunday morning, or his daughter of

[1] See ch. II above, pp. 47–8.

[2] The objection was in fact made by an acute member of the audience at the lectures on which this book is based.

eighteen reading *Lady Chatterley's Lover*, or his son voting Labour when the family has always voted Conservative, or his Rotary Club having Bertrand Russell, who has been four times married, to address them on Problems in Modern Philosophy. That is the sort of thing he will 'draw the line at', very firmly and often very unpleasantly; and will never see, and will never be persuaded to see, how perfectly arbitrary and perfectly irrational it all is: how the things that do shock him bear no recognisable relation to the things that do not shock him; how it is possible, in short, to be thoroughly hard-headed and hard-boiled and 'unconventional' (in Callicles' sense) about most things, yet to be at the same time thoroughly soft-headed—sloppy and sentimental and stupidly 'conventional'—about other things.

This, I suggest, is what Plato has in mind when he shows us Callicles drawing the line at the catamite. Of course it is arbitrary and of course it is irrational: Callicles' being shocked at the image of the catamite bears no recognisable relation to Callicles' *not* being shocked by, but on the contrary condoning with equanimity, the brutalities of the tyrant who puts into practice the might-is-right doctrine. But that, precisely, is the point—that it *should* be arbitrary and irrational, Callicles being the sort of man he is; and that is what makes the brilliant psychological truth of the catamite image in this context.

But there is still one further twist in the situation, one last turn of the screw. Callicles, we remember, repudiated the moral laws established and maintained by what he called 'convention', the refuge of the weak—those who insist (for instance) that to do injustice is a greater evil than to suffer it because they are themselves too weak to do injustice; and he acclaimed the laws of what he called 'nature', the laws established and maintained by the stronger, and especially by the strongest, that is, the tyrant.[1] Yet here we find Callicles himself reacting in a thoroughly conventional way to the image of the catamite, expressing all the shock and loathing that an

[1] See ch. II above, pp. 44–5.

ordinary unsophisticated conventional man would express because (according to Callicles' doctrine) he was 'too weak' to practise the dangerous pleasures of the catamite.

This is the first point, which is already full of pleasant irony. But there is a further and final irony to be discerned. Callicles (Plato desires us to see) is in fact *right*, morally right, to be shocked by the image of the catamite. The life of a catamite *is* terrible, foul and miserable; and it is a last sign of grace in Callicles, we are meant to see, that he should recognise this. But according to Callicles' own doctrine, the moral law that condemns the pleasure of the catamite is conventional, the law that condones it is natural (since 'by nature', Callicles has explained, *every* pleasure is legitimate, and the more unjust or injurious the more legitimate). Yet what convention prescribes in this instance turns out *by Callicles' own admission* to be morally *right*, what nature prescribes is morally *wrong*. In other words, Callicles' crucial distinction is seen to have been quietly and unobtrusively stood on its head: what was conventional and therefore wrong is now conventional but right, and what was natural and therefore right is now natural but wrong. And this complete reversal of Callicles' doctrine, this complete transvaluation of his values, has been achieved by the strictest adherence to the rules of the dialectic, the last and nicest irony in this charged little situation in the *Gorgias*.

It will be evident from this brief account of the main principles of the Socratic dialectic that there are formidable difficulties in the way of the modern reader who seeks, however earnestly, to arrive at a complete and perfect, an 'ideal', reading of the Platonic Dialogues. I have stressed the importance of relating every particular argument in a given Dialogue to its total context; but the sheer difficulty, at this distance in time, of possessing oneself of the total context of a particular argument must always be great, and will often no doubt be unsurmountable. There is the difficulty, to begin with, of discerning all the finer shades of the false opinions that are being exposed in any particular Dialogue. To grasp these fully would require the sort of topical knowledge of Athenian history—practically its day-to-day history, history almost as current affairs—which it is not easy even for the scholar to acquire and practically impossible for the amateur reader of Plato. And the lack of this sort of detailed knowledge of the historical context would make it impossibly difficult also to determine the exact nature and extent of the common ground between Socrates and the adversary, upon which the dialectical validity of the arguments so often depends.

But, besides these, there are the still more intrinsic difficulties arising from our imperfect understanding of the Greek system of logic, the so-called 'two-valued logic' that Socrates and Plato habitually use, which, according to modern logicians, is one of several possible logics, and is open to certain damaging objections whose significance the literary reader of Plato will not easily grasp for lack of sufficient formal training. There is, it is true, at least one elementary point about this two-valued logic that the literary reader may be expected to grasp. It accounts (we are told) for the constant postulation in the typical Socratic argument of only *two* alternatives: the adversary is asked to choose between two, and always *only* two, 'contradictories' which are assumed to be exhaustive. There is no doubt that to know even this helps a little. It at least helps—or ought to help—to check our frequent desire to dispute, in so many of the Platonic arguments, this very assumption that the two alternatives proposed *are* exhaustive. We can so often, we know, think of a third or even a fourth alternative, and would like to see the adversary proposing them, instead of giving his usual meek assent to the alternatives proposed. But this objection, we are made to understand, is illegitimate because within the framework of a two-valued logic two, and only two, alternatives are permissible; and this is certainly to know something, not nothing, as Socrates would have said. But no literary reader will dare to doubt that there is more to two-valued logic than just this;

and for lack of further light on the matter, he must assume that he is likely to miss at least some of the finer points of at least some of the Socratic arguments.

These are the disabilities that the modern reader of Plato labours under; and their bearing on the problem of the sophistical argument in the Socratic dialectic should be obvious. Since it is likely that many seemingly sophistical arguments would appear less sophistical or not sophistical at all if our knowledge of the total context were more complete, it would seem to be a wise policy not to be too rash in dismissing a particular argument. Where it seems to be sophistical, it will always be wise to give Socrates the benefit of the doubt; and then, conscientiously and patiently, to seek out whatever help may be available for its better interpretation. But the first condition of these better interpretations of the Socratic arguments is an understanding of the principles of the dialectical method; and though to understand the principles will not by itself enable one to make the right interpretation of any particular argument, it will, or ought to, prevent one from making wrong interpretations—the sort of wrong interpretation that springs from an imperfect understanding of the rigid conditions or rules which govern this whole remarkable method of instruction. And this, one would like to think, is something gained for the better understanding of *The Republic* and the other Platonic works that the literary reader is likely to venture upon.

THE SOCRATIC PARADOX: THE REDEMPTION OF THE COMMON MAN

It remains to say something about that most complex and most elusive feature of the Socratic dialectic, the so-called Socratic paradox. This turns upon the systematic exploitation of the ambiguity of terms, and has a very important bearing on the question of what is possible in the way of positive affirmation within the framework of the dialectic.

I stressed the point[1] that the master of dialectic is not able within the framework of the dialectic to prove his own position to be true; he is only able to prove his adversary's position to be false because self-contradictory. Now certainly the master of dialectic, so long as he confines himself to dialectics and does not illegitimately slip into didactics, can in no circumstances *prove* his own position to be true. But he can *affirm* it; and though he cannot affirm it explicitly, he can affirm it implicitly; and the implicit affirmation of positive doctrine within the rigid framework of the dialectic is what the Socratic paradox is, I believe, chiefly designed to accomplish.

The simplest but (I suggest) also the most comprehensive way of viewing the Socratic paradox is to see it as a metaphor expressing a fundamental aspect of the Socratic vision of life, the experience of the permanent contradiction and clash between appearance and reality. 'Knowledge is virtue'; 'He who has knowledge of justice is a just man'; 'Archelaus, the tyrant of Macedon, so far from being the happiest of men, is the most miserable of men'; 'It is a greater evil to do injustice than to suffer it'; 'The good man cares nothing about saving or being saved [that is, cares nothing about self-preservation, about mere survival]': the first is perhaps the most famous of the Socratic paradoxes, the rest are instances (all moral in content) drawn from the *Gorgias*. They are all paradoxes in the first and most important sense that they flatly contradict the common beliefs or opinions of common unreflective men. Indeed, to the common unreflective pre-Christian men who are Socrates' adversaries in the *Gorgias*, they are extravagant and perverse to the point of seeming quite insane.[2] Yet Socrates is able to show by the dialectical method that to deny each of these propositions involves a fatal self-contradiction; therefore they must be in some sense true; and if they are true, the contradiction they seem to express must be apparent and not real.

This, precisely, is what Socrates succeeds in intimating

[1] Pp. 308–9 above.   [2] See ch. II above, pp. 36–7.

with the utmost clarity and force. These paradoxes seem extravagant or perverse or insane when, and only when, the crucial terms 'knowledge', 'virtue', happiness', 'saving', 'being saved' are used to signify the (false) appearances of the thing signified, but cease to be so when they are used to signify the thing in its (true) reality. Thus knowledge *is* virtue when 'knowledge' is used to signify, not opinion, which is only apparent knowledge, but real knowledge, knowledge perfect and complete—such real knowledge (insight, wisdom) being indeed the necessary condition and the guarantee of real virtue (goodness), virtue perfect and complete. And the man who possesses such knowledge of any particular thing—for instance, justice (morality)—will indeed be a just, or perfectly good, man. Again, when the pursuit of power and pleasure are seen to be the appearance, not the reality, of happiness, it becomes clear why Archelaus the tyrant of Macedon *is* the most miserable of men; and when mere self-preservation, mere survival, is seen to be not the reality of salvation but its false appearance, the seeming contradiction in the good man's caring nothing about 'saving' and 'being saved' vanishes.

It is not necessary that the modern reader of Plato should accept the 'real' meanings of these terms 'knowledge', 'happiness', 'virtue' and the rest that Socrates may be supposed to have had present to his mind when he propounded these moral paradoxes. It is not necessary even to believe that they *have* a real meaning as distinct from this or that apparent meaning. For his limited purpose, which is merely that of understanding the *modus operandi* of the paradoxes in the Socratic dialectic, it is necessary only to see how their force depends upon the constant juxtaposition of the world of reality and the world of appearances as Socrates understands these matters. Recalling the diagrammatic image of the two moral worlds (Socrates' and his adversaries') as two overlapping circles,[1] a Socratic paradox occurs, one might say, in

[1] See ch. II above, pp. 26–7.

the overlapping area of the two worlds; and occurs with the greatest, the most explosive, force ('knowledge is virtue', for instance) at the points of intersection of the two worlds. And if one may imagine the world of appearances wholly superimposed upon the world of reality (the condition, one must suppose, of the dwellers in the deepest and darkest part of the cave), then the whole field becomes a field for paradox, and there is nothing, literally nothing, the master of dialectic can affirm that is *not* paradoxical.

I do not suggest that this is the only possible analysis of the Socratic paradox, but I believe that it is a true analysis of Socrates' own intention in propounding his paradoxes. What he sought to do by means of his paradoxes was to bring into violent collision the world of appearances and the world of reality as a challenge to the dwellers in the cave who happened to be his adversaries of the moment. Then, having thrown down the gage and induced in them the kind of perplexity, bewilderment and general confusion of mind that would (at least) ensure their attention to what he had to say, he proceeded to show that the contradiction arose always and only when the terms were used with the meanings belonging to them in the world of appearance, but vanished the moment they were used to signify the realities. And that is how Socrates uses his paradoxes to intimate, again and again, the ultimate incoherence of the world of appearances, the ultimate self-coherence and self-completeness of the world of realities.

This is the general intention of the Socratic paradoxes. Their method turns upon the deliberate and systematic exploitation of the double meaning of the crucial moral terms. 'Knowledge', 'justice', 'happiness', 'virtue', 'salvation': in the language of common discourse, *the same terms are always used to signify both the appearance and the reality.* But the apparent meanings and the real meanings are always different, for the most part, indeed, so different as to be diametrically opposite. And Socrates persistently in his dialectical arguments exploits this fundamental ambiguity of the language of common discourse as one of his most important devices for inducing his adversaries to repudiate the apparent and embrace the real.

This Socratic device has, more than any other, been regarded as vicious by those who believe (with Aristophanes) that Socrates is essentially as sophistical as the sophists he condemns. They see the deliberate exploitation of the ambiguities of language as an illegitimate play on words by which the master of dialectic traps his adversary into assent to a proposition which he, the adversary, granted in one sense, the apparent sense, but the master takes in the other, the real sense—thus using the adversary's concession in a sense he did not intend to convict him of self-contradiction.[1] On the view I have suggested, however, these ambiguities, so far from being vicious, should be seen rather as an intensely economical way of simultaneously exposing the false and affirming the true. In the proposition, 'He who has knowledge of justice is a just man', for instance, the apparent meanings of the terms 'knowledge' and 'justice' are shown to involve the adversary Gorgias in a fatal self-contradiction; and at the same time the real meaning, which is there all the time (co-present, as it were, with the false) is being pressed upon the adversary as the only possible basis of a self-coherent and self-complete position.

This simultaneity of statement, if one may so call it, is a persistent feature of the Socratic paradox; and its virtue is of a kind that students of literature are perhaps especially qualified to appreciate. For Socrates' exploitation of the ambiguities that make this kind of simultaneity of statement possible operates in the Platonic Dialogues, I would suggest, in a manner analogous to the operation of metaphor in poetry, in particular the so-called metaphysical metaphor or conceit. Recalling again[2] T. S. Eliot's definition of the metaphysical

[1] This exactly is the charge that Callicles directs against Socrates in the *Gorgias*. See *Gorgias*, 483 A, and ch. II above, p. 44.

[2] See ch. II above, p. 49.

conceit, 'heterogeneity of material compelled into unity by the operation of the poet's mind', and Dr Johnson's, 'the most heterogeneous ideas...yoked by violence together', it is not difficult to see the parallel. There are surely no two more disparate, more heterogeneous, elements than appearance and reality, and none that, if yoked together at all, would *have* to be more violently yoked together. These features, the heterogeneity, the unity and the violence, are all to be discerned in the Socratic paradox on the analysis I have suggested; and together they do much to account for the extraordinary impact of the paradoxes, which on this view are so effective pedagogically because so effective poetically and dramatically.

There is still one final aspect of the Socratic paradox to be remarked, and this perhaps its deepest and most interesting. The Socratic paradox expresses the Socratic irony in its profoundest form; and to understand the way in which the irony operates here is to receive a confirmation, as illuminating as it is unexpected, of the final gap or defect in Socrates' redemptive vision.[1] For what it exhibits is at once the grandeur and poignancy of Socrates' position as one of the greatest Christian missionaries before Christ, seeking to redeem the common unreflective man by way of his reason, and the necessity and yet the insufficiency of the dialectical method as the instrument of this redemptive effort. Socrates *had* to argue by the dialectical method, with all its restrictions, because the common unreflective man cannot be 'taught'; and he had to *argue* because he could not preach; and he could not preach because he had no revealed God and no revealed Gospel. As the eloquent intimations of immortality and the fable of the judgment-day in the *Gorgias* (to mention no other evidences) so clearly show, Socrates' whole system was pressing—travailing, one might almost say—towards the affirmation of just such a final source of certainty and authority. But the moral and religious tradition from which he drew his

[1] See ch. II above, pp. 57–9.

inspiration could not yield what he sought, and his own genius was powerless, it seems, to reach so far by its own unaided effort. His mind was filled with the knowledge of God, and he burned with the true redeemer's passion to make his knowledge accessible to all men for their salvation; but for lack of the final certainty and the final authority of a revelation, he had no way of affirming his saving knowledge except by way of his paradoxes. Because he could not say, as Jesus could, 'I and my Father are one', and 'He who seeth me seeth the Father', he had no alternative but to resort to the linguistic mechanism of the paradox to affirm the superiority in dignity and power of reality over appearance. And because he knew that this was what he was doing and why he was doing it, and his adversaries, the men he was seeking to redeem, did not know and could never be made to understand, the Socratic paradox stands as the profoundest expression of the Socratic irony.

APPENDIX B

TWO MEANINGS OF 'DIALECTIC'

THE connexion between the dialectical *method* discussed in Chapter II and Appendix A, and the *study* called 'dialectic', which Plato describes in Book VII and part of Book VI of the *Republic*,[1] is not immediately apparent; and it may accordingly be useful to set out briefly the main points of Plato's analysis and suggest how it is connected with the dialectical method we have observed in operation in the *Gorgias*.

It will be remembered that the ascent of the soul to the apprehension of the Form of the Good, which is the consummation of the philosopher's quest for truth, is accomplished by an arduous programme of studies arranged in an ascending order of abstractness. The highest, most general, study is what Plato calls dialectic; the study immediately below dialectic in the hierarchy is geometry; and Plato introduces his account of dialectic by an analysis of geometry and geometrical reasoning.

The main features of geometrical reasoning appear to be the following. (1) The starting-point of every piece of geometrical reasoning is what Plato calls a *hypothesis*, what the modern geometer would call an axiom: for example, parallel lines never meet. (These specifically geometrical axioms are to be distinguished from the more general axioms of logic, such as 'the whole is equal to the sum of its parts', or 'if *A* is greater than *B* and *B* is greater than *C*, *A* is greater than *C*'.) (2) The defining feature of these geometrical axioms or hypotheses is that they are themselves never demonstrated to be true, they are simply assumed as true and used in all geo-

[1] *Rep.* 511–12; 533–4.

metrical reasoning. (3) Geometrical reasoning is purely deductive. The geometer infers all kinds of properties of triangles, circles, planes and other geometrical entities from these axioms, which are few in number and simple compared with the theorems that may be deduced from them. (4) Since it is no part of the task of geometry as such to examine its own axioms or hypotheses, no piece of geometrical reasoning, no geometrical argument, can result in a re-examination of the axioms or hypotheses of geometry: the result of a geometrical enquiry cannot show them to be either true or false, cannot either establish or undermine their validity.

Now the important, indeed the defining feature of dialectic is that it undertakes to do precisely that which geometry cannot, and must not, attempt to do. It undertakes to examine the validity of those very hypotheses which geometry takes as axiomatic; and not only of the axioms of geometry, but those of *all* the special sciences. Dialectic is the 'science of sciences'—the science that takes for its subject-matter, and submits to a critical examination, the very foundations of each of the special sciences; hence it is the supreme *logical* study performing the function which would nowadays be called the analysis (or critique) of concepts.

But dialectic for Plato is also the science of sciences in another sense, the metaphysical, in that it seeks to discover a single unifying principle, which Plato calls a Form, in the light of which the hypotheses or axioms of the special sciences may be examined and proved to be true or false. To 'prove' a hypothesis of a special science to be true or false means to show that it is or is not deducible from that single unifying principle. If it is deducible, it is thereby proved to be true, if not deducible, it is proved false. And once proved true in this sense, it ceases to be a hypothesis, merely assumed, and becomes a principle really known to be true.

This view of the task of dialectic presupposes that a single unifying principle, a Form of Forms, can be discovered—that it is there to *be* discovered. This assumption will not commend itself to anti-Platonists; but since we are not concerned in this discussion to criticise Plato's view of the dialectic, only to understand it, this is an objection that need not be pursued.

The further peculiarity of dialectic, viewed still as a study and not yet as a method, is that it alone of all the studies in Plato's hierarchy concerns itself with what he calls 'intelligibles' as distinct from 'sensibles'. Plato explains that, though the geometer reasons about triangles, circles, planes and so on as intelligibles or abstract entities (not about *this* triangle, *that* circle, but about *the* triangle, *the* circle), yet the sensible is present in those pictorial representations of the geometrical entities which he uses to assist him in his reasoning. And though he may dispense with their assistance (as, it seems, advanced mathematicians in fact do), yet the fact that the geometrical entities admit of pictorial representation at all establishes their link with the sensible. Thus geometry, though the most abstract of the studies before dialectic, is yet seen to be not wholly independent of the senses, not wholly ideal. This complete independence of the senses, complete abstractness or ideality, belongs uniquely to the subject-matter of dialectic in its metaphysical aspect. And that is how dialectic viewed as a metaphysical study comes to take for its specific subject-matter the Forms of all objects, these Forms being pure intelligibles or 'ideas'.

Having in mind this account of the dialectic, how (we may now ask) is it related to the dialectical method that Socrates practised as a method of instruction? The crucial link seems to be in that feature of the dialectical method which stresses that the truth about any disputed matter can only be discovered by an intensive and systematic examination of the various relevant opinions (hypotheses); from which it follows that the dialectical method is essentially *a method of examining all hypotheses including its own*. An example of the way in which it works in practice is the enquiry into the nature of justice in the first books of the *Republic*. The object of the dialectical quest is the Form of Justice. Socrates proceeds, we remember, by examining the various hypotheses presented by his adversaries—first by Thrasymachus, later by Glaucon and Adeimantus. The examination is conducted by the question-and-answer method—a method that is at once searching and systematic; and the result of this intensive enquiry is the emergence at the end of Book IV of the true nature of justice, which is the Form of Justice.

This enquiry would seem to satisfy the main points of the definition of dialectic set out in Book VII of the *Republic*. First, as to subject-matter: since it is possible to give no visual or sensible representation of justice (any more than of temperance, wisdom, courage or any of the moral virtues), it is purely an intelligible, an idea, in a way in which even 'triangle' and 'circle' are not pure intelligibles. Second, as to method: what makes it clear that this enquiry into the nature of justice is a dialectical, not a geometrical, enquiry is that *it takes nothing as axiomatic*. The hypotheses which are the starting-point of the enquiry are not accepted as true without proof; on the contrary, they are subjected to the most searching examination for the purpose of discovering whether they are or are not true; and they are successively discarded as it becomes evident that they are self-contradictory and therefore false. And while in a geometrical enquiry the final result of the demonstration (its conclusion) can never lead to any modification of the hypotheses upon which the whole depends, exactly the opposite is true of this dialectical enquiry into the nature of justice. The hypotheses with which the enquiry began—which were its starting-point in the sense that the whole enquiry depended on them, just as the axioms in geometry (which Plato also calls hypotheses) are the starting-point of a geometrical enquiry in the sense that every geometrical argument presupposes ('depends' on) them—are radically modified by the conclusion, namely, the discovery of the true definition of justice. They are seen to be either limited, imperfect, incomplete, or completely false; and such an outcome, which is impossible in geometry[1] or any of the special sciences, is the distinctive feature of dialectic alone.

What is true of the enquiry into the nature of justice in the *Republic* is equally true of the several enquiries in the *Gorgias*: that into the nature of rhetoric with Gorgias himself; that into the nature of power, which is the real subject of Socrates' exchange with Polus; and the culminating enquiry into the nature of the good—whether it is or is not the same as pleasure—which is the real subject of Socrates' exchange with Callicles. In each instance, the master of dialectic is seeking to discover the real nature, the Form, of pure intelligibles; he proceeds by the intensive examination of the hypotheses concerning the nature of rhetoric, of power, of the good, which were the starting-points; and the conclusion of each enquiry is the emergence of the true definition, in the light of which the original hypotheses are either radically modified or discarded.

[1] The *reductio ad absurdum* proof is the exception to this rule. But since this is generally regarded as a departure from the regular type of geometrical proof, Plato's account of the geometrical method would seem to be substantially correct. It may be of historical significance that the *reductio ad absurdum* proof in geometry is in fact identical with the typical proof in dialectics.

APPENDIX C

THE LAMBETH CONFERENCE, 1958: THEOLOGY OF SEXUALITY

THE importance of the deliberations and resolutions concerning 'The Family in Contemporary Society' contained in the published Report of the Lambeth Conference of 1958[1] is by now generally recognised. To many, indeed, and especially perhaps to those who are neither members of the Anglican communion nor even Christians, this will seem the most important and impressive part of the whole Report. It abounds in pronouncements on this most complex and difficult of topics which are as informed, intelligent and incisive as they are wise and compassionate, and accordingly command assent equally by their truth of feeling and their truth to the facts of experience. One of the most impressive and moving sections is that on 'Christian Family Ideals',[2] in which the bishops show that a profound insight into the psychological and moral needs of children in contemporary (as in any) society can be perfectly accommodated within a framework of firm Christian principle; another is the whole discussion of 'The Family in an Industrialised Society',[3] which shows, besides a knowledge of actual conditions that a professional sociologist could hardly better, a most tender 'inward' understanding of the suffering, material and moral, to which even in a Welfare State so many are still condemned. Apart from the details, however, this part of the Report combines an exemplary open-mindedness, fairness and scrupulousness in the treatment of some of the most controversial problems of

[1] *The Lambeth Conference, 1958: The Encyclical Letter from the Bishops together with the Resolutions and Reports* (S.P.C.K. and Seabury Press, 1958).

[2] *Ibid.* II, pp. 151–3.

[3] *Ibid.* II, pp. 157–63.

modern life with positive knowledge, positive principles, energy in enquiry, and resolution in seeking (and finding) practical solutions. In an age in which the simplifications of unqualified, uncompromising dogma, whether religious or secular, offer an illusory solace to the divided mind and tormented spirit of modern man, the work of the bishops at the Lambeth Conference represents a triumph of civilisation as well as true spirituality.

For the religious Humanist, however, the discussion of 'Theology of Sexuality and the Family'[1] is the most profoundly interesting, challenging, and—with the qualifications to be mentioned—inspiring section of this part of the Report. Here the bishops undertake a radical review of the three 'ends' of marriage set down in the marriage-service of the Church, and in their final interpretation indirectly confirm at least one vital point of the Humanist critique set out above,[2] namely, that these ends of Christian marriage *as they stand* and as normally understood by Christians are seriously misleading, and likely as a consequence to distort and falsify the true nature of the marriage bond. Arguing first (justly, it would seem) that the formal order in which the three ends or purposes are set down in the marriage-service—first, 'for procreation', second, 'as a remedy against sin', third, 'for mutual society, help and comfort'—is not to be regarded as necessarily an order of priority, the Committee then proceeds to urge the vital importance of the third end:

> It has been common, in Christian theology, to mention the procreative function first, as if to say that it is the ruling purpose. So it is, in the sense that no marriage would be according to God's will which (where procreation is possible) did not bear fruit in children. But it is clearly not true that all other duties and relationships in marriage must be subordinate to the procreative one. Neither the Bible nor human experience supports such a view.[3]

From there the Committee passes on to make its crucial pronouncements on the 'theology of sexuality'. Having re-

[1] *The Lambeth Conference, 1958*, II, pp. 142–57. [2] Ch. x, pp. 277–81.
[3] *Ibid.* II, p. 144

affirmed, with all possible emphasis, the importance of the procreative function, it goes on to say that, nevertheless,

> The procreation of children is not the only purpose of marriage. Husbands and wives owe to each other and to the depth and stability of their families the duty to express, in sexual intercourse, the love which they bear and mean to bear each other. Sexual intercourse is not by any means the only language of earthly love, but it is, in its full and right use, the most intimate and the most revealing; it has the depth of communication signified by the Biblical word so often used for it, 'knowledge'; it is a giving and receiving in the unity of two free spirits which is in itself good (within the marriage bond) and mediates good to those who share it. Therefore it is utterly wrong to urge that, unless children are specifically desired, sexual intercourse is of the nature of sin. It is also wrong to say that such intercourse ought not to be engaged in except with the willing intention to procreate children.[1]

This is followed by a statement on contraception, which is declared legitimate and proper as a means of family planning on the sound, sober, and thoroughly Christian ground that 'scientific studies can rightly help, and do, in assessing the effects and the usefulness of any particular means; and Christians have every right to use the gifts of science for proper ends'.[2] This view of the legitimacy of using scientific methods of contraception is, however, strictly qualified in the passage that follows; and since this is the passage I particularly want to take issue with, I will quote it in full:

> Continence, self-control, and chastity have often been advocated on the basis of a view of life that identified the principle of evil with the 'material' or 'the flesh'. Though we can no longer accept the dualism expressed in Puritanism and in the theology of St Augustine, yet the Church holds as strongly as ever that continence, chastity, and self-control are a positive and creative element in Christian living. They are indeed an ingredient in an heroic and sacrificial response of man to the costly redeeming love of God. If Christian living were to be so influenced by current hedonism as to allow free reign to biological and sexual urges, it would lose the dimension of holiness and its power to challenge 'the world'.
>
> In the man-woman relationship, not only before marriage but in it,

[1] *Ibid.* II, p. 147.

[2] *Ibid.* II, p. 147.

chastity and continence are virtues of positive worth, sustained by the grace of God, for they release creative power into other channels. If the sexual relationship is to be truly an expression of partnership, the male has to recognize that his sexual urge may be the stronger and therefore he has more consciously to exercise self-control. Nothing that is said hereafter about the use of contraceptives in family planning takes away from the beauty and strength of abstinence mutually accepted.[1]

The last point is reiterated in the passage that follows which sets out the means of birth control 'not acceptable to Christians', of which the first is 'the wilful withholding of one partner from intercourse with the other, sometimes misnamed "continence"'. This paragraph ends with the parenthesis,

(This, of course, does not refer to a mutual decision of husband and wife to agree to abstain from intercourse for a time as a particular and special offering to God.)[2]

The rest of this section ('Family Planning') touches on various other difficult and delicate problems such as abortion, sterilisation, and artificial insemination, setting out its resolutions with moderation and firmness; and it ends with a splendid reaffirmation of the finer, nobler possibilities of the marriage relation disclosed in our time by 'the new freedom of sexuality':

Marriage is a vocation as well as an estate of nature; it is an essay in responsible freedom; and we have no more right to expect it to be without its problems than we might expect good citizenship or personal integrity to be painless.... Freedom is also the way towards the attainment of all that is excellent and true. And, perplexing though the choices in contemporary marriage are, it must also be said that the new freedom of sexuality in our time is also, and equally, a gate to a new depth and joy in personal relationships between husband and wife. At a time when so much in our culture tends to depersonalize life—to erode and dissolve the old, clear outlines of human personality—Christians may well give thanks for the chance given us to establish, in marriage, a new level of intimate, loving interdependence between husband and wife and parents and children, freed from some of the old disciplines of fear.[3]

[1] *The Lambeth Conference, 1958*, II, pp. 147–8. [2] *Ibid.* II, p. 148.
[3] *Ibid.* II, pp. 149–50.

It remains to add, for the completion of this summary account of the Committee's resolutions, that on the question of divorce and the readmission to Holy Communion of divorced persons ('the Church's discipline in marriage'), it reaffirms the resolutions of the Lambeth Conferences of 1948 and 1930, namely,

> that the marriage of one whose former partner is still living may not be celebrated according to the rites of the Church, unless it has been established that there exists no marriage bond recognized by the Church;

and

> that in every case where a person with a former partner still living is re-married and desires to be admitted to Holy Communion the case shall be referred to the bishop, subject to provincial or regional regulations.[1]

In taking issue with this account of their theology of sexuality, as the bishops call it, I hope it will not be supposed that I am joining in the easy game of twitting the Church of England on its propensity to 'compromise', 'have its cake and eat it', 'sit on the fence' and so on. No doubt it has sometimes, perhaps even often, deserved to be so twitted; but this, in my judgment, is not a case in point. In this instance, what moves one to criticism is rather the disappointment one experiences on finding that, having gone so far in the right direction, having given us so much that is admirable, true and profound, the Church can yet fail to go far enough. In drawing attention to some of the confusions, contradictions and evasions contained in this part of the Report it is accordingly in the interests of truth, not polemic, that I shall once again proceed on the Socratic assumption that a position which is in serious points self-contradictory exposes itself as false, or at least as gravely imperfect and incomplete.

The first faint misgiving is felt when one reads, in the passage quoted above, of 'the *duty* [of husbands and wives] to express in sexual intercourse the love which they bear and

[1] *Ibid.* II, pp. 170–1.

mean to bear to each other'. To do what is one's duty is not, one knows, necessarily incompatible with a spontaneous joy and delight in doing it. Yet the normal usage of the word, if it does not positively exclude them, certainly does not emphasise the joy and delight; and since it is this precisely that the bishops do emphasise, implicitly in their repudiation of the false Augustinian and Puritan dualism and explicitly in their welcoming of 'the new freedom of sexuality in marriage in our time' as 'a gate to a new depth of joy in personal relationships between husband and wife', the word 'duty' in this context does have an odd, chilling sound.

This sense of misgiving deepens when we read that sexual intercourse is 'a giving and receiving in the unity of two free spirits which is in itself good (*within the marriage bond*) and mediates good to those who share it'. The phrase in parentheses, we feel, surely begs the question, even conceals an evasion. If by 'the marriage bond' is meant here essentially the bond of mutual tenderness, love, care and responsibility of two free souls—'a union, life-long and life-deep, of the two in "one flesh"', as the bishops beautifully put it—without reference to the particular social and legal forms, whether civil or ecclesiastical, by which the bond is publicly solemnised; if, in other words, it is the love, thus understood, that creates and sustains, indeed *defines*, the marriage, not the marriage, civil or ecclesiastical, that defines the love, then there is, of course, no essential difference between the Christian and the Humanist view of the *intrinsically* redemptive power of this love which (as the bishops not only grant but insist upon) is, in the first instance and the last, sexual—rooted in, sustained by, and consummated in the love of the body. And this, one feels bound to add, is the only meaning of the phrase 'within the marriage bond' that is properly consistent with the bishops' explicit denial of the Augustinian and Puritan view, that there is, in any sexual relationship—whether or not, one must presume, sanctified by the ritual of the Church—an intrinsic evil.

But this, it may be safely assumed, is not what the bishops mean by the phrase 'within the marriage bond'; or, if it is part of what they mean, it is certainly not what they chiefly mean. 'The marriage bond' for them must mean marriage within the Church—otherwise there is no sense whatever to be made of the Church's 'discipline in marriage', namely its laws concerning divorce and the readmission to Communion of divorced persons. Therefore, sexual intercourse is 'a giving and receiving in the unity of two free spirits which is in itself good. . . and mediates good to those who share it' when and only when it has been mystically sanctified by the marriage rites of the historic Church. And what this surely implies is that sexuality as such *is* after all, in some sense, 'evil', being redeemable, in the last analysis, only by the marriage rites of the Church which render it 'in itself good and capable of mediating good to those who share it'; and Christian marriage remains accordingly (as Augustine and the Puritans said) 'a remedy against sin and to avoid fornication, that such persons as have not the gift of continency might marry and keep themselves undefiled members of Christ's body'.[1]

It should perhaps be mentioned that this criticism is in no way, either direct or indirect, intended to disparage the marriage rites of the Church of England or of any other Christian church. The need for some appropriately serious, significant (and, if possible, also beautiful) form of public

[1] It should be mentioned that in the 'revised' Prayer Book of 1928 (published under the title *The Book of Common Prayer with the Additions and Deviations proposed in 1928*) the wording of this second 'end' of Christian marriage was changed to the following: 'Secondly, it was ordained in order that the natural instincts and affections, implanted by God, should be hallowed and directed aright; that those who are called of God to this holy estate, should continue therein in pureness of living.' This definition, it will easily be seen, expresses much more exactly than the old Augustinian formula the freer, braver, nobler view of the physical basis of marriage set out by the bishops in some of the passages quoted above. Since, however, a Resolution proposing to authorise the use of this Book in all Churches was twice (in 1927 and 1928) defeated in the House of Commons, it must be presumed that communicants of the Church of England are still married in accordance with the old formula.

solemnisation of the marriage bond is recognised by the Humanist equally with the Christian. The main object of this criticism is (as I explained) to expose a self-contradiction in the bishops' position that seems to me serious, particularly in view of its connexion with their views on sexual abstinence to be discussed below. If it has a further object, it is to intimate that the deepest contradiction of all in the bishops' theology of sexuality is that between their own truest, wisest and most inspiring statements about the nature and function of sexuality in marriage and their emphatic reaffirmation of the Church's law concerning divorce and the readmission of divorced persons: their reaffirmation, that is, of the literal indissolubility of marriages, however bad; and their persistence by implication in regarding the failure of a marriage, not as a tragic mistake (which it should be the Church's main endeavour to help to remedy, by the kind of pastoral advice and guidance that could make a second union for each sufferer as blessed as the first was wretched), but as in some sense a mortal 'sin' which it is the Church's business to 'punish' by excluding the offenders for an indefinite period from Holy Communion. I do not propose, however, to pursue this matter further here, having already briefly examined the Humanist view of the Church's discipline in marriage.[1]

To press so hard on a parenthesis might nevertheless still seem a trifle disproportionate; and certainly the contradiction it implies, if it went no further than this, might be thought a mere lapse in consistency which time and further reflection might well correct. But it goes much further and deeper; and just how far and deep it goes may be discovered by examining more closely the bishops' pronouncements on continence, self-control and chastity.

First, it must be clearly understood that when the bishops speak of 'continence' and 'chastity' they do not mean only temperance—that is, the exercise of moderation in the enjoyment of sexual life, the avoidance of excessive indulgence in

[1] Ch. x, pp. 280–1 above.

what C. S. Lewis called 'the highest bodily pleasure'. They mean also, as they say explicitly, *abstinence*; and (as we saw in the passages quoted above) they proclaim such abstinence to be a positive virtue, not only before marriage, but in it:

> The Church holds as strongly as ever that continence, chastity and self-control are a positive and creative element in Christian living. They are indeed an ingredient in an heroic and sacrificial response of man to the costly redeeming love of God....
>
> Not only before marriage but in it, chastity and continence are virtues of positive worth, sustained by the grace of God, for they release creative power into other channels.
>
> Nothing that is said hereafter about the use of contraceptives in family planning takes away from the beauty and strength of abstinence mutually accepted.
>
> The wilful withholding of one partner from intercourse with the other, sometimes mis-named 'continence', cannot be endorsed.... (This of course does not refer to a mutual decision of husband and wife to abstain from intercourse for a time as a particular and special offering to God.)[1]

Leaving aside the Humanist's specific doctrinal grounds for denying the virtue of such abstinence, and confining ourselves entirely to the bishops' own expressed views, is there not (one asks) a palpable contradiction between this insistence on 'the beauty and strength of abstinence mutually accepted' and the view of sexuality they themselves propose? If, as they say, 'sexual intercourse...is a giving and receiving in the unity of two free spirits which is in itself good (within the marriage bond) and mediates good to those who share it'; if 'the new freedom of sexuality in marriage in our time...is a gate to a new depth and joy in personal relationships between husband and wife', if it establishes 'a new level of intimate, loving interdependence between husband and wife and parents and children, freed from some of the old disciplines of fear'—if sexual life is or yields all this, what intelligible moral or religious reason can there be for abstaining from it 'as a particular and special offering to God', or as part of 'an

[1] *The Lambeth Conference, 1958*, II, pp. 147–8.

heroic and sacrificial response of man to the costly redeeming love of God'? Would it be thought a suitable offering to God (during Lent, for instance) for a mother to abstain from the natural normal expression of her love for her child—except on the Puritan hypothesis, that every natural affection is a form of self-indulgence and therefore in some sense evil, which the bishops elsewhere so vigorously repudiate? Is a Christian pastor at any time asked to abstain, by mutual decision any more than one-sidedly, from exercising his love and care of his brothers in Christ 'as part of a heroic sacrificial response of man to the costly redeeming love of God'? If it is the expression of love, not lust, that we are talking about—and it *is* love, explicitly and insistently, that the bishops refer to—what, one asks, is there in the consummating expression of sexual love that sets it so far apart from the corresponding expressions of parental or pastoral love as to make abstinence from it (but not from them) 'a particular and special offering to God'?

The answer is all too plain. In spite of their statements to the contrary, sexual love for the bishops is still, it seems, physical, unspiritual, 'carnal' or 'sensual' in a way that parental and pastoral love are not, and for this reason to be placed on a level with other forms of sensuous pleasure—eating, drinking, smoking and so on—as a suitable offering to God at all times, and in particular during those periods in the Christian calendar especially set aside for such offerings. To be more exact: it is the *pleasure* that sexual intercourse yields (like eating, drinking, and smoking, only in a far greater intensity) which is isolated as the 'particular and special offering to God' made by a husband and wife mutually consenting to abstain from it for a given period; it is abstinence from it *qua* pleasure, *qua* indulgence, that is thought a suitably 'heroic and sacrificial response of man to the costly redeeming love of God'. But is this a view of sexual love that the bishops can consistently take? Are they not, on the contrary, by all they themselves have said, with so much insight and eloquence, about the redemptive power of sexual love within the marriage bond, committed to a view diametrically opposite to this? Was not the whole point of the marriage sacrament *in the Church's sense* (leaving aside, for the present argument, the Humanist's sense) to 'sanctify' the physical, carnal bond—that is, so to transform its 'natural' character as to make the physical pleasure an integral part of the whole experience of communion ('a giving and receiving in the unity of two free spirits...', a 'depth of communication signified by the Biblical word so often used for it, "knowledge"...'), therefore precisely *not* separable from it as pleasure, and therefore in no valid sense to be compared with such pleasures as eating, drinking and smoking? That the bishops should find it possible to make this strange equation suggests that the old Augustinian bias—in this connexion, at any rate—has not yet been properly exorcised. Sexuality within the marriage bond may no longer be 'intrinsically evil', but it is still, it seems, despite the Church's claims for the transforming power of the marriage sacrament, 'concupiscential' or 'appetitive'; as such it is still (like eating, drinking and smoking) a suitable sacrifice to God; and there is still the greatest 'beauty and strength' in abstaining from it.[1]

[1] It might be argued in reply that this transformation or sanctification of the concupiscential by the marriage sacrament is indeed the Christian *ideal* of sexuality in marriage; but it is (alas) too rarely the *actuality*; and since the 'transformation' in actual Christian marriages, even the best, is always only incompletely and imperfectly achieved (as what is not by fallen man?), it is surely only realistic to postulate the presence of an unredeemed concupiscential element in every sexual relation between every Christian husband and wife, and accordingly reasonable to recommend abstinence from sexual pleasure as a suitable 'offering to God'. The answer to this is substantially the same as that given to another hypothetical defence of the Church's 'realism' (ch. x, p. 278 n. above). Invoking again Mr Eliot's admirable definition, I would suggest that the Church's attitude in this, as in all matters of vital importance to moral and spiritual life, is to have 'high—indeed absolute—ideals and moderate expectations': which means here, as elsewhere, always to show charity and mercy to all lapses from the ideal but never to *condone* them (and what is the false realism appealed to here but a principle of condonement?), and to base its spiritual direction rather on the degree of perfection actually attainable by men and women, especially with the help of the Holy Spirit acting through their spiritual directors, than (as in this instance) on the residual imperfection that *ex hypothesi* can never be eliminated.

The reason for this vestigial Augustinianism in the bishops' theology of sexuality is suggested by another short but significant passage. Speaking of the traditional view of the primacy of the procreative function in marriage, the bishops admirably repudiate the fear and mistrust of the sexual on which they believe this view to be based:

> Where it has been held, the reason generally lay in a fear of the misuse of the sexual relationship or in a false sense that there is, in any sexual relationship, an intrinsic evil. Neither fear nor a false sense of what is 'evil' is a helpful guide for humanity, in this or any other matter.[1]

Yet when presently, in an attempt to explain (and justify) their insistence on continence, chastity and self-control as an ingredient in an heroic and sacrificial response of man to the costly redeeming love of God, they write

> If Christian living were to be so influenced by current hedonism as to allow free reign to biological and sexual urges, it would lose the dimension of holiness and its power to challenge 'the world'

do we not detect in this a note of a similar fear (here, of modern 'hedonism'), and a strong suggestion of the un-holiness of 'biological and sexual urges'? The Humanist believes with the Christian that there is indeed plenty to fear in modern hedonism; and he believes too that the biological and sexual urges, like all human urges, whether formally good (like maternal love) or formally bad (like acquisitiveness, pride, power-seeking and so on), are perpetually in need of moral guidance and control. What he does not believe is that sexual abstinence in marriage in any way augments the 'dimension of holiness' of a Christian or any other life, or in any way strengthens its 'power to challenge "the world"'. A false ideal of freedom is not to be met by a false ideal of restraint; and modern hedonism will not be vanquished by the illusory beauty and strength of the abstinence recommended by the bishops.[2]

[1] *The Lambeth Conference, 1958*, II, pp. 144–5.

[2] This is perhaps the point at which to take up briefly the bishops' particular claim that 'chastity' and 'continence' within marriage are 'virtues of positive

From what has been said in the last chapters of this book about the Humanist's view of the redemptive power of sexual love, the grounds on which he repudiates the claim for the beauty and strength of sexual abstinence will be plain enough. What it occurs to him to ask, however, is whether this exaltation of sexual abstinence is not also repudiated, in the most powerful and decisive way, by the Christian scheme itself. With the pronouncements of the bishops still fresh in his memory, with the word 'communion' echoing in his mind, and recalling now also the words of the bridegroom to the bride in the marriage service, 'With my body I thee worship', the Humanist may well ask whether it is not the Incarnation (rather than the Virgin Birth) that is the relevant Christian image in this connexion. Is it not the mystery of the Incarnation that most fully and most powerfully illuminates, expresses, indeed *defines*, the mysterious and wonderful communion of the spirit achieved by a husband and a wife in the bodily consummation of their love; and is not therefore the act of sexual union in the profoundest sense a 'figure' of the Incarnation—the Word, which is love, made flesh? Likewise,

worth, sustained by the grace of God, for they release creative power into other channels' (p. 341 above). When in an earlier note (ch. x, p. 280 n. above) I explained that in rejecting the Roman Catholic dogma about virginity as the highest state, the Humanist did not reject sexual abstinence as such as 'a purely practical expedient in special circumstances, for the accomplishment of special tasks and for special types of people', I had in mind chiefly of course the religious orders, but also the scores of secular priests and dedicated Christian pastors of all denominations who have remained celibate because (as some would readily admit themselves) they would not, they knew, have the strength to combine the proper fulfilment of their duties and responsibilities as pastors or missionaries with the proper fulfilment of the duties and responsibilities of husbands and fathers, and as a consequence, given their special vocation for the pastoral or missionary life, would (as St Paul says) fail in their proper service of the Lord. But to accept celibacy as a necessary evil, so to speak, for those who are *too weak* to accomplish special spiritual tasks except by the conservation of energy thus achieved is quite different from acclaiming celibacy (or, in marriage, continence) as a positive virtue, that is, as a positive power or *strength*, as the bishops do. The fact that they can view it in this (to the Humanist) false light is of course a direct consequence of their antecedent belief discussed above, that sexual life, even in marriage, is a form of carnal pleasure or indulgence, and that there is accordingly a special beauty and strength in abstinence mutually accepted.

is not Holy Communion—the sacrament by which Christians commemorate and mystically participate in that one Death which, uniquely, blossomed into life eternal—the Christian ritual that most fully expresses the experience of death issuing in life; and where more intimately, more intensely, more spontaneously, and more universally than in the act of sexual union between a husband and a wife is this experience relived and re-enacted—the 'dying' to the world by a complete giving up of each self to the other, and the 'rising' again into life, new-born, replenished, full of love and joy drawn from the divine plenitude itself?

The Incarnation (Christians seem sometimes to forget) is a very carnal affair. If therefore the analogy proposed is true to Christian experience, we may glance again for the last time at the beauty and strength of abstinence to ask, Would not, or ought not, the Christian to find it as unthinkable to abstain as a particular and special offering to God from worshipping *with his body*, expressing his passionate love of and joy in the woman with whom he is *one flesh*, as in the same circumstances to abstain from expressing his passionate love of and joy in Christ by the mystical eating of his Flesh and drinking of his Blood in the sacrament of the Eucharist? Indeed, with the Incarnation, the Crucifixion, and the Resurrection more intensely and vividly present to him, one imagines, at these times than at others, it is not abstinence from sexual communion, but rather (one would suggest) the fullest, most joyful, most *grateful* expression of it that becomes at such times his truest deepest response to the costly redeeming love of God. The true virginity is not (as the Church has for so long held) the power to renounce bodily love. It is rather the power to rediscover and relive, each time afresh, the peace, power and joy of this most intimate of unions, to experience, each time afresh, its inexhaustible wonder and mystery. It is the man and the woman to whom the act remains, each time, as fresh and beautiful as it was the first time; who are able to sustain and perpetuate their first sense of its glory in the midst of the sober or bleak or sordid realities of day-to-day life, and who can feel, afresh each time, a boundless gratitude for each other and for this blessed source of sweetness and strength—it is they who are the truly 'virgin', the truly pure and chaste; and (on the Humanist hypothesis) it is they who are the remnant selected by grace to be the true spiritual seed of the risen Christ.

This, I recognise, is probably not a view that any Church Council could accept. Yet, having in mind the modifications proposed by this Lambeth Conference of the older theology of sexuality, it does not now seem to me so wildly, preposterously remote from a position that the Church might imaginably adopt if it pursued these modifications to their logical conclusion. In any case, to the religious Humanist, who has received his first life from the Judaeo-Christian religion and is condemned to nurse his redemptive hope in solitude between the emancipated irreligious on the one side and the orthodox religious on the other, these resolutions of the Lambeth Conference will afford the greatest encouragement and consolation. Viewed in the light of this need, the bishops' positive achievement is immeasurably more important than their shortcomings and lapses.

INDEX